FERGAL KEANE OBE was born in London and educated in Ireland. He is one of the BBC's most distinguished correspondents, having worked for the corporation in Northern Ireland, South Africa, Asia and the Balkans. He has been awarded a BAFTA and has been named reporter of the year on television and radio, winning honours from the Royal Television Society and the Sony Radio Awards. He has also been named Reporter of the Year in the Amnesty International Press Awards and won the James Cameron Prize and the Edward R. Murrow Award from the US Overseas Press Association. He was also given the Index on Censorship Award for Outstanding Commitment to Journalistic Integrity.

Visit www.AuthorTracker.co.uk for exclusive information on your favourite HarperCollins authors.

From the reviews of *All of These People*:

'This memoir from Keane charts his eventful journey from Ireland in the Sixties to the pinnacle of his trade, by way of gruelling experience in various hellholes. Many were in Africa, a continent which he clearly loves with a passion . . . Keane's writing captures the spell that Africa casts on those who make the effort to meet it halfway . . . A moving narrative runs through the book . . . Powerful and commendably candid'
Daily Mail

'The first part of Keane's memoir buoys the reader with hilarious accounts of his newspaper apprenticeship . . . The serious stuff begins in Africa, reporting first for the Irish broadcaster RTE. He sees the killing of innocents and is

determined to make sure their stories are told ... A profoundly honest book'   *Observer*

'When a writer's prose flows as smoothly as a pint of
"SmoothFlow" beer, you can't help but be a bit irritated with
the man. Writing for the rest of us is like breaking rocks. But
for Fergal Keane, whole paragraphs come perfectly formed
with a head of cream. He talks as well as he writes and his
gift is somehow unfair and unnatural. So it's a tribute to the
strength of this book, and his genius for storytelling, that my
jealousy was outgunned by my enjoyment'
                                JOHN SWEENEY, *Literary Review*

'Fergal Keane will add greatly to the many fans of his TV
reporting with this wonderful memoir ... It overflows with
hope and optimism ... The words bounce from the page
with emotion, pathos, integrity ... Compelling reading'
                                            Irish Independent

'*All of These People* is a better book than we have a right to
expect ... I admired the book's reporting passages which
also seemed honest and down-to-earth ... [Keane's] real
distinction was in his reporting talents which, as this book
shows, are considerable '   *Evening Standard*

'*All of These People* is a fascinating memoir ... As a portrait
of growing up in Ireland in the shadow of alcohol, this has
rarely been bettered'   DERMOT BOLGER

'Beautifully written and poignantly observed'
                                            Glasgow Herald

FERGAL KEANE

All of These People

A MEMOIR

HARPER PERENNIAL
London, New York, Toronto and Sydney

Harper Perennial
An imprint of HarperCollins*Publishers*
77–85 Fulham Palace Road,
Hammersmith, London W6 8JB

www.harperperennial.co.uk

This edition published by Harper Perennial 2006

1

First published by HarperCollins*Publishers* 2005

A catalogue record for this book
is available from the British Library

ISBN-13   978 0 00 717693 9
ISBN-10   0 00 717693 7

Set in PostScript Linotype Sabon by
Rowland Phototypesetting Ltd, Bury St Edmunds, Suffolk

Printed and bound in Great Britain by
Clays Ltd, St Ives plc

For My Parents

CONTENTS

ILLUSTRATIONS

SECTION I

Page 1:

With parents and godmother, London, January 1961. (Author's private collection)
On the beach in Ardmore. (Author's private collection)
In Ardmore, aged around two years. (Author's private collection)

Page 2:

My Kerry grandparents, Bill and Hanna Keane. (Author's private collection)
Michael Collins. © Sean Sexton Collection/Corbis

Page 3:

Fr Davy O'Connor. (Author's private collection)
My father, Éamonn Keane. (Author's private collection)
My mother, Maura Hasset. (Author's private collection)

Page 4:

A photograph taken on my first Holy Communion, sometime in the late 1960s. (Author's private collection)
With Brother Jerome Kelly, headmaster and visionary. (Author's private collection)

Page 5:

With my uncle John B. Keane. (Listowel Writers' Week Committee)

Page 6:

As a young reporter in Ireland interviewing Charles Haughey. (Irish Press)

All of These People

PROLOGUE

Early in the new year, 2004, I was due to meet a friend for coffee in Chelsea. As I waited an elderly man entered and went to the front of the line. I felt a flash of annoyance and tried to attract the attention of the staff. 'He's jumping the queue,' I said. But nobody heard me. The manager came and showed the man to a table. He turned, slowly, and I looked into the face of my father.

In the fourteen years since his death he had not changed. My father did not recognise me but I knew him: those poetic lips, the melancholy vagueness of the old king fighting his last battle, the same shock of greying black hair, the thick-rimmed glasses, the tweed hat and scarf I gave him once for Christmas, the aquiline nose – the Keane nose! Crossing O'Connell Bridge in Dublin one day Paddy Kavanagh had turned to my father, his friend, and remarked: 'Keane, you have a nose like the Romans but no empire to bring down with you!'

The man in the coffee shop was not, of course, really my father, but it was his face I saw. After being seated at a table near the window he had begun to talk to himself. I heard him. An English accent – upper class, not at all like my father's. 'I want to admire the magic,' he said, and made a grand, kingly gesture, waving his hand. The manager laughed.

They both laughed. It was the kind of language Éamonn, my father, would have used. Expansive. *I want to admire the magic . . .*

~

This book began as an attempt to describe my journalistic life and the people and events which have shaped my consciousness. I had come through several traumatic personal experiences and arrived at middle age – a time when men often collide with their limitations and feel the first chill of mortality. I needed to take stock of where I had come from, examine the influences which had formed me, and to look at where I might be going. There were also certain resolutions to be made in the way I lived my life. Chiefly they concerned the risks I was taking in different conflict zones of the world.

What I did not understand then was that another imperative would emerge. This book would also become a journey in search of someone I had loved but with whose memory I was painfully unreconciled. When I tried to describe my journalistic life and world, I found my father waiting for me at every corner; the past intruded so acutely on the present that I found myself pulled constantly towards a man who had been dead for more than fourteen years. For much of my adult life I had lived in confusion about my father: thoughts of him made me feel both angry and sad. I could never understand him or the manner in which our relationship had affected my life.

When I look now at my journalism, at the preoccupations which have remained constant – human rights, the struggles for reconciliation in wounded lands, the impulse to find hope in the face of desolation – I know that I am largely defined by the experiences of childhood. Since much of that childhood was framed by the realities of growing up in a household dominated by my father's alcoholism, it might be assumed that

I found my father's influence to be a wholly negative one. This book acknowledges the pain of the past, but writing it has revealed to me that *both* my parents gave me gifts that were profound and lasting. Their passionate natures and belief in justice were my formative inspiration. They were, above all, people of instinct. I doubt that either of them had a calculating bone in their bodies.

I did not always realise the good they had handed on; I too often saw the past through the prism of an angry, alienated child. But a personal crisis in the closing years of the last millennium set me on a journey towards understanding my father. I travelled part of his road of suffering and found that I was more like him than I knew.

Two physical landscapes dominate this book. One is the country in which I grew up and which, for all my exile's tendency to criticise, I love and feel very proud of. I was a child of the Irish suburbs. The familiar worlds described in the conventional Irish narratives – misery in the tenements, a happy romp through the fields to school – were not mine. I was born of middle-class parents and grew up in the 1960s and '70s amid the death throes of traditional Catholic Ireland. I saw the emergence of a modern state at a time when one part of the island was descending into sectarian war and the other, my own country, was experiencing a social revolution unprecedented in its history.

The other landscape of this book is Africa, a place I loved from a distance as a child and which would draw me back again and again as an adult. Ireland and Africa are bound together for me. Events in Ireland have often helped me to make sense of what I saw in Africa, and my experiences in Africa, particularly in the age of apartheid, helped to illuminate possibilities of change in my homeland. I regard both as home in the larger sense of that word: they are places where I can feel a sense of belonging. In Africa I witnessed the death of people I knew. I saw friends taken away before their time. I saw the very worst of man and felt death brush my own shoulder. But I also met the best friend of my adult life, a man whose willingness to forgive was an inspiration.

Writing this book I have also tried to answer some fundamental questions: why was I willing to risk my life repeatedly? How did war change me? Why did I go to the zones of death? I have found that the motivations were as complex as the consequences. By the time I drove into Iraq during the war of 2004, a perilous drive from the Jordanian border to Baghdad, I had been a journalist for twenty-five years, fifteen of which had been spent reporting conflict.

I recently wrote down as many of these war zones as I could remember – Afghanistan, Algeria, Angola, Albania, Burundi, Congo, Cambodia, Colombia, Eritrea, Gaza, Northern Ireland, Sudan, Philippines, Rwanda, South Africa, Sierra Leone, Liberia, Lebanon ... all places where circumstances had reduced the daily lives of men and women to misery. I found that as I travelled the zones of conflict there was much that seemed familiar, echoes of the history of my own country. As a boy in primary school I had listened to legends and half-truths. I had heard the stories of an Irish war handed down by former combatants in my family. I was conscious too of the stories we were not told – of civil war and atrocity, the lies of silence used by our leaders to bury the past. Those echoes became louder as I wrote this book.

I have been well rewarded for my travels. My reporting of war has won plaudits, awards, public attention. Yet I found the longer I stayed on the road the more I became aware of the psychological backwash of war. This, of course, touched the participants and victims most of all, but for the professional witnesses there was also a high price to be paid, not mitigated by the fact that we had chosen to put ourselves in the line of fire.

Prologue

For me the greatest consequence of life at war, particularly after the Rwandan genocide of 1994, was a feeling of guilt. The cataclysm which engulfed the Great Lakes region of Africa in the late spring of 1994 left many of the witnesses with lasting feelings of responsibility, or in some cases a rumbling but impotent rage. Sometimes you could experience all those feelings within seconds of each other. We had watched the unimaginable – the slaughter of nearly a million people in one hundred days – and we had survived. All of my friends who covered Rwanda came away with something more than memories: we were, in different ways and with varying degrees of intensity, haunted. In my case the story followed me for a decade. It follows me still. Rwanda led me into two extraordinary relationships: one an encounter of love, the other a confrontation with a man whom I felt myself loathing and fearing, and who in the end I would have to face in a courtroom in the middle of Africa.

While writing this book I have been surprised by the number of times I laughed at the recollection of this or that event and how inspired I have felt at the memory of certain individuals. Even in the worst of situations there have been kind gestures, compassionate acts; often these kindnesses have come from those who have been most abused, people who insisted, when we met, on recognising our shared humanity.

The title of this book, *All of These People*, comes from a poem by the Ulster writer, Michael Longley, one of the most sensitive chroniclers of the pain caused by the Troubles. It is his tribute to those who have inspired him; I carry a little photocopy of this poem wherever I travel in the world.

All of these people,
alive or dead,
are civilised.

The civilised are those who can love, forgive and hope. The world is full of them. My mother was one such person. My father too.

In this account there are individuals whom I have left out, either because they would not wish to be included, or because doing so might put them in the way of harm. In describing the relationship with my father, I am conscious that it is only my version of events, my direct conversation with somebody who is long gone but whose presence remains a constant in my life. Others will see him differently and remember different things about him.

I hope that anyone reading this book will come away from it with a sense of optimism. I am an optimist. I believe there is more good in humanity than evil, and that we are capable of changing for the better. This is the continuing lesson of my personal life as much as the public sphere in which I have operated. I make my claim on the entirely unscientific basis of one man's lived experience: it is the view from the long journey, not blind to the madness but awake to our finer possibilities.

CHAPTER ONE

Echoes

Ideal and beloved voices
Of those who are dead, or of those
who are lost to us like dead.

Sometimes they speak to us in our dreams;
sometimes in thought the mind hears them.

And for a moment with their echo other echoes
return from the first poetry of our lives –
the music that extinguishes far-off night.

'Voices', C. P. CAVAFY

Here is a memory. *It is winter, I think, some time in my seventh or eighth year. There is a fire burning in the grate. Bright orange flames are leaping up the chimney. The noise hisses, crackles. On the mantelpiece is a photograph of Roger Casement gazing at us with dark, sad eyes. My father loved Casement. An Irish protestant who gave his life for Ireland. In this memory my father sits in one chair; my mother is opposite him. They are rehearsing a play,* Rosencrantz and Guildenstern Are Dead *by a man called Tom Stoppard. It will open at the Gate Theatre in Dublin in a few weeks' time. I* hear my parents' voices going back and forth. My father's voice is rich, deep. It rolls around the room, fills me up with wonder. My mother's is softer, but so intense, the way she picks up when he stops. Never before have I seen such concentration, such fidelity to a moment. I don't really understand this play. Two men are sent to kill another man. It's about Hamlet, my mother explains. The two men are in the Shakespeare play. But who is Hamlet? It doesn't matter. I am enchanted. I feel like part of some secret cell. I don't want them to stop. I want this to last forever. Us being together in this calm; the words going on, softly, endlessly. Years and years later I try to find his voice, her voice, as they were on that night, when there was calm. If I will it hard enough I can hear them. My parents, the sinew and spirit of me.

My mother is pretty. She smells of Imperial Leather. Her hair is brown – long, and she asks me to comb it. Six pence for ten minutes. Half a crown for twenty. My father is darker and in the sun his skin tans quickly. Like a Spaniard. He says the Keanes are descended from Spanish sailors who were wrecked off the west coast of Ireland during the Spanish Armada. Such pictures he paints of our imagined beginnings along the rocky coast of Galicia, the great crossing of Biscay, the galleons smashed on the black rocks of Clare, the soldiers weighed down by their armour, sucked down into the cold. 'Only the toughest survived,' he says.

His eyes are green like mine: 'Like the heather,' he says. When he poses for a publicity photograph for one of his productions my father looks like a romantic poet, a man who would sacrifice everything for his art. He wore a green tweed jacket; I remember the scratch of it when he embraced me. And the smell of John Players cigarettes, the ones in the little green boxes with the sailor's head on the front, and I remember how the smoke would curl above his head. Sometimes in the mornings I would see him stooped over the bathroom sink

*in his vest, peering into a small mirror as he shaved. After-
wards he would have little strips of paper garlanded across
his face to cover the tiny razor cuts. He used to tell a joke
about that:*

*A rural parish priest goes into the barber's and asks for a
shave. The barber is fond of the drink and crippled with a
hangover. His hands are shaking. Soon the priest's face is
covered in tiny little cuts.*

*Exasperated, he says to the barber: 'The drink is an awful
thing, Michael!'*

The barber takes a second before replying.

*'You're right about that, Father. 'Tis awful. Sure the drink,
Father . . . it makes the skin awful soft.'*

~

I have a cottage by the sea on the south-east coast of Ireland.
Every year I go there in August, the same month that I have
been going there for over forty years. I am well aware that my
addiction to this place is a form of shadow chasing. It was
here, on the most restful of Irish coasts, that I enjoyed my
happiest hours of childhood. What else are you doing, going
back again and again, but foraging for the ghosts of lost
summers?

Last August I went to a party at the house of a friend
overlooking Ardmore Bay. We had sun that day and the horizon was clear for miles. In Ireland when I meet older people,
they will frequently ask one of two questions: 'Are you anything to John B. Keane?' or 'Are you Éamonn Keane's son?'
Yes, a nephew. Yes, a son. My father and his brother were
famous and well-loved figures in Ireland. Éamonn, the actor,
and John B, the playwright. Although they are both dead, they
are still revered. In Cork city people will usually ask if I am
Maura Hassett's boy: 'Yes I am, her eldest.' They will say they

remember her, perhaps at university or acting in a play at one of the local theatres. 'She was marvellous in that play about Rimbaud and Verlaine.'

At the party in Ardmore I was introduced to an elderly man, an artist, who had known my parents when they first met. In those days he was a set designer in the theatre. My parents were acting in the premiere of one of my uncle's plays, *Sharon's Grave*, about a tormented man hungry for land and love: 'I have no legs to be travelling the country with. I must have my own place. I do be crying and cursing myself at night in bed because no woman will talk to me,' he says. He is physically and emotionally crippled, a metaphor for the Ireland of the 1950s.

Stunted and isolated, Ireland sat on the western edge of Europe, blighted by poverty, still in thrall to the memory of its founding martyrs, a country of marginal farms, depressed cities and frustrated longings, with the great brooding presence of the Catholic Church lecturing and chiding its flock. My parents were children of this country, but they chafed against it remorselessly. The artist told me that he'd sketched them both during the rehearsals for the play.

'What were they like?' I asked him.

'The drawings? They were very ordinary,' he replied.

I said I hadn't meant the drawings. What had my parents been like?

'Well, you could tell from early on they were an item,' he said.

We chatted about his memories of them both. He praised them as actors, and talked about the excitement their romance had caused in Cork. The love affair between the two young actors became the talk of Cork city. The newspapers called it, predictably, a 'whirlwind romance'. The news was leaked to the papers by the theatre company. Éamonn and Maura married after the briefest courtship. The love affair caught the imagination of literary Ireland. For their wedding the poet Brendan Kennelly gave them a present of a china plate decorated with images of Napoleon on his retreat from Moscow, and there were messages of congratulation from the likes of Brendan Behan and Patrick Kavanagh, both friends of my father. When the happy couple emerged smiling from Ballyphehane church, members of the theatre company lined up to cheer them, along with a guard of honour made up of girls from the school where my mother taught.

Once married they took to the road with the theatre company with *Sharon's Grave* playing to enthusiastic houses across the country. In a boarding house somewhere in Ireland, a few hours after the last curtain call, I was conceived.

~

Several weeks after I met the artist who sketched my parents a brown parcel arrived at my home in London. Inside were two small photographs of his drawings. They looked so beautiful, my parents. My father handsome, a poet's face; my mother, with flowing brown hair and melancholy eyes. Looking at those pictures I remembered a line I'd read somewhere about Modigliani and Akhmatova meeting in Paris: *Both of them as yet untouched by their futures.* The artist had caught them at a moment in their lives when they believed anything was possible. There is a poem by Raymond Carver where he remembers his own wedding. This remembrance comes after years of desolation, amid the collapse of his marriage.

> *And if anybody had come then with tidings of the future*
> *they would have been scourged from the gate*
> *nobody would have believed.*

That was my parents in the year they met, 1960. I was the eldest of their three children, born less than twelve months after they were married and we would live together as a family for another eleven years.

I showed the sketched images of my parents to my eight-year-old son. He looked at them briefly and then wandered off to play some electronic game. I felt the urge to call him back, to demand that he sit down and contemplate the faces of his grandparents. But then, I thought, why would he want to at eight years of age? To him the past has not yet flowered into mystery. Anyway, he knows his grandmother well. Maura is a big figure in his life. He never met his grandfather whose gift for mischief he shares, and whose acting talent has already come down along the magic ladder of the genes.

He is occasionally curious though. 'What was your dad like?' he asks. 'My dad and *your* granddad,' I always say. Usually a few general words suffice, before his mind has hopped to something else. But I am sure the question will return when he is older. Just as I ask my mother about her parents, and wish I could have asked my father about his, my son will want to put pieces together, to find out what made me and, in turn, what shaped him.

~

My parents were temporary exiles from Ireland when I was born. After the successful run of *Sharon's Grave*, Éamonn was offered the role of understudy to the male lead in the Royal Court production of J. M. Synge's *The Playboy of the Western World*. They lived in a small flat in Camden Town from where my mother could visit the antenatal clinic at University College Hospital in St Pancras. In those days Ireland had no national health service and an attempt to introduce a mother and child welfare scheme had been defeated by the Catholic hierarchy. They considered it a first step on the road to communism.

In London my mother was given free orange juice and milk and tended to by a doctor from South Africa and nurses from the West Indies. Remembering this she told me: 'It was the best care in the world. It was the kind of treatment only rich people could afford at home.'

On the day of my birth my father was out drinking and my mother went to hospital alone. It was early January and it had been snowing. A taxi driver saw her resting in the doorway of Marks & Spencer and offered her a free lift to the hospital. By now she would have known a few of the harsher truths about the disease of alcoholism. For one thing an alcoholic husband was not a man to depend on for a regular income or to be home at regular times. Éamonn appeared at the hospital later on and, as my mother remembers it, there were tears of happiness in his eyes when he lifted me from the cot and held me in his arms for the first time.

A week or so later I made my first appearance in a newspaper. It was a photograph of the newly born Patrick Fergal Keane taken as part of a publicity drive for a forthcoming film on the life of Christ. The actress Siobhan McKenna was playing the role of the Virgin Mary in the film and the producers decided that a picture of her with a babe in arms would touch the hearts of London audiences. McKenna was the foremost Irish actress of her generation and was also playing the female lead in *The Playboy of the Western World*. As a favour my parents had agreed to the photograph. In the picture I am held in the arms of McKenna who gazes at me with a required degree of theatrical adoration.

The declared reason for the embrace had nothing to do with film publicity. The actress had agreed to become my godmother. Strictly speaking this involved a lifelong commitment to ensuring my spiritual wellbeing. I was not to hear from

Siobhan McKenna again. Holy Communion, confirmation and marriage passed by without a word.

Thirty years later I met her at a party held in Dublin to celebrate the work of the poet Patrick Kavanagh. My father had come with me. It was a glorious summer's evening and Siobhan looked radiant and every inch the great lady of the stage. My father approached her and introduced me: 'This is Fergal. Your godson.'

Siobhan smiled and threw her arms around me, and the entire gathering of poets and playwrights seemed to stop in their tracks as she declaimed: 'Sure it was a poor godmother I was to you.' She stroked my cheek and then stepped back, looking me up and down: 'But you turned out a decent boy all the same.'

My father laughed. I laughed.

'That's actors for you,' he said.

～

Éamonn and Maura both loved books. Our home in Dublin was full of them. I remember so vividly the musk of old pages pressed together, books with titles like *Tristram Shandy, The Master and Margarita* and *1000 Years of Irish Poetry*. I have that last one still, rescued from the past. My father liked the rebel ballads:

Oh we're off to Dublin in the Green in the Green . . .,
Where the rifles crash and the bayonets flash
To the echo of a Thompson gun.

My mother would sing 'Down by the Sally Gardens'. Her voice trembled on the high notes.

Down by the Sally Gardens,
My love and I did meet,
She passed the Sally Gardens,
With little snow-white feet.
She bid me take love easy
As the grass grows on the weir
Ah but I was young and foolish
And now am full of tears.

My parents were the first to foster in me the idea that I might someday be a writer. The first stories they read to me were Irish legends. As I got older they urged me to read more demanding works. I believe my first introduction to the literature of human rights came when my mother gave me a copy of George Orwell's *Animal Farm* when I was around ten.

My father wrote plays and poems, but it was his gift for interpreting the writings of others which made him one of the most celebrated Irish actors of his generation. Sometimes when my father was lying in bed at night rehearsing his lines I would creep in beside him. After a while he would switch out the light and place the radio on the bed between us. We would listen to a late-night satirical programme called *Get An Earful of This* which had just started broadcasting on RTE. *Get an earful of this, it's a show you can't miss*. The show challenged the official truths of Ireland and poked fun at its political leaders. My father delighted in this subversion. In my mind's eye I can still see him beside me laughing, his face half reflected by the light shining from the control dials of the radio, the red tip of his cigarette glowing in the dark and me falling asleep against his shoulder.

~

Nothing in either of my parents' natures fitted the grey republic in which they grew up. Sometimes my father's outspokenness could get him into serious trouble. Once he was hired to perform at the annual dinner of the Donegalmen's Association in Dublin. The usual form was for the President of the Association to speak, followed by a well-known politician, and then for my father to recite poems and pieces of prose.

On this particular night the politician was a narrow-minded Republican, Neil Blaney, who in 1957 was Minister of Posts and Telegraphs, the department which controlled RTE, my father's place of employment. At the time the government of Éamonn de Valera was making strenuous efforts to bring RTE into line after some unexpected outburst of independence on the part of programme-makers. My father later claimed that Blaney had denounced the drama department at RTE in the course of his speech to the Donegalmen. The historian Professor Dermot Keogh went to the trouble of researching the old files on the incident. He published the official memorandum, a dry account of what was surely an incendiary occasion:

> Before the dinner started Mr Keane left his own place at the table and sat immediately opposite where the Minister would be seated. When the Minister arrived, and grace had been said, Keane began to hurl offensive epithets across the table at the Minister and had to be removed forcibly from the Hall. Mr Keane was suspended from duty on 22nd November.

Quoting a civil service inter-departmental memorandum, Professor Keogh wrote:

> Described as 'a substantive Clerical Officer' who had been 'seconded to actor work as the result of a competition held in 1953', Keane submitted 'an abject apology in

writing for his behaviour.' He said he had been feeling unwell before the dinner and had strong drink forced on him to settle his nerves, with the result that he lost control of himself and did not realise what he had been saying.

The memorandum added tartly:

The action did not appear to Mr Blaney to be that of a man not knowing what he was doing. Mr Blaney said that Keane came very deliberately to the place where he knew the minister would be and that when Keane arrived in the hall he did not appear to have much, if any, drink taken.

Blaney was vindictive. My father lost his post as an actor and was sent to work as a clerical officer in the Department of Posts and Telegraphs. He didn't last long and left to work as a freelance actor in Britain. Years later my father told me what he had said to Blaney. Drink was definitely involved but I think my father would have said what he had in any case. He told the minister that his only vision of culture was his 'arse in a duckpond in County Donegal'. Keeping with the marshy metaphors he said that as a minister Blaney was as much use as 'a lighthouse in the Bog of Allen'.

There was uproar. My father told me it was a price well worth paying. His verdict, nearly thirty years later, was: 'That ignorant gobshite! What would he know about culture?'

Years later Blaney would achieve notoriety when he was sacked from the cabinet amid allegations that he had been involved in smuggling arms to nationalists in Northern Ireland.

~

My first memory of childhood is of clouds. They are big black clouds and they sit on the roofs of the houses in Finglas West. I see them because I have run out of the house. I cannot remember why. The garden gate is tied with string. I cannot go any further, so I stand with my face pressed against the bars and watch the clouds. The bars feel cold and I press my face even closer, loving that coldness. I keep watching the clouds, wondering if they will fall from the sky, what noise they will make when they hit the ground. But the clouds just sit there. Then I hear my name being called.

'*Fergal, Fergal.*'

It is my mother's voice.

After a while she comes out and leads me back into the house.

There is silence inside. My father is upstairs. At this age I know nothing. But I can sense things. There is something about this silence that is not like other silences, not like the silence of very early morning, or the silence of a house where people are sleeping. It is the silence after an argument, as if anger has changed the pressure of the air. I have already learned to live inside my head; in my head there are ways to keep the silence at bay. I stand in the room and feel the silence for a moment and then I go deep into my head and start to dream, back to the clouds and the noise of rain, loud enough to fill the world with sound. This is how things have been from the moment I can remember.

I go to bed and stay awake as late as I can, lying in my room, listening for the sound of his homecoming: footsteps outside the front door, shuffling, a key scratching at the lock, and a voice that sings sometimes, and other times shouts, and other times is muffled, a voice being urged to quietness by my mother.

Drinking. What do you know about drinking when you are six years of age? More than you should is the quick answer.

Drinking is someone changing so that their eyes are staring out from some other world to yours, flashing from happy to angry to sad, sometimes all in the same sentence; eyes that are far from you, as if behind them was a man who had been kidnapped and held prisoner; drinking is a mouth with a voice you know but cannot recognise because it is stretched and squashed, like a record played backwards, or the words falling around like children on ice, banging up against each other, careening across the evening with no direction, nothing making sense except the sound of your own heart pounding so loud you are sure every house in the street can hear it. *Boom, boom, boom.*

You imagine the noise travelling out of your bed and knocking on all the doors, waking up those sane, clean-living Irish families and spilling your secret. You are ashamed. Of that one thing you are certain. Shame. It becomes your second skin. You are sure other people know. Someone will have seen him come home, or heard him making a noise. They can read it in your eyes, in your silences and evasions, in the way you twitch and fidget. After nights lying awake for hours you go to school half sick for want of sleep, your mind miles away. The teacher speaks your name in Irish:

'*Are you listening, O'Cathain? Are you paying attention? Come up here and explain to the class what you were thinking about.*'

'*Nothing, Bean Ui Bhanseil. Nothing.*'

'*Don't mind your nothing. What was I teaching just now? What did I read?*'

'*I can't remember. I'm sorry.*'

Tabhair dom do labh. Give me your hand.

There. Now go back to your seat and pay attention. Don't be crying like a mammy's boy.

Other kids say that too. *Mammy's boy*. They know how to get me going. A boy called Grant, a big fellow, always in trouble with the teachers, shouts at me one day: 'Your mammy's a pig.' I attack him. I have no idea where the strength comes from but I go for the bastard and hurt him, until he gets over the shock and starts to hurt me. Punch, kick, punch. I am left sitting on the ground crying. Grant is right. I am my mother's boy. I cling to her. I am her confidant.

As I get older I often sit up late with her. I have learned to make calculations. I know that if teatime passes, and homework time, and there is still no sign of him, there is a chance that my father is drinking. And if the evening news comes and goes without him I know it is a certainty. My mother corrects school homework. I watch the television. We wait. After the national anthem has played on RTE my mother switches off the television.

I have grown used to this tension and fear. It is my homeland. And here is the hardest thing to admit: I love being this boy who stays up late, this child who imagines himself as his mother's protector, the boy who can listen to confidences, who is praised for being so mature. That's me: Little Mr Mature. You could tell him anything.

My father always smiles when he sees me. He pulls me towards him, always gently, and I smell the smell that is half sweet and half stale, fumes of hot whiskey breath surround me and fill the room. He tells me that he loves me and he hugs me, again and again. If he is in a happy drunk state he tells stories about people he met on the way home – impossibly sentimental stories of kindnesses given and received; but if he's angry he will curse some enemy of his at work, some actor who is conniving against him, some producer who doesn't know his arse from his elbow. He can rage bitterly. I don't know why sometimes he is happy and other times angry. My father has never raised his hand to me. Nor can I remember him ever being consciously cruel to me. It is his anger that scares me, the violence that takes over his voice. Through it all I keep an eye on my mother, until she signals that I should go to bed, and reluctantly I climb the stairs.

Sometimes from upstairs I hear a louder voice. It echoes up the hallway. This voice is beyond control. I keep my eyes on the lights of cars flashing their beams across the ceiling. I put my hands to my ears. Downstairs I hear the sound of my childhood splintering. Only when it is quiet, long after it is quiet, do I sleep.

It is still a few years to their separation. At this point nothing is determined. I do not sense that a sundering is close. I am not afraid that they will break up. In this Ireland families do not break up because of drink. Families like us stay together. Instead I have this fear that they will both die. It comes to me in dreams. I dream that they are killed in a car crash and I wake up crying.

CHAPTER TWO

Homeland

Many young men of twenty said goodbye.
On that long day,
From the break of dawn until the sun was high
Many young men of twenty said goodbye.
'Many Young Men Of Twenty', JOHN B. KEANE

I had come back to Ireland with my parents in 1961, as thousands of their fellow countrymen were heading the other way. Our people clogged the mail boats to Holyhead with their cardboard suitcases and promises of jobs on the building sites. Éamonn and Maura lived in a succession of flats and boarding houses. They had little money. My father had acting work but if he started drinking there was no money. There were days of plenty and days of nothing. By now my mother was pregnant again. Two more children would follow in the next two years. Saving money for a deposit on a house was out of the question. Eventually they were given a house by the Dublin Corporation in one of the vast new council estates being built to the west of the city, in Finglas. In those days the tenements of inner-city Dublin were being cleared and the residents moved to vast new housing estates on the fringes of the city. One nineteenth-century writer described Finglas as a village where 'the blue haze of smoke from its cottages softened the dark background of the trees'. But by the time we arrived there there were no cottages or trees. The green fields had been turned into avenue upon avenue of concrete.

In keeping with the nationalist ethos of the Republic many of the streets on the new estates were named after heroes of rebellions against the British. Go onto any council estate in Ireland and you will find streets named after guerrilla leaders. My parents were given the keys to a two-bedroom terraced house on Casement Green, named after Sir Roger Casement.

Éamonn and Maura would have stood out among the residents of Finglas. They were neither Dubliners nor working class. Both were well educated. Most of those they lived among had grown up on the hard streets of the inner city and left school at an early age to find work. It was said then of Finglas, and not quite jokingly, that it was so tough even the Alsatians walked around in pairs.

~

Our next-door neighbour was Breda Thunder. At dinner time her house smelled of boiled bacon ribs and cabbage, and chips with salt and vinegar. Breda was a handsome woman with auburn hair and laughing eyes – a native Dubliner, from Charlemont Street near the Grand Canal. Her husband Liam was a thin and wiry redhead and came from Rathmines on the other side of the canal. Breda and Liam arrived on the estate a few weeks after my parents. Years later Breda told me: 'The first time I saw you, you were standing on your own in the garden near our fence, a lovely little boy with blond hair, just standing there and smiling. That's how I'll always see you.'

I loved her because she seemed so fearless. You felt safe around Breda. She was the first person I knew who showed no fear when my father was drunk. Breda had grown up in tenement Dublin, on some of the toughest streets in Europe, in an atmosphere where women learned early how to deal with men who drank, and where the only dependable wage for many was the 'shilling a day' earned in the service of the British military. Her own father, Jamesy Harris, had served in both world wars, and her grandfather fought in the Boer War. Breda had a good soldier's courage.

Breda and Liam had five boys and had fostered a girl – the daughter of Liam's brother Paddy who had been killed serving with the Irish Guards in Aden. Her sons were my first play-mates. They were boisterous and noisy and loyal. The neigh-bourhood bullies knew to give the Thunder boys a wide berth. Pick on a Thunder or on any of their friends, and you had the whole clan to deal with. Once, a young policeman collared Breda's second youngest son, Sean, for cycling on the pave-ment outside her house. The child was about five, and quite obviously too young to head out onto the open road. Breda looked out the window and saw the very tall policeman har-anguing her child. Seconds later she was bearing down on him:

'Where are you from?' she demanded.

He replied that he came from County Mayo.

This triggered an automatic resentment in Breda's heart. She was a proud Dubliner, convinced that the city had no equal anywhere in the world and believing that visitors to the city owed a debt of respect to the natives. Any public official from County Mayo or any of the remoter rural areas would initially have been regarded with suspicion by Breda and her neighbours. Only after proving themselves as decent souls would they be welcomed. To have a *culchie* – a country person – even if he was a policeman, tell her son he couldn't cycle on Dublin concrete was an appalling insult.

'*Well, fuck off back there, you big ignorant gobshite!* This is my town and I won't have some *culchie* in size twelve boots frightening my child.'

The policeman departed soon after, followed by a hail of abuse.

Breda's was a house of relentless noise, a great deal of which was laughter. One of her daily trials was raising her sons from their beds and hunting them out to school. None of them liked the Christian Brothers School in Finglas; all waited for the day when they could quit and go to work, and each morning there was the same vaudeville: Breda would stand at the bottom of the stairs and roar at her sleeping boys above. When this failed to rouse them she would run upstairs and shake them out of bed. She would then go back downstairs to prepare the breakfast and school lunches. The boys merely continued to sleep where they had fallen, or crept into another bed.

～

I have fragmented memories of that time. I remember walking with Breda to the shops on a misty morning in winter and seeing the horses of travellers grazing on the green, the owners camped nearby under plastic sheeting and their red-haired children running out to look at us. We called them 'the tinkers'. My father said they lost their land when Cromwell drove the Irish into Connaught.

There were other mornings, standing in the hallway of Breda's house, when her husband Liam would stop by with a trayful of cakes from the bakery where he worked. 'Pick any one you want,' he would say. There were sugary doughnuts, chocolate éclairs, custard slices and thick wedges of dark cake called 'Donkey's Gur'. The back of Liam's van smelled of warm bread: turnover and batch loaves, fresh from the baker in Cabra. As he drove away other kids would run after the van. 'Mr Breadman. Mr Breadman. Gi's a cake, will ya.' And I remember Breda's happiness on a weekend night, when the work of feeding and cleaning was done, and she would sit in the small front room and tell stories about her father fighting the Nazis, before switching into song: *The Roses are Blooming in Picardy* . . .

My mother told me stories about our neighbours.

Near to the shops lived a family I will call the Murphys. Joe worked in a factory and Mary cleaned offices in the city. Such work involved leaving home every morning shortly after six and rushing home in the late afternoon in time to make dinner for the family. Mary spent her life on her knees, polishing the long floors of the Royal College of Surgeons for pitiful wages. In Mary's case, cooking was a problem. She was a devoted mother but her ignorance of all but the basic rudiments of cooking shocked Breda. There was much resort to tins and packets in Mary's house. So Breda Thunder took it upon herself to teach Mary how to prepare roast chicken and potatoes for Sunday lunch.

The following Monday, Mary knocked on Breda's door. The chicken and spuds had been a triumph. Mary described in detail how the chicken had been divided:

'You know, I had a leg for Joe, a leg for Peter and a leg for myself and for Martina, there was a leg for Mick too when he came in from work, and there was even one left over to give the dog in his bowl.'

Astonished at the profusion of legs on one chicken Breda declared: 'Are you sure it was a chicken and not a fuckin' centipede you cooked!'

As I grew older other neighbours and their children entered my field of vision. There was a woman called Sadie Doyle who lived on the opposite side of the street. Sadie wore a fur coat and her blonde hair in a beehive. She had a family of seven crammed into a tiny council house. When she came into Breda's house the boys would start singing a Beatles song: *Sexy Sadie, what have you done? You made a fool of everyone* . . . Sadie would make to clip them on the ear and then burst out laughing.

Like Mary and Joe and Breda and Liam, Sadie worked all hours to keep her family fed and clothed. Sadie and Breda were much less romantic in their ideas about men than my mother. Both were immensely protective of Maura. They saw her as a lost innocent who had blundered into the world of marginal choices and needed protection if she was going to survive. My mother spoke with a different accent and was clearly a child of the Irish middle classes. But Breda and Sadie were immune to resentment or class bitterness. When she came to them Maura was thin and haggard, strained with the effort of caring for the man she married and her growing family. They saw a young woman in trouble and responded in the only way they knew.

~

With Breda acting as childminder my mother was able to go to work. She found a job on the other side of the city at a placed called Clontarf, an old, established suburb on the shores of Dublin Bay. 'Clontarf is where Brian Boru was killed by the Danes when the Vikings invaded Ireland,' she told me. A big Dane called Broder came into the King's tent and murdered him.

My mother taught English and French to boys who had no interest in either. But she was alive in a way that these boys had never known a teacher to be. She told them stories and helped them to find something they did not know they had: their better nature. The headmaster was a strict man, a man of his time and place. I met him once and he surprised me, after what I had heard about him, by taking me to the basement and opening the door onto a room where he kept a huge train set. The room was dusty, smelled of chalk and ink, and the train sped around and around, through tunnels and past mountains, like the train to my grandmother's house in Cork. I imagined him standing there after the school had emptied watching the endless journey of his tiny locomotives, a hard lonely prisoner of Ireland in the 1960s.

Now that my mother had a job there was regular money. She was saving every month, putting by a little into a special account because she dreamed of owning a house of her own. For my mother, coming from the comfortable world she did, it was not unusual to aspire to ownership. But for her neighbours, Breda and Liam, the money they were busy saving represented an unimaginable social change. In the old Ireland people like them didn't get to own houses. They went from generation to generation in crumbling tenements or lived in hope of a flat in one of the new tower blocks. Liam Thunder had other ideas.

Finglas was getting tougher all the time. If he kept his sons there, there was a good chance at least one of them would get into trouble. Squad cars already called at other houses in the area. The police were becoming the enemy. In the years to come parts of Finglas would become notorious for drug dealing, as cheap heroin flooded into Dublin and boys from the area would become addicts, pushers and gangsters.

My mother kept saving. I think there may also have been part of her which believed that a move might somehow change my father. Once she had saved the deposit she started hunting for houses, far away in Terenure on the south side of the city. She found a handsome redbrick on a quiet street named Ashfield Park and we moved there in the middle of the 1960s.

After Casement Green this house seemed huge to me: downstairs it had a living room, a dining room, a breakfast room and a kitchen; upstairs there were four bedrooms. I had one all to myself. Outside the room in which my parents slept there was a huge willow tree which swayed back and forth whenever the wind blew. At first it frightened me, and then my father told me that the willow was a lucky tree.

Shortly after we moved in, Breda Thunder and the boys came to visit. I remember Breda wearing a black fur coat and filling our new dining room with laughter, astonished like us at the size of the place. Not long afterwards she and Liam and the boys left Finglas too for a bright new home of their own on the western approaches to the city. For a while it looked as if all our luck was turning.

~

My father's career as an actor began to blossom. By the mid-sixties he was in demand on radio, television and stage. I was about six years old when I first entered a radio studio. It was the old RTE building on Henry Street in Dublin, near the riotous noise of Moore Street market with its vegetable and flower sellers, and right next to the General Post Office – still pockmarked with bullet and shrapnel marks from the fighting of 1916.

To a child's eye Henry Street was a deep and gloomy building which smelt of floor polish and cigarettes. In the actors' greenroom men and women lounged on sofas and chairs mumbling to themselves as they read great sheaves of paper. These were called scripts, my father explained, and you had to learn them off by heart. The actors, producers, writers, and an army of sound engineers, turned out everything from Chekhov to one of the Republic's first soap operas, *The Kennedys of Castleross*, about a family in a seaside village whose tribulations – very minor by the standards of today – kept the nation entranced for years. In one of those studios I watched, mesmerised, as my father and the other actors read their lines. Never before had I seen such stillness, or concentration. As soon as the recording was done, the actors started chatting. The spell was broken. How could they go from such magic to behaving like boring adults?

Acting was always my father's greatest love. He committed himself totally to every performance; it tormented him of course, and criticism of any kind tore into him like a steel claw. When reviews were bad he would retreat into himself as if the words were directed at him the person and not the actor on the stage; he was a man who could never divide the actor from the self. On those days he was angry and short tempered, storming out of the house at the smallest excuse.

Luckily the bad reviews were rare. As the sixties progressed he had a string of successes. He appeared as the lead in a triumphant revival – 'the hit of 1968' – of Dion Boucicault's melodrama *The Shaughraun* at the Abbey Theatre. Movie offers started to come in. He appeared in two American films that were made in Ireland. He started to talk about Hollywood. After all, there other Irish actors like Barry FitzGerald and Milo O'Shea who had already blazed the trail. My father's first film appearance was in *Underground*, set in France during the Second World War. There was a role for a child in this film and my father arranged an audition for me. When the day came I was taken down to the National Film Studios in County Wicklow. But I was seized by terror and ran out of the film company offices. A few months later I was again convulsed by stage fright during a school play. I knew the words but my throat went into spasm from fear. Any temptation to follow my father onto the stage disappeared in those agonising moments.

～

Ireland was changing now. Playwrights such as my Uncle John B. Keane and Brian Friel were writing an alternative narrative to that offered by Church and State. Éamonn and Maura relished the new atmosphere, the challenge to the old order that was being thrown up. My awareness of the wider world was shaped by my parents' non-conformism and, in both of them, a blazing sympathy for the underdog in Irish life. One of my earliest memories is of my father inviting in a group of travelling people – the eternal outcasts of our society – and sitting them down to tea.

I doubt if he checked whether we had the food to give them, and he certainly wasn't the person who cooked, but it was an important example for me. It was the gesture that mattered. Many other doors on our street would have been slammed in their faces. Years later, when I read Nadine Gordimer writing about apartheid in South Africa, there was a phrase which reminded me of my parents. It was the duty, said Gordimer, of every person faced with injustice to make the 'essential gesture'. It would be different in every life. Some would go to jail for their beliefs; others would do something as small as writing a letter to their local newspaper, or signing a petition. But what gave the gesture its power was that it came from the heart.

My parents filled their lives with 'essential gestures'. They were people of the heart. When she was teaching Keats's 'Ode to a Nightingale' my mother went and dug out some library books on the poet, and in the course of her research discovered that Shelley had come to Dublin to campaign on behalf of the Catholic poor. With great flair she conjured up an image of the poet, shivering on the streets of nineteenth-century Dublin, as he pressed his pamphlets on the uninterested gentry and the bemused proletariat. 'Oh, the courage of that,' she would say.

My mother taught English and French for forty years. She worked long hours. At night when the school day was over she would sit marking mounds of copybooks, laughing to herself at the mistakes, calling me over to read when a pupil had written something particularly good. Her work ethic was an inspiration. Long before the idea of extra-curricular activities became fashionable she was spending hours in cold school halls rehearsing her pupils through the plays of Shakespeare, or taking her senior class to art-house cinemas to watch films such as Ingmar Bergman's *The Virgin Spring*, and Fellini's *La Dolce Vita*. I was taken along to that particular double bill, and was bored out of my mind, developing a lifelong aversion to black-and-white Scandinavian films. Years later I asked my mother why she took a young child to witness the grimness of Bergman. 'I thought it might be good for you,' she said, without pausing to explain why.

Troubled children were drawn to my mother. So too were the slow learners. I remember resenting the amount of time she gave to her army of timid, abused, or struggling pupils. But in a society where the idea of talking your troubles out with a therapist was hardly known, the sympathetic teacher was often the only option. Some of these pupils are still her friends today.

Maura was the second eldest of nine children, a bright, determined child. She excelled at school and went on to study English literature and French at university. She was the first member of the family to travel abroad, going to work as an au pair in France after graduating from school. At the age of eighteen she hitchhiked from France to Italy and back to Ireland, a journey of exceptional daring for a child of middle-class Ireland. My mother was her family's rebel. She teamed up with a 'radical', though not by today's standards, group of students and dated a 'notorious' communist, a rare species in Cork, 'Red' Mick O'Leary, who later went on to become Deputy Prime Minister of Ireland and signed the Sunningdale Agreement to create the first power-sharing government in Northern Ireland.

Largely her life then seemed to involve dancing to American rock and roll and walking barefoot through Cork in solidarity with the oppressed masses of the world, reading the work of people like Jack Kerouac and Allen Ginsberg and ambushing with eggs and flour the stuffy students of the Medical Department when they paraded through town. In those days the medical establishment was fiercely reactionary, dominated by conservative Catholics and paranoid about state intrusion into its private demesne. My mother and her friends were the Beats of Cork, though not likely to bring the stuffy Republic crashing to its knees.

Some strange characters floated through our home. Among the more exotic visitors in the late 1960s was a leader of the IRA. This was before the revival of the Troubles. The man was a dour character who was steering the movement away from nationalism towards Marxism. The nationalists despised him and soon afterwards the movement split. There was murderous feuding and our guest was, for a period, avoiding the bullets of his former comrades. I remember only a long night of tea drinking with the IRA boss droning on, his political lecture delivered half in Irish, half in English. A remark of my father's has stayed with me from that night. 'Jesus, that fellow could bore the British out of Ireland,' he said.

My father knew many different politicians but he was never a party political person. Instead great causes appealed to him, so he would turn out to act in a play about apartheid in South Africa, or the murder of Patrice Lumumba in the Congo. At different times he could be a romantic nationalist, a socialist visionary, a worshipper of Parnell and Collins, and sometimes all of these things at once.

~

In the summer of 1968 we went to London. My father had a part in the Abbey Company's production of the George Fitzmaurice play *The Dandy Dolls* at the Royal Court in Sloane Square. The play and my father's performance in particular were well received. Those are among the happiest days of my childhood memory.

We all travelled over by boat, arriving at night into a city that seemed on fire with light and roaring with noise. This was the first return to the city in which I'd been born and my parents seemed excited and happy. We stayed in a guesthouse on Ebury Street in Pimlico. There was no end of novelties. We had orange juice and bacon for breakfast, travelled on red buses and on the Tube, motored down the Thames on a riverboat and ate takeaway curries at night. A theatre critic over from Dublin asked me one day: 'Do you know at all what a great man your father is?' I told him I did. I was passionately proud of him. My father wasn't drinking and seemed genuinely happy. At night he took me for short walks, my hand in his, guiding me through the night.

We had good days, my father and I. They are so precious to me now that I remember the smallest details. On my birthday in January 1971, in Dublin, he took me into town on the bus. The Christmas lights were still up, reflected on the dark Liffey and in the pools of rain along O'Connell Street. He held my hand as we walked down into Henry Street, past the hawkers back from their Christmas break, flogging off the last of the tinsel and crackers, shouting 'apples, bananas and oranges', and every so often I would notice someone recognising my father. Sometimes they came up and asked for his autograph. Other times they whispered to the person they were with: 'It's your man off the telly. Your man the actor.'

By this time Éamonn was a public figure. He was always kind to the people who asked him to sign something or who wanted to have a moment of his time. I would stand there, holding his hand, while he listened to them praising his performance in some play or other, or sharing some anecdote from their own lives.

But on the day of my birthday nobody stopped us. We were *unstoppable*! My father had been sober for a while now, and we strode through the city with confidence. We went to a café behind the Moore Street market. 'You can have anything you like,' my father said. Double burger and chips followed by doughnuts it was, then. Then we went to see the great film of the moment, *Waterloo*, starring Rod Steiger. I cheered when the Emperor returned from Elba and was re-united with his army. At the end of the film I wept at Napoleon's defeat and was comforted by my father. 'Able was I ere I saw Elba,' he said. 'That's the same sentence even if you spell it backwards.'

We travelled home across the bridge over the Grand Canal and into Harold's Cross where the road divided for Terenure and Kimmage. On the bus home I pressed close to him and he put his arm around me and told me jokes.

My memory is hungry for the happy moments. I realise now that I have hoarded them over the years. They are my version of the family silver. I remember a night around Christmas time when the car became trapped in a bog on the way to my father's home place in Listowel. There was a heavy mist. But I wasn't fearful. My mother was calm at the wheel. My father kept talking to keep our spirits up.

By the time we got there the lights were out in my grand-mother's house on Church Street. I staggered sleepily upstairs to bed in the footsteps of my parents. When I woke early and looked outside the street was glistening with frost and I saw the first donkeys and carts rattle past, laden with milk cans on their way to the creamery.

CHAPTER THREE

The Kingdom

*Kerry, as we intimated, possesses pre-eminently, one dis-
tinction for which it has long been famous, the ardour
with which its natives acquire and communicate knowledge. It is by no means rare to find among the humblest
of the peasantry, who have no prospect of existing except
by daily labour, men who can converse fluently in Latin
and have a good knowledge of Greek.*

From *Listowel and its Vicinity* (1973)
by FATHER J. ANTHONY GAUGHAN

My father's country begins on the shores of the River Shannon.
The river is wide here where it meets the Atlantic and the
currents twist and race as fresh water, from the distant mountains, washes into the ocean. On one shore there are the hills
of Clare, on the other the flatlands of North Kerry. Kerry and
Clare are separated only by a few miles of water. But they are
immeasurably different. The Clare people – my wife's people
– are quiet, modest and watchful, they wait before sharing
their opinions. To me there is something stolid, almost puritan
about them, born of generations of tough living on small, flinty
farms.

On the other side of the river, my father's side, are people who call their county 'The Kingdom' and regard it as just that: not a collection of townlands and villages, mountains and rivers, but a place set apart from the rest of Ireland, by virtue of its beauty and its characters – writers, politicians, footballers and dreamers. Football and politics are the twin religions here. In his youth my father was a good footballer. He played for Listowel in fierce matches against teams from neighbouring villages.

There is a photograph of my father, taken when he would have been around seventeen, playing for Listowel. He is standing in the middle of the group, but I recognise the expression in his eyes. He is with them, but he is far away, already thinking of elsewhere. Soon after the photograph was taken he left Listowel to find his dream in Dublin. 'He just upped and went,' an aunt remembered.

But the villages of childhood rang in his memory. Names shaped by Irish words, names such as Moyvane, Duagh, Lisselton, Knocknagoshel, Asdee, Finuge, Ballylongford, Cnoc an Oir, the mountain of gold where Finn McCool fought the King of the World. The Norsemen ravaged here, and the Normans after them, followed in time by the armies of Elizabeth and Cromwell, and later still the Black and Tans. A country of ruined castles and crumbling abbeys, all the history of conquest and dispossession poking out from beneath thickets of brambles.

When my father spoke of Kerry there was always a tenderness in his voice, a caressing of the names which took him back to a world before the city. The city was the only place to be if you wanted to be an actor. But my father was always a countryman, never truly at ease with the noise and pace of Dublin.

As a child I would sense the beginning of that magical country through the sweet smell of burning turf, watching from the car window the smoke curling from the chimneys of isolated cottages; the ricks of freshly dug peat stacked near the roadside, or standing like the cairns of some lost civilisation across the acres of bogland; the black surface of the bog, crisscrossed with pathways made by generations of turf diggers, interspersed with clumps of snipe grass, and sometimes, in the right season, white wisps of bog cotton.

For several miles after Tarbert it was a country of small horizons; I remember the distant shimmer of the Atlantic against low clouds and then the road pushing inland, the bog giving way to small farms as we climbed into the hills above the River Feale, travelling back to my father's beginnings. Coming down into the valley, I would see the river, and badger my father to take me fishing there. There were deep pools upriver, he said, where if you fell in you would never be seen again. But in those pools were the biggest salmon. Once I followed him with siblings and cousins up the path by the river, across the ditches, and along the edge of Gurtenard Wood. This landscape had been a place of escape for him as a child. He had wandered there alone, reciting aloud the poems of Wordsworth and Shelley, already planning a life on the stage, burning with belief.

There was a place where the trees leaned over the water and a small, sandy beach extended almost to the middle of the river. This was one of the salmon pools, he said, and my heart thrilled. We fished with a line, a tiny hook and a worm I'd rooted out from the bottom of a ditch. How long passed without a bite that afternoon? It might have been one hour, two hours, more. I didn't mind at all. I loved the sight of him there, happy in a place he loved, with the river dreaming its way past us. And then there was a bite. A flicker on the line and my father became alert, slowly moving to the edge of the water. 'Sssh,' he said. Then whispering, 'We have one.'

He tugged hard and brought it in. It was a brown trout, small, the brackish colour of the river. When it was directly beneath us, twisting at the end of the line, my father said, 'Watch this' and put his finger under the white stomach of the fish. I swear that after a few moments of him stroking it stopped its frantic movement, and sat suspended between his hand and the surface of the water. I remember feeling so proud of him then, my father, the least practical of men, metamorphosed into a skilled hunter on the river. We cooked it later in my grandmother's kitchen, sizzling in butter, tiny now that the head and tail had been removed.

Before a trip to Kerry he was excited, like a child. Coming into town he would point out the Carnegie Library, where he dreamed over books, and St Michael's College, where his genius for language won him first prize in Greek in the national examinations; the cemetery where our people were buried, and the police barracks where the Royal Irish Constabulary mutinied against the British in 1921.

My grandmother's people farmed at a place called Lisselton, a few miles away in the green valley between Listowel and the Atlantic Ocean. To get there you drove down a small brambly lane and into a wide whitewashed farmyard. This was in the time before Irish farms were mechanised, and I milked cows by hand and saw the curd churned into butter. My instructor was one of the gentlest men you could hope to meet, an old IRA man, my grand-uncle, Eddie Purtill.

After the day's work had been done cards would be played in the kitchen, and then stories would be told. There was no television; the magic box hadn't yet colonised the homes of much of rural Ireland. It was a large and airy room and life congregated around the big hearth where food was cooked and clothes dried. My father told stories too. I asked him to tell me those I had heard a thousand times before. 'Tell me about the Knight of Kerry's castle, Da.' And he would. They were true stories and made-up stories; stories he had heard from his own father or the men and women who'd told their legends of ghosts and old battles around the firesides of his youth. He could keep an audience spellbound, whether they were farm labourers or the Dublin intelligentsia.

Kerry was my father's inspiration, a country of magic. But I could tell he was haunted by it too. It was the place where he had known uncomplicated happiness but it was also the source of much of his pain.

~

Éamonn was born there in 1925; his parents, Bill Keane and Hanna Purtill, had married in 1923, the same year the Irish Civil War reached its terrible apogee. The country of his birth was devastated by war. His mother had fought with the IRA against the British and been a marked woman. She smuggled guns and communications. Her brother Mick led the IRA Flying Column in North Kerry. A Black and Tan named Darcy called the beautiful farmer's daughter 'the maid of the mountains'. When she refused to go walking with him he gave her twenty-four hours to leave town. Hanna laid low but refused to leave Listowel.

In the civil war that followed the British withdrawal, my father's people took Michael Collins's side. They were tired of war and believed the Treaty he signed with the British was the stepping stone to freedom that Collins promised. Hanna worshipped Collins. When he was shot by his former IRA comrades she wept inconsolably. Years after, when the IRA began attacking meetings of Collins's supporters, she joined an outfit called the Army Comrades Association, better known as the Blueshirts.

Depending on who you talk to the Blueshirts were a legitimate self-defence organisation forced into being by IRA intimidation, or a quasi-fascist legion imitating the Blackshirts of Italy and the Brownshirts of Germany. I believe the truth is somewhere in between. The movement disintegrated after their leader, a pompous buffoon called General Eoin O'Duffy, led a brigade off to Spain to fight for Franco in the Civil War.

In Kerry a general warning was sent out that anybody seen in the Blueshirt uniform would be attacked. Hanna was told the IRA would rip the shirt off her back. So she put on her blue shirt and walked up Church Street staring into the faces of the IRA supporters. Nobody dared attack her.

I called my father's mother Granny Kerry. She would meet us at the door like a proud queen, with her neighbours looking on. She had one son a famous playwright, another a famous actor, another studying to be a teacher in Dublin, a daughter a nun in Cahirciveen, and other sons and daughters all taken care of, married or working. There were no idle Keanes, which in that time and place was something to be said.

Hello, Granny Kerry, it's lovely to see you. She would embrace me at the door to the house on Church Street. *Wisha, child, 'tis lovely to see yourself.* She was still a handsome woman. Her hair was dark and her skin sallow. Like a Spaniard. Her family name was Purtill. *It used to be Purtillo*, my father said – his Spanish connection. In her youth she had been an aspiring actress, before becoming a guerrilla fighter, and then mother of the Keanes.

Her house smelled different to a city house. You could start at the door where Joan Carroll – modest, quiet Joan who gave me money for sweets – rented a room from my grandmother. Joan ran a hairdressing salon from the room and the scent of her shampoos and lotions overflowed into the hall, sweeter than I'd ever smelled in my life. There was a door with a glass window through which you could see the matrons of Listowel being primped and clipped. On the wall were photographs of beehive hairdos and perms.

The heart of the house was the parlour, a small room with

-a large open fireplace at its centre. Dominating the fireplace was a big steel range into which turf was poured at frequent intervals. My grandmother cooked on this range and dried clothes beside it. It filled the room with the musk of the peatlands. When the window was open to the back yard, other smells blew in and mingled: the smell of meadow and river, of hedgerows and brackish water, of donkey droppings in the lane between the house and the Major's Field.

It was a country house. The long narrow stairs, three storeys high, creaked and sagged as you climbed up to bed, the voices of the adults growing fainter as you turned one corner, and then another, until you were left with the sound of your own footsteps and the groan of the floorboards.

Across the landing from where I slept was a locked door. It was shut tight with a length of wire from a coat hanger. Behind it lay the stairs to the attic, where Uncle Dan used to live. Dan was a bachelor, my grandfather's brother. My father said: 'Your uncle Dan used to talk to the crows. They could understand him, I swear. They would come in through the eaves into the attic and sit on the edge of the bed and Dan would be talking away to them.'

In Dan's attic there were wisps of cobweb hanging from the rafters and the only light was that from a paraffin lamp, throwing shadows around the shoulders of my father and his brothers as they listened to Dan's stories. He sat on the bed, an uncle remembered, 'with his cap askew and his collar undone and his lips ringed with the brown stain of porter'.

My father and his brothers would sit in the attic and listen to his stories for hours. But Dan could not easily communicate with adults, except at the cattle fairs where he made a few pounds acting as middle man between the sellers and buyers. It was said that Dan was a good man to make a deal. But he never owned a cow himself. Apart from fair days his one excursion was to Mass. Dan didn't care too much for appearances. On Sundays he would march to the top of the church and find the seat where the most pious matrons of the town were ensconced. Dan would force them to squeeze in and accommodate him. There would be furious muttering. But Dan ignored it all. If the sermon displeased him he would chatter away to himself, conducting a personal dialogue on the finer points of theology. Eventually the parish priest could stand no more and rounded on him, screaming:

'Dan Keane if you don't shut up I'll turn you into a goat and put two horns on you.'

To which Dan replied: 'And by God if you do I'll fuckin' puck you.'

Now that Dan was dead and gone the door to his attic room was locked.

What's up there now, Granny Kerry?

Yerrah, only old stuff, boy. And dust. A power of dust.

But I did not believe it. My child's imagination told me that Dan was still there, surrounded by his crows, a muttering old storyteller whose feet I could hear creaking across the floorboards at midnight. I wanted so badly to open that door. It would not have taken much. A few twists on the wire and I'd be through. But my courage failed me every time. Suppose Dan really was there? Hidden away by the family because he had gone mad. Suppose the crows were there protecting his lair, waiting to peck the eyes out of any intruder. There were safer places to go adventuring.

Out the back was a big turf shed. My grandmother would ask: 'Will you go out and bring in a bucket of turf, boy?' Granny Kerry knew I loved the big shed. The dried turf smelled of dead forests, of Ireland before history. My father said the Tuath de Dannan, the mythical people said to have been supplanted by the Celts, had buried great treasures in the bog, and that 'You never know what you might find in the turf.' I looked for jewels or a golden crown in the dried-out turf. I pulled away the sods and smashed them open. I never found anything there though, except once a sixpenny bit on the floor. I suspect my father put it there. Down below the turf was a cobbled floor that must have been centuries old. Under that, my father swore, lay a great fortune.

~

Our holidays in Kerry always seemed to begin with laughter. But as I got older I sensed the tension between my father and grandmother. Mostly the conversation between them seemed to revolve around horse racing.

'What do you think of Glencaraig Lady at Cheltenham?'

'Yerrah? I'm not so sure about that one.'

They would sit at the table next to the range, the newspapers spread out around them. It was the time they seemed most at ease with each other. But he could not stay long with her before something she said, some change of tone or inference would set his nerves twitching. And then he would be gone. Out the door and up the road to Gurtenard Wood or down to the fields by the river, walking his anger away.

Hanna would look up from her paper and shake her head: 'What did I say wrong?' Usually it had something to do with her praising another member of the family, or some words my father would interpret as criticism. And after that there would be no more ease in the kitchen, no swapping of tips for the horses, only waiting for the next offending word.

I believe the source of the friction between them was love. She loved him. But in his eyes it could never be enough. He craved her approval, and anything less than total and constant affirmation sent him into despair.

As a child my father had been bright and precocious. But somewhere in childhood there was a sundering between him and his mother. I think it happened slowly. As more children arrived Hanna was forced to divide her attention. My father responded by throwing tantrums. He became the troublesome one; he gave cheek and stayed out late, but ended up alienating his mother.

Enter the figure of Juleanne Keane, the spinster sister of my grandfather. She lived with the family and acted as my father's champion. When he was chastised by his mother, Juleanne would step in to shield him. In her eyes Éamonn was faultless. The violent scenes he staged to attract the attention of his mother were rewarded by Juleanne with smothering kisses, trips to the sweet shop, the protecting embrace of her shawl.

But though she tried, I do not believe Juleanne could replace my grandmother. By the time he left home my father was already an angry young man. He was angry with the Church, with the bitter politics of the time, and angry with his mother. He had also started to drink. He found that it gave him courage and took away his anguish.

∽

Hanna Purtill had sad eyes. Even at six or seven I could see that. Her smile was like my father's smile: generous, warm, but always flushed through with something melancholy.

On her bad days my grandmother would stay in bed, and we would be warned to leave her in peace. *She gets the bad nerves sometimes.* That was how some uncle or cousin explained it. In Ireland people who got bad nerves often took to the bed. Trays of food would come and go, be picked at and sent back downstairs. Often the nerves would be explained as an illness. A trapped nerve. A bad stomach. A stiff knee. A bad back. But everybody knew what it really was: something that descended on the mind. Like coastal fog it could sit for days.

Granny Kerry was silent when she took to the bed. But light or dark she was always kind to me. I went into the room once to give her the paper and she motioned to me to come closer. She put her two arms out to hold me. Close to her, tighter than she'd ever held me. When I stood back up I saw she was crying. I went out of the room and found my mother.

'What's wrong with Granny Kerry?'

'She feels sad. It's not her fault.'

'Oh.'

When the nerves struck an Irish house people talked in low voices. Children were told to go out and play and stay out. A doctor might come and sit with the patient, prescribe some tablets and shrug his shoulders or nod his head, sympathetically, as a family member showed him out of the house: *Time is the best cure, you know. Just give it time and she'll be grand again.*

And after a few days she would be up. I would come downstairs and Hanna would be in the small kitchen peeling spuds or marking the racing pages in the parlour. She would smile and put her hand on my head and tell me to sit down and eat my breakfast. And that would be the end of the nerves. I never knew what brought on the sad hours. I simply came to accept it as part of our family inheritance.

Now there are things I know that explain part of the sadness. Some of it, at least, had to do with the hard circumstances of life. My grandmother reared nine children on a country schoolteacher's paltry pay. For much of the time she lived under the same roof as her parents- and brother- and sister-in-law. It was a house without retreat or space for the young mother in a country where women were told that suffering was their noble duty.

I did not know my grandfather, Bill Keane. He died when I was a baby. My mother remembers: 'He used to sit you on his knee when you were a baby and tell stories to you. By that time he was sick with throat cancer. Very sick. And he could only really swallow things that were very soft. He used to drink ice cream that had melted but it was still agony for him. He was a lovely man.'

Everybody I ask says the same thing. *A lovely man.* Bill taught at Clounmacon school, seven miles outside Listowel. He walked there and back every day of his teaching life. A few years ago I met two elderly nuns who remembered him. One of them said: 'He was a gentle teacher. You know, in those days some of them could be wicked blackguards. They beat the children something terrible. But your grandfather wasn't like that. He loved teaching and he loved words. The way he could get across those words of great writers to you was something magical. He had a great way of talking.'

I formed a picture in my mind of Bill Keane in that country classroom, before him the children of the surrounding farms, many of them boys who would soon leave to plant their father's fields or to work as labourers on other farms, barefoot children of a pre-industrial Ireland held in thrall by the teacher's stories.

Next to the kitchen in Church Street he kept a small library. My father and Uncle John B were introduced to the great writers like Hardy and Dickens through that little cupboard. The Keane house also had a name as a place where visiting actors were sure of a welcome. At that time theatrical companies still toured Ireland bringing the works of Shakespeare to the small towns and villages. The great Anew McMaster came and recited verse in the small parlour and inspired my father to become an actor. Words filled that house.

But my grandfather Bill was not what you would call a practical man. The best description I have of him comes from a poem written by my uncle, John B.

When he spoke gustily and sincerely
Spittle fastened
Not merely upon close lapel
But nearly blinded
Those who had not hastened
To remove pell-mell.
He was inviolate.
Clung to old stoic principle,
And he dismissed his weaknesses
As folly.
His sinning was inchoate;
Drank ill-advisedly.

Bill would stop for a drink on his way home from school in the houses of people who knew and loved him (*Yerrah, Bill, come in for the one*). He stopped at crossroads where he met the local characters (*I can only stop a few minutes*). At Alla Sheehy's pub next door (*I must be off now in the name of God. Well, just the last one so*).

My grandfather worked through to his retirement. He cared for his family and every one of them remembered him with love. He was a thinker but also a dreamer. Sometimes he could spend money on drink that Hanna depended on to pay bills and provide for the children. It was not a permanent crisis but it added to the pressure on my grandmother.

He clashed with the Catholic priest who was the ultimate manager of Clounmacon school. Part of my Uncle John's later aversion to organised religion sprang from what he felt was the unforgiving attitude of the Church towards his father. He told me once of how the priest had arrived at the house and gone upstairs to where my grandfather was lying sick in bed and harangued him to get up and go back to work.

Bill Keane did get revenge of sorts, or at least he proved he was not cowed by the Church imperial. Once when seeing a particularly unpleasant priest – a man with a reputation for brutality in the classroom – on the main street, Bill walked past without doffing his cap, the customary greeting. As John B's biographer describes it:

'The priest rounded on him. "Don't you know to salute a priest when you see one?"'

To which my grandfather replied: '*When* I see one.'

My uncle wrote a play about his father. It may have been the bravest thing he ever wrote. In those days autobiographical drama was rare in Ireland, the fear of bringing shame on a family in such a small community was too great. In *The Crazy Wall* John B describes a man attempting to build a wall in his garden. But the builder, clearly modelled on his father, is not a practical man. The wall twists and turns. It is badly made and eventually crumbles. John B later told an interviewer: 'When things were not going his way, my father built a symbolic wall around himself, to shut out the harsh realities of the world; he once dreamed he was going to take off around Ireland, but it came to nothing. He wanted to write the great book, and that, too, became a futile exercise.'

The relationship between my grandparents went through difficult times. Hanna must have suffered when her husband retreated into himself and when the bills came and there was no money to pay them. But when they walked out together, well into old age, those who saw them remember a couple in love, strolling arm in arm along Church Street and out towards the country lanes. They were alert to the higher values – love, compassion, the beauty of words – but hemmed in by the Free State and its poverty, the puritanical hectoring of the Church, the leeching bitterness of the Civil War and the exceptional demands of rearing many children in a small place. When I visualise my paternal grandparents I imagine two sensitive people, people of restrained nobility. But somewhere in that large family with its many pressures I believe my father became lost.

~

I cannot understand my grandparents, or my father, without looking at the country in which they lived. My father grew up in a state ruled over by former guerrilla fighters, men who had fought the British and then fought each other. In war photographs they are dressed in peak caps and trench coats, country boys with expressions that are half eager, half desperate, men with a price on their heads, who would be shot out of hand if captured, wild rebels in the mountains. But in my father's country they were transformed. Éamonn de Valera had helped spark the Civil War by rejecting the Treaty with the British and providing political leadership for the IRA; his successor, Seán Lemass, was a man who had shot dead an unarmed British agent at point-blank range. But now they wore grey suits and dark hats; their rebel years behind them, they said their prayers and listened carefully to the raging whispers of the bishops.

When I was younger I judged them harshly, our spent revolutionaries. But after seeing war myself, especially the self-murdering insanity of civil war, I see them in a different light. I think they were tired men, trying as best they could to create a country after nearly a decade of conflict, battered by the economic depression that followed the Wall Street Crash, and then allowing themselves to be dragged into an economic war with Britain which they could not win. In the original shooting war against the British they had been hunted like wild animals; they had killed and been killed; in the Civil War men who had fought together, in some cases members of the same family, turned their guns on each other. The Civil War overshadowed everything in my father's country. How could it not: that

44

memory of ambush, executions, torture? It may be fanciful to believe, but I think some of them were more than tired; they were in a state of lingering shock, frightened by what they had discovered in themselves during those terrible years of war.

My father said: 'We hated each other more than we ever hated the British.' I don't know how true that was. But he did grow up listening to stories of atrocity: men shot dead as they surrendered, others tied to landmines and blown to pieces. By the time my father was politically aware, he would have known that two parties dominated the landscape: there was Cumann na nGaedheal, the party of Collins's people, and Fianna Fáil, the party of de Valera. They barracked each other with bitter words. 'Murderers'. 'Free State traitors'. 'IRA assassins'. The toxic rasp of hatred went on and on in the lives of the people. They fought about it at political meetings, football matches, anywhere crowds gathered.

Yet both parties were profoundly similar. They were deeply conservative, both bended the knee to the Catholic Church and both would, in time, use fierce repression to protect the new Irish state from would-be revolutionaries. More than anything our new state suffered from a chronic failure of imagination. Having achieved freedom, our leaders were too tired or too blinkered – or a combination of both – to do much more than manage the shop. Innovation and inspiration were decades away.

Though they were devout supporters of Collins, the Keanes were independent-minded enough to recognise the absurdity of the political situation. During one particularly bitter election campaign my Uncle John B and his friends decided to put up a mock candidate who went by the name of Tom Doodle. The idea was to inject laughter and reduce the bitterness of the hustings. Doodle was the pseudonym given to a local labourer. His slogan, depicted on posters all over the town, was: 'Vote the Noodle and Give the Whole Caboodle To Doodle.'

John B had organised a brass brand and a large crowd to accompany the candidate to his election meeting. He travelled to the square standing on the back of a donkey-drawn cart. It was a tumultuous affair. In a speech that satirised the clientelist, promise-all politics of the time, Doodle declared his fundamental principle: 'Every man should have more than the next.'

~

Some time in the 1940s, not long before he left the town, my father was wandering around Listowel square, thinking and dreaming. It happened that there was a mission under way in the Catholic Church. The visiting Redemptorists were well known peddlers of hellfire and damnation and would send scouts into the square to round up any locals who malingered outside the church. When one of the priests approached my father, warning him to get into the church fast or face an eternity roaring in the flames, Éamonn responded with a remark that would earn him the status of local legend.

'My good man,' he said to the raging priest 'your fulminations have the same effect on me as does the fart of a blackbird on the water levels of the Grand Coulee dam.'

With that he said goodnight and walked away. It was typically opaque, a very 'Éamonn' response.

My father's country was a place of paradox. It was full of poetry and music, there was laughter and satire, but also repression and darkness. For every story told there were a hundred suppressed. There was magic there, but madness too.

Éamonn nurtured a dislike of the clergy all of his life. There were individual priests and nuns whom he liked but he loathed the organised Church. These gentlemen lived in fine palaces and generally behaved with all the humility and decorum you would expect of imperial pro-consuls. In 1937 de Valera

framed and succeeded in having adopted a new Irish constitution. For the first time in Irish history the pre-eminent
position of the Catholic Church 'as the guardian of the faith
professed by the great majority of the citizens' was guaranteed
by law. This meant the Catholic hierarchy could exert influence on everything from football matches (it succeeded in
banning a visit by a team from communist Yugoslavia) to the
welfare of mothers and children (it stopped a state-sponsored
scheme to provide free healthcare to new mothers and babies
on the grounds that it was socialist). In my father's home town
the parish priest shut the gates of the local church against the
coffin of an unmarried girl who had died after giving birth.

There were more immediate personal issues at play too. At
school my father and uncle witnessed and experienced terrible
brutality. The local secondary school was run by priests, among
them a notorious brute, Father Davy O'Connor. Under any
normal state of affairs he would have been jailed but was instead
treated with fawning respect by the cowed townspeople. It says
much for the place that even a Catholic priest, writing in the
still conservative early 1970s, described St Michael's College
as a place with 'an unenviable reputation for strict discipline'.

When my father remembered his worst story of Davy
O'Connor his mouth tightened. He carried the shame of it like
a hump on his back. I heard it, how many times? It was as
if by telling he might talk away the pain. But he could not.
Even in his last years, the memory of what happened in that
classroom burned within him. O'Connor screamed and beat;
he used his fists and his boots and a leather strap. My father
said that one of his favourite punishments was to take a boy
and place his head on the windowsill, facing out towards the
fields. He would then lower the window so that the boy's head
was jammed outside. With his victim trapped O'Connor would
then pull the boy's trousers down and thrash him on the
backside.

So a boy like Éamonn would stand there facing the trees, hearing the noise of birds and the rush of the river only a field away, and be trapped as the leather slashed at his body, the class trapped too by the shame of it, the sheer terror that any wrong move or word could lead them to the same place.

John B told of how O'Connor had once asked boys during English class to recite any poems they knew. My uncle was already writing his own poems, and he stood and recited from memory a poem called 'The Street':

> *I love the flags that pave the walk*
> *I love the mud between*
> *The funny figures drawn in chalk.*

When he had finished Father O'Connor asked him who had written the poem. John B replied that it was his own work. The priest immediately lashed out, knocking him to the floor. Another boy who tried to intervene was also knocked over. O'Connor proceeded to punch and kick my uncle before throwing him out of the class. On that day John B vowed he would be a writer and that no man would shut him up again.

Such incidents were not anachronistic. They reflected the dominant reality of the time. My father and my uncle were comparatively fortunate. They were not inmates of one of the Church-run industrial schools where children were not only beaten but raped as well.

It was in matters of sex that the Church really got to work and screwed up the minds of several generations. The physical and mental damage inflicted on children in the borstals has been well publicised. But the rest of the population was subjected to perverted brainwashing. Contemplate this extract from a booklet produced by the Catholic Truth Society, propagandists for the hierarchy:

... the pleasure of sex is secondary, a means to an end and to make it an end in itself, or deliberately do this is a mortal sin ... Let a tiger once taste blood and it becomes mad for more ... the poor victim is swept off his feet by passion, and decides, for the time being at any rate that nothing matters except this violent spasm of pleasure ... Happier a thousand times is the beggar shivering in his rags at the street corner if his heart be pure, than the millionaire rolling by in his car if he be impure ... the boy and girl have to avoid whatever of its very nature is morally certain to excite sexual pleasure. That is why they are warned about late hours; about prolonged signs of their God-given affection which cheapen so easily, about wandering off alone to certain places where they are morally certain to succumb to temptation.

The writer, in all likelihood a priest, went on to chastise girls who wore revealing clothing:

So girls of all sorts, the short and the stocky, the fat and the scraggy, the pigeon-chested and the knock-kneed, insist on exposing their regrettable physical misfortunes to the ironic gaze of the easily amused world around them ...

His final blow is directed at morally suspect mothers. It is profoundly revealing of that twisted sensibility which governed the moral order in Ireland:

How any mother can allow her small daughter to romp and play with her brothers without knickers on is incomprehensible and quite disgraceful.

My father never talked about sex. That was not unusual for his Irish generation. Sex was the deed of darkness. But Éamonn was a romantic. He dreamed of loving the Protestant parson's daughter. He went into the woods and wrote poems to her. But he kept these to himself. In Listowel, as in the rest of Ireland, love was something schoolboys sniggered about.

And God help the boy whom Father Davy O'Connor or one of his type found walking with a girl. These princes of the Church roamed the lanes with blackthorn sticks in hand ready to beat any would-be lovers. I think of them when I hear the snivelling apologists for our Catholic past. *Sure it wasn't that bad at all.*

It was only a few years ago that I learned my father had suffered from a bad stammer when he was a boy. Fear had been the cause. Fear of Father Davy O'Connor. For my father who dreamed of being an actor the stammer might have been an impossible hurdle. But through force of will he overcame it. On his own in the woods or upstairs in Church Street he read the poems of Keats and Shelley over and over, training his voice until it was strong enough to leave the town and face the harsh judges of the Abbey School of Acting in Dublin. And when they heard him and accepted him it must have seemed to Éamonn that he could conquer the world.

When he came back to Listowel as an adult, my father was one of Ireland's most successful actors. Walking down the main street with him, hand in hand, could take an hour or more. People wanted to stop and talk with him. Some of them were tourists who recognised him from television or the stage. But mostly the people we chatted with were locals. They called him 'The Joker' or 'Ned', two nicknames from his childhood. For all the tension that existed between him and his mother, he felt proud on those streets and I remember most of all the firm, confident grip of his hand. In those days he was going places.

CHAPTER FOUR

Tippler

The next planet was inhabited by a tippler. This was a very short visit but it plunged the little prince into deep dejection.

'What are you doing there?' he said to the tippler, whom he found settled down in silence before a collection of empty bottles and also a collection of full bottles.

'I am drinking,' replied the tippler, with a lugubrious air.

'Why are you drinking?' demanded the little prince.

'So that I may forget,' replied the tippler.

'Forget what?' inquired the little prince, who already was sorry for him.

'Forget that I am ashamed,' the tippler confessed, hanging his head.

'Ashamed of what?' insisted the little prince, who wanted to help him.

'Ashamed of drinking!'

The tippler brought his speech to an end, and shut himself up in an impregnable silence. And the little prince went away, puzzled.

'The grown ups are certainly very, very odd,' he said to himself, as he continued on his journey.

The Little Prince, ANTOINE DE SAINT-EXUPERY

One day we were crossing the bridge over the River Feale. My father stopped in the middle. 'Do you see that there?' he said.

He pointed to a spot directly in the middle of the bridge.

'That is where a distant relative of yours fell into the river. Do you know how it happened?'

I shook my head.

'He was drunk and he got up and sat there and he thought he was riding the winner in the Grand National. And you know what happened then?'

'No, I don't,' I said.

'He fell off into the river. That's what drink does to us.'

We laughed together.

~

I had my first drink on the way home from the creamery. Willie Purtill sat beside me on the cart, the reins of the donkey wrapped loosely around his hands, and behind us the empty milk churns rattled as we plodded home towards the Purtill farm. I was a city child and entranced by that world of haystacks, milking parlours, trips to the creamery and all the pungent scents of the countryside.

On this day, coming back from the crossroads, we stopped at a thatched pub. Willie pulled on the reins and brought the donkey to a stop. He went in and emerged a short while later with some lemonade and 'porter', a dark brew in a tin mug. (Porter was made by Arthur Guinness & Son.)

I wanted to try the black beer. Given what alcohol was doing to my childhood it might seem a strange request. But the impulse had nothing to do with logic. I was only aware of this intense curiosity and of a strange excitement. *Give me a try of it, Willie. Go on. Give me one try of it.*

Willie Purtill was my third cousin. He was a big, good-hearted farmer's son. After a lot of pestering he relented. I drank the dark liquid slowly. It tasted bitter and I grimaced. Willie took the drink back and laughed. I didn't like the taste, but I would later grow to love the feel of pubs and the smell of them – the peat from the fire, the tobacco, the faintly sweet aroma from the beer that had been spilled on the counter and floor and which had worked its way into the permanent odour of these places.

~

Next door to my grandmother's house on Church Street in Listowel was Alla Sheehy's pub. Alla was bald and plump and kind, a laughing man who gave me free lemonade and exchanged tips for the horses with my grandmother. I loved being in that pub with its rows and rows of beer and spirit bottles, and the farmers on fair day bunched up together at the counter, their voices filled with argument and laughter. There were beers like Time, Phoenix, Double Diamond, all now extinct, and the ubiquitous Guinness. Above the bar was a stuffed fox about to devour a stuffed pheasant, the two of them suspended forever in the moment of surprise.

I had my next drink when I was about eight years old. It was Halloween and my mother had cooked a turkey. There was a big flagon of cider on the table. I think my mother may have reckoned that cider would be less damaging to my father than beer or whiskey. On this Halloween night my mother lit a fire. The shadow of flames flickered and danced on the walls. And reflected against the fire the liquid in the cider bottle took on a deep golden colour. My parents were in the kitchen talking. I poured a small measure from the flagon. I sipped at first. It tasted sweet, delicious. I swallowed. The liquid hit my stomach and I felt warm. The warmth spread out from my stomach, along my arms and legs, up my neck and into my head.

I took the flagon by the neck. It was heavy and I struggled to raise it to my lips. One swallow. More of that lovely warmth. My feet left the ground. I walked on air. I felt so good, a feeling like laughter that went on and on. I never forgot the power of that first draught of cider. It felt as if a warm rainbow had exploded in my head. It took me away from the present, and that was the best feeling in the world. I didn't drink again for years after that night with the cider. But my body had registered the magic of booze. In time I would return to alcohol and nothing I saw as a child would be powerful enough to pull me away from it.

~

Another memory.

My father drinks too much that night. And he keeps drinking. Through days of remorse and promises, and nights, so many nights, of that voice filled with rage and pain. My father is being pulled further away from us. My twitching has got much worse. It begins with my eyes blinking quickly. I can't stop them. Then it becomes a tightening of the neck muscles. They tighten and loosen, tighten and loosen. I feel like a freak.

I have only one photograph of those days. It was taken on the day of my Holy Communion. I am standing in the garden of our house in Dublin and blinking into the sunlight. I am a small dark-haired boy in a navy blazer and white shorts. In my mind's eye I see him still, that strange little boy. He is always on the edge of crowds in the schoolyard, always thinking, always somewhere else, a dreamer like his grandfather and his father. In front of strangers he is quiet. He says 'please' and 'thank you' too often. 'Stop saying "thank you" all the time,' a woman tells him. 'It's very irritating.' Silly old cow. What does she know of his world? People who know the family remark to his mother on how well behaved he is. But it isn't good behaviour. He simply does not know how to behave as an ordinary child.

So if he is angry he does not show it. And if he is sad, if something happens that reduces him to tears, he goes upstairs and hides away to weep. The boy lives inside his head because it is by far the safest place he knows.

From there he makes all kinds of journeys; he reads the Ladybird Book of David Livingstone *and sees himself crossing the African plains. Africa will become the place of escape. The pictures show a genial old white man surrounded by smiling natives. The colours are so vivid! Outside on the grey slate roofs of Terenure rain is falling and the clouds brush the chimney pots. But in Africa the sun is shining and the sky spreads forever. He puts his hands over his eyes and imagines he is with Livingstone. The old man is kind to him. He tells the natives to carry the boy because his legs are tired. They cross mountains and rivers, and they reach the Great Falls together.* Moise e Tsunye. *He tries to say it but his mouth swallows the words. Then Livingstone vanishes into the spray and the boy is back in Dublin, promising himself that one day he will go there.*

He goes to the library in the school where his mother teaches and finds anything he can on Africa. There is a book of world history: Man's March through Time, *though it doesn't say much about the Africans, only the white explorers. He reads about Hannibal, the most famous African general, who crossed the Alps and challenged Rome.*

In another book Stanley is in the Congo and the natives are blacker than in any of the other books. There is also a book with a picture of Cecil Rhodes on a horse and the ground around him covered with diamonds. The boy in the Communion photograph dreams of being a hero. He wants to save people from fires, rescue them from drowning. He sees himself back in the days of the Irish revolution.

Danger is everywhere, but he always survives. Patrick Pearse becomes his hero. And Michael Collins too. They teach him in school that dying for Ireland was a glorious thing. He wants to die for Ireland. Gloriously like Cuchullain strapped to the stump of a tree, the hero light flashing above his head and he fighting back the armies of Queen Maeve. A man called Leo Maguire teaches the class singing. He has his own show on the radio where he says: 'If you must sing a song, sing an Irish song.' Mr Maguire has a deep, hoarse voice. The boy sings the 'Bold Fenian Men' and 'Roddy McCorley' and his favourite 'The Foggy Dew': 'Twas down the glen came marching men . . .

In all of these worlds he enters – the Africa of exploration, the Ireland of revolution – he is brave. There is no hint of weakness about him. There is nothing to be ashamed about. Nobody can mock him in these worlds.

Years later he reads a story by Frank O'Connor called 'The Ugly Duckling' and he is taken back to the world of childhood:

> Because of some inadequacy in themselves – poverty and physical weakness in men, poverty or ugliness in women – those with the gift for creation built for themselves a rich interior world; and when the inadequacy disappeared and the real world was spread before them with all its wealth and beauty, they could not give their whole heart to it.
>
> Uncertain of their choice, they wavered between goals; were lonely in crowds, dissatisfied amid noise and laughter, unhappy even with those they loved best.

~

I know now that in order to live with my fears and anxieties, I created a parallel world in which I was brave and unafraid.

(Many years later in different war zones I would enter a world where I would test my fear again and again.) But I also learned how to please, anticipating what the adults might say, or even think. I could read their faces, sense the changing of moods like one of those sensitive weather machines that detects the coming of a storm from thousands of miles away. I was not an honest child. I told people what I thought would please them. I found my comfort in being the 'best boy' in the eyes of adults. In the playground I was a coward. I ran from fights. On the rugby pitch at Terenure College I was useless, because I was afraid of the pushing, shoving, the boys who came at you with an aggression you could never hope to summon up.

~

My father fought to become well. At some point towards the end of the 1960s my father was admitted to hospital in Dublin for treatment for his alcoholism. He went to the main treatment centre for men with the 'good man's fault'. In his poem 'Dawn at St Patrick's' Derek Mahon, a former patient there, conveys the atmosphere:

> *One by one*
> *The first lights come on,*
> *Those that haven't been on all night.*
> *Christmas, the harshly festive, has come and gone.*
> *No snow, but the rain pours down*
> *In the first hour before dawn,*
> *Before daylight . . .*
> *Television, Russian fiction, snooker with the staff,*
> *A snifter of Lucozade, a paragraph*
> *Of Newsweek or the Daily Mail*
> *Are my daily routine*
> *During the festive season.*

> *They don't lock the razors here*
> *As in Bowditch Hall. We have remained upright –*
> *Though, to be frank, the Christmas dinner scene,*
> *With grown men in their festive gear,*
> *Was a sobering sight.*

I went to visit him. It was the first of many visits to many hospitals. They would go on for thirty more years, in one part of the country or another. The hospital was halfway between the Guinness brewery and Heuston railway station where we used to catch the train to visit my maternal grandmother in Cork. Éamonn didn't look sick. In fact he looked better than I remembered him being for a long time. In hospital he couldn't drink. He was sharing a big room with some other men and seemed to be popular with them.

My father could have charmed the Devil himself. His way was to start out very quiet and humble, and then dazzle people with a few stories or recitations. Before long the whole place would be talking about what a great character he was. In Ireland people love a good storyteller. Éamonn was a gifted mimic and would mock the more pompous consultants (the power of the Irish consultant class was matched only by its self-regard). But what I could not see then, and did not understand for decades, was that my father was trying to fight back; his hospitalisation was not a weakness, nor should it have been something to be ashamed of; it was a brave attempt to change.

In those days our national attitude to alcohol was extraordinarily perverse. There was hardly a family in the country that did not count an alcoholic somewhere among its members. The hospitals were crammed full of men, and women, suffering from alcohol-related illnesses. Recognising the crisis as far back as the mid-nineteenth century, the Catholic Church campaigned for the cause of temperance. Regular appeals were made for men to join the Pioneer Movement, a church group which promoted total abstinence from alcohol, and children in secondary school were urged to take the pledge not to drink.

Yet awareness of the problem did not extend to honest public discussion, or any campaign by the state to provide treatment for the alcoholics who were victims of our most pernicious national disease. Nor was there any state support for women who were the victims of physical or emotional violence. 'You made your bed now lie on it,' a priest told my mother once. Alcoholism belonged in the land of silence. If there was a drunk in the family they were all urged to shut up and get on with the suffering. Most families did. It was a nowhere land where nothing could be confronted, where a woman dare not leave because of social pressure, or the simple fact that she had no job and depended on the man for economic survival.

My mother was lucky in that she had a profession. And when she could take no more, when it seemed as if my father could not succeed in giving up alcohol, she decided to leave.

~

We left at the beginning of January 1972. We were moving south to the home of my maternal grandmother in Cork. The last Christmas was harrowing. My father drank heavily. I see a toppled Christmas tree, a broken chair, fish and chips scattered on the ground; I hear his voice raging downstairs alone, mad at everything. There were bitter, painful scenes. And afterwards there was regret and apologies and the promise of better times. But I no longer believed. I feared him then. I was angry with him. I wanted to run away. I did not want to say goodbye. I was so lost, so screwed up and scared, that more than anything else in the world I wanted peace.

How long does it take for a heart to break? Mine did not break instantly. It broke every day. Year after year. So that by the time I was old enough to understand that word – ALCOHOLIC – I took it as the definition of everything broken and hopeless. My hope departed incrementally. Year after year, slowly, surely, definitely, a little more went.

And how long does it take for the habits of a lifetime to form? My own: lurking anger, the habit of sadness, and that fear which goes on even now. All of my life I have been quietly afraid. I can still lie in bed, after my wife and children are asleep, and feel full of anxiety; this in a house full of ease and warmth. To this day the sound of a key turning in a door at night, feet shuffling on the street outside my window, can set my heart racing.

Now, I would give anything to know, to be able to talk with him about what he felt when he looked into my eyes then. What did he see looking back at him? Did he see the twitching eyes, the strange, strange child I had become? So many times I wanted to shout: 'In Jesus name why can't you stop?' But I was never bold enough for that.

For me the story of my father and I doesn't have 'sides'. There isn't his side of it or my side of it; a wrong or a right side; a good or a bad side. There is what I lived through and what I remember of him. I loved him every day. I was proud of him. But I was also scared of him. Can you understand that? To be all those things at once, the negative not cancelling the positive, but all of it so muddled up that I couldn't tell light from dark. I had no lamps, no compass, no maps, and there were no explanations. In those days I practised survival not analysis.

Da. That's what I called him. *Da.* It's a softer word than 'Dad' or 'Daddy' or 'Father'. *Da* lingers, a solitary syllable at the end of the world, a word to convey everything I felt about him in those days, a word full of tenderness and loss. I can't describe the impossible loneliness I felt at the moment of goodbye. Lucky for me he was asleep when I looked in and saw him. I mouthed the word 'Goodbye'.

CHAPTER FIVE

Shelter

> *. . . You had a lovely hand,*
> *Cursive, flourishing, exuberant, grateful, actual, generous.*
>   'Daddy Daddy', PAUL DURCAN

My father used to write to me regularly. He had beautiful handwriting. His script was neat and flowing. He wrote about the plays he was performing or the film parts that might be coming up, he asked about how I was getting on at school. The letters *d.v.* appeared a lot.

'What does that mean?' I asked my grandmother.

'It means *hopefully*,' she said.

Every fortnight he would send magazines along with a postal order for pocket money. The magazines were *Look and Learn* and *World of Wonder*. They were packed with articles about history and adventure. I have them to this day. Once I showed them to my son Daniel. He read them with intense curiosity, seeing them as I had all those years before. 'Gosh,' he said. 'He gave you a lot, didn't he?'

Usually I would see him at Christmas, Easter, the summer holidays. I waited for him in hope. You didn't always know if he would make the visit. He would want to, I know that now. But somewhere between his best intentions and the railway

61

station, alcohol might intervene. I would watch the crowds coming off the train, and search for his face, heart beating with excitement. If the crowd passed by without any sign of my father it could mean he was still sitting on the train which in turn meant he was probably drunk. Or it could mean that he hadn't made the journey.

If he was there, but drunk, I would panic. What if he met my school friends in town? They might see him stumble, or come over to say hello and hear him slur or smell the whiskey. I learned the power of shame. I knew people saw. I wanted to hide my father. I wanted to make him better. The last thing on earth I could do was accept him.

When he was sober we had happy times on his visits. They shone like the brightest diamonds. He would come to my grandmother's house for tea, laden with presents and stories. Once in Killarney he bought me fishing gear and we wandered across the fields to a quiet spot and lay on the grass for hours under the hot sun. I cannot remember what we talked about, but I do know that I wished those hours would last forever and that when it came time to say goodbye I experienced the fiercest grief. That was how the world was after separation. I had my moments with him but we were far from each other, my father and I.

~

Through all of these times my Cork grandmother's house was the port of shelter. I had been going there since I was a baby. Some of my earliest memories of smell and colour come from her garden. In autumn it smelt of blackcurrant and apple. I pressed my face to the bushes, sweet and musty, and saw the apples scattered on the grass. Never before had I seen so many. They were green but a lighter green than the grass. I picked one up and bit hard. My teeth stuck in the skin. Suddenly I was spitting, bits of peel spewed out. I yelped at the bitter taste. That would have been in the early 1960s when my grandmother, May Hassett – or May H as I called her – was still a young woman, in her early fifties, and only recently widowed.

All the other pictures of the garden are from a later time: the three apple trees, two on the left hand side, the other in the middle of the garden, and the ground always covered with fruit from the end of August until deep into October. *Come on, lads, for the love of God, pick them up before they're spoiled. I'll make apple jelly.* The high hedge between us and Freddie Cremin's garden – busy Freddie who lived in fear of marauding children trampling his garden and who we swore cut his grass every day, rain or sun, and who was kind to my grandmother. Beyond Cremin's was White's where young Brid White lived, a year older than me with dark hair and wide excited eyes, and to whom I silently swore eternal love.

Behind the trees was the green shed where I smoked my first cigarette. My late grandfather had used it for keeping his tools. May H saw the smoke curling out of there, and said nothing. That was her style, by and large. Where her grandchildren were concerned my grandmother was mellow; not lax or careless but knowing when the blind eye was wisest. May was softhearted but never sentimental. I think suffering had made her a pragmatist; she lived for what happiness the present could bring. She was the family's first real traveller, heading off to visit her relatives in America and travelling by Greyhound bus from New York City to the deserts of New Mexico, carried along by an unshakeable conviction that if she was nice to people they would be nice to her. She travelled several times to America and to her relative's summer home in Barbados.

I longed to emulate her. On Sundays a group of us children from the road would cycle up the hill to Cork airport and hope a plane might take off or land while we there; I saw those departing planes of childhood as a promise. Some day, I told myself, I will climb on board. I will be going somewhere.

My parents gave me the passion of idealism. May H encouraged common sense and warned me against taking myself too seriously. 'If you can't have a laugh you're finished,' she would say. The greatest enemy, she said, were the 'dreaded *nadgers*'. By this she meant 'nerves', as Irish people were apt to call any kind of emotional disturbance. If I worried too much, or failed to see the lighter side of a predicament, my grandmother would caution me against the *nadgers*.

'Jesus Mercy, think of poor Auntie Katie above on the Lee Road with her wonderful education, one of the cleverest women in Cork, and where did it get her?' My grand-aunt Katie was my grandmother's sister-in-law and had been a progressive and highly admired national school teacher and one of the first women headmistresses in the city. But in her later years she was overtaken by mental illness, and ended her days in the city's mental hospital, a place that would have sat well in Stalin's Gulag.

My grandmother's antidote to *nadgers*, and the inevitable incarceration that would follow, was to believe that no situation was so bad that it could not be remedied with the application of common sense, humour and a cup of Barry's Gold Blend tea. Over the long term, that faith was challenged by the death of a beloved child, but even afterwards and up to the end of her life my grandmother retained a gift for laughter. Her voice is with me constantly, especially when I am agonising over some drama in my adult life. *The only thing you can't get over is death. All the rest you can manage.*

~

She was born May Sexton in Cork city in 1910 when Ireland still dreamed of Home Rule and a future as loyal subjects within the Empire. May lived in a neat terraced house looking down on the city in the middle-class suburb of Ballinlough. Her father was an accountant with an old Cork firm; her mother was an orphan from a moderately well-to-do family, whose guardian before her marriage was a major in the Indian army.

My great-grandfather, John Sexton, was a quiet, gentle man, who went on the very occasional skite and once terrified his family by disappearing on the night the Black and Tans tried to burn Cork. He had been trapped, unable to get home from the pub because of the roadblocks. 'I remember we watched the red glow of buildings burning that night. We were terrified. We were sure the Tans had got him. My poor mother was distracted with worry,' May recalled.

May had one sister, Grand-aunt Kitty, who helped to radicalise my political consciousness. I spent an unhappy couple of weeks with her one summer and we spent hours arguing over politics and religion. Kitty was a generous person but well to the right on issues of faith and fatherland. She stoutly defended Mussolini and General Franco as 'fine Catholics' and regarded my political views as communist and blasphemous (by then I was a teenage socialist).

My grandmother and her parents were people of Cork's genteel suburbs and, like the majority of their class, lived comfortably enough in the embrace of the Empire. Cork had been a British military and naval base for two centuries. There were several British military barracks in the city and nearby at Crosshaven and Cobh were the great naval bases of Haulbowline and Fort Camden. The harbour was also an important stopping point for transatlantic liners from the Cunard and White Star lines. It was here that the *Titanic* made her last stop before heading out to disaster in the North Atlantic.

My grandmother grew up in the world of dry sherry in crystal glasses, china cups for the visiting priest, the lace table cloth at Easter and Christmas, and the voice of Count McCormack on the gramophone. *When you and I were seventeen and life and love was new./ That golden spring when love was King and I your wonderful Queen . . .*

She saw McCormack once, on the day he sang at the Eucharistic Congress in 1932; it was the largest public demonstration in the history of twentieth-century Ireland, an assertion of papal power in the still young independent state. May travelled up by train with her husband-to-be, a young car mechanic and veteran of the War of Independence, Paddy Hassett. 'You could hear a pin drop that day. I never heard a voice so sweet.'

McCormack sang the Panus Angelicus and a grateful, pious nation swooned. On the way back to Cork my grandparents had an argument. When she spoke about it later May could not remember what it had been about, but she gave him back his ring. The estrangement lasted until they reached Cork and, undone by his sad, apologetic face, she asked for the ring once more. 'We never argued again after that,' she said.

I never knew Paddy. He died when I was a baby. I have only the things my mother has said to me over the years. They are impressions of character, and specific images: *He was the kindest man. I never heard him raise his voice. He worked so hard. He only went out once a week to play cards at the Catholic Young Men's Society, that was his entertainment. He loved the opera. When they came on tour he'd go and sing along because he knew all of the arias. You should have seen him there with the tears streaming down his face and the passion in his voice . . .*

Both May and Paddy were passionate about their home city. Visitors call Cork people clannish, slow to welcome the outsider. 'They're only jealous because there's none like us!' May would say. The city is divided by the River Lee. In the middle there is an island connected by several bridges and on either side hills rise up, giving the whole place an atmosphere of closeness that locals find intimate and reassuring, and visitors often condemn as claustrophobic. More than any other place I have lived, it is Cork I regard as my home. It is my city and though I may never live there again, I have great sympathy with something my father told me the writer Frank O'Connor had once said: 'I could never get over the feeling that although I had left Cork, Cork had never really left me.'

The fierce local pride displayed by my grandmother, passed on to my mother and in turn to me, is at least partly the consequence of the city being constantly, and unfavourably, compared to Dublin. Corkonians have never really accepted a 'second-city' status. The city's merchants boasted that Cork had the deepest natural harbour in Ireland. As trade flourished with Europe grand mansions sprang up along the valley of the River Lee; they were the homes of merchants who summered in southern Europe and came home to christen their new suburbs with Italian names like Montenotte and Tivoli.

My grandmother's city was Cork but her country was the home, and when she married my grandfather Paddy Hassett in 1936 she settled into domestic life. Paddy built their house, St Declan's, on one of Cork's southern hills. It had ivy-covered walls and fine gardens at the front and back; there were four bedrooms, a kitchen that was almost entirely constructed of glass, so that even on the bleakest Irish days it threw light back into the dining room, and a genteel sitting room, usually kept locked until important visitors came. There was a lovely woman called Minnie, who first came in the 1930s as a housekeeper but who had become a member of the family. 'Min' was my grandmother's rock and loved us as if we were her own children.

I lived with my grandmother for more than a year after my parents' separation and spent each August with her in a cottage she rented at Ardmore, my grandfather's birthplace, on the County Waterford coast. Those days roaming the rock pools of the foreshore were the happiest of my childhood; they left me with a lifelong addiction to pottering around at the edge of the sea, and a committed belief in the healing powers of the landscape of west Waterford. Always when I am troubled, or returning from some unpleasant place, I head for Ardmore.

It was May's courage that left the deepest impression on me and encouraged me to get on with things whenever I was tempted to feel sorry for myself. By the time I went to live with her she had already experienced tragedy. Of her nine children, one died shortly before she was due to give birth, another when he was a baby of two months. Her sixth child, my Uncle Ben, was born with muscular dystrophy. My grandmother took him to Lourdes in the hope of a holy cure. She was a devout Catholic (though never a craw thumper), but there was no cure. Ben was fourteen years old when he died at home on a summer afternoon.

Ten months later her husband, Paddy Hassett, died. I believe his death was the direct result of stress. Paddy had got into financial difficulty in the early 1960s, essentially the victim of his own niceness. He owned a garage business in Cork but was undone by his willingness to give financial credit. When hard times came his debtors refused to pay up. Paddy's nerves gave out. He had fought for his country in the War of Independence and worked hard to provide the best for his family. Yet now he felt that he had failed as a man. Paddy retreated into silence. My grandmother would ask him to talk but he could not. He was forced to sell the business and then the cottage he had built near Ardmore, the place where he was born. As his world collapsed Paddy suffered a stroke and was hospitalised. A few months later he had another stroke and died. For a while it looked as if my grandmother would lose St Declan's, until an uncle stepped in and bought it from the bank.

It was the death of my uncle Michael, her fourth child, which fully revealed the extraordinary depths of my grandmother's courage. Mike had emigrated to the United States in the late

1950s. He started out working with General Motors but his heart was set on becoming a theatre director. Mike worked until he'd saved enough money to go to college. After graduating he went on to teach drama at Columbia University, and was building a reputation as a promising director off-Broadway. Mike was drafted for Vietnam but got a deferment because of his studies. He'd protested against the war and had no intention of becoming cannon fodder for Richard Nixon. As the sixties came to an end he started to miss home. In a last letter he'd told my grandmother about a job that had come up at Dublin's Abbey Theatre.

I had met Michael only twice. One summer a few years before he'd come to visit us at a house my grandmother rented by the sea. It was his first visit home from the States in nearly a decade. I remember that Mike had dark hair and wore a plaid jacket and blue jeans, and looked like a character from a Simon and Garfunkel song. My grandmother laughed a lot around him. Mike was always up and moving about, he filled the little house with his gestures and voice; he told stories about America and sang 'The Red River' when he shaved in the morning, *Come and sit by my side if you love me/Do not hasten to bid me adieu . . .*

He threw me into the waves at Goat Island and when I bawled with fright he raced in and smothered me with apologies and carried me on his shoulders up and down the beach until I'd completely forgotten the anguish of a few minutes before. A few weeks later I saw him again as he was getting ready to leave Ireland. He was taking a train which would in turn take him to the plane. The carriages were crowded with football supporters. They were friendly but boisterous and Mike had to push to make his way to the window to wave goodbye. He smiled, he always smiled, then waved as the train pulled away taking him back to America.

~

In those days when an Irish person was killed abroad it was usually a substantial item on the news. But Mike's death was overshadowed by a national crisis. We were sitting by the fire in St Declan's watching television when the main evening news came on. The headline said that thirteen people had been shot dead by the British army in Derry. There were black-and-white pictures on the screen of soldiers shooting and then a priest waving a white handkerchief leading some men down a lane-way. The men were carrying a body. I'd never seen a real body before. There was a statement from the Irish government condemning what had happened.

I remember my grandmother saying 'Mother of God, this is desperate.' Even to a child living in the far south of Ireland, largely cut off from the politics of the day, I knew that these black-and-white images represented a moment of significance. If my gran was angry it meant something serious had happened. Then there was a knock on the front door. My mother went to answer. I heard my Uncle Barry's voice. 'Lads, I have some bad news for ye.' And after that there were muffled sounds. Doors opened and closed. Then I heard a woman's voice crying. My mother told me that Uncle Michael was dead. 'Be good now because we have to mind Gran,' she said. The rest of that night passed in a procession of grown-ups coming and going.

On the night of the fire Mike had been out with friends in Greenwich Village. He came home and fell asleep, possibly with a candle still lit. The firemen found him near the door where he'd crawled trying to escape. *The New York Times* carried a short paragraph:

Michael Hassett was killed in a fire in his apartment on Spring Street in Manhattan. Police are investigating the cause of the blaze.

There wasn't really much to investigate. It was an accidental death a long way from home. The coffin came home a week or so after we got the news of his death. It was the first coffin I'd ever seen for real, a big steel coffin, and it scared me and made me sad, because until it arrived I thought that there might be a mistake and Mike might still walk through the door.

The day of the funeral the wind and rain belted in from the coast. I went with an uncle and stayed at the back of the church. Then we followed in the procession to Ballyphehane graveyard where Michael was buried next to his father and his younger brother Ben. I have no memories of my grandmother on that day. She was surrounded by people and I could not catch a glimpse of her. I remember my mother dressed in the black of mourning with a veil covering her face. Underneath she glistened with tears.

May Hassett's house had been a place of ease and security. I was afraid now that grief would take her away from me. It was an inchoate fear, spurred by the utter change I was witnessing in somebody I had always known to be strong. She retreated, slept during the daytime, and wept when she did not think I could see her. But I was by then attuned to the secret strategies of adults. I could always tell.

Then, after several weeks my grandmother emerged from mourning. She struggled to take her place again at the centre of the family. It wasn't a swift transformation. But May knew we were all watching her, and slowly she found a way to laugh again. It was only years later that I understood how much she fought to prevent grief from overwhelming her. By then I'd started work on a newspaper and bought my first car. I was taking my grandmother on a long drive through the countryside on a Sunday afternoon when she began to talk about Michael.

She talked about what he had been like as a child, mischief-loving and easygoing, how heartsick she'd been when he took the ship to America, and how the break-up of his marriage had been a relief to her: 'They weren't suited to each other at all, you know.' May talked about the letters he'd sent describing his successes at Columbia and then off-Broadway. He'd sent her a book on the American theatre in which his production of a Strindberg play had been analysed and praised. Then my grandmother began to sob. I hadn't seen her cry in years. 'He was so young,' she said. And she repeated this several times. We drove on in silence for several miles. Then she asked me if I believed in heaven.

'What makes you ask that?' I asked.

'Because I wonder if I'll see him again,' she replied. 'I would give anything to see him just once more.'

In those days I did not know what I believed in, if anything, but I told her I was sure there was a heaven. Then this devout woman told me that when Michael had been killed she wondered if there was any God. She said she'd kept on going to Mass but she struggled with faith, asking how her child could have been taken in such a way. When I asked her why she didn't crack up, go under, become a heart-broken recluse, her explanation was that she hadn't any choice but to keep going. 'What else was I going to do?'

Love carried her through. The love for her children, the love she gave in taking care of myself and my siblings. The light of my grandmother's life was my younger sister, Niamh. Barely two years my junior she was born with coeliac disease and was seriously ill as a baby. Given the troubled state of things in our home May H offered to look after Niamh in Cork. Niamh was effectively reared by my grandmother and her presence helped May H greatly as she fought to emerge from her grief over Michael.

Though she would have abjured such a notion herself, I believe my grandmother was the first heroic person I knew.

CHAPTER SIX

'Pres' Boy

. . . Yet he was kind; or if severe in aught,
The love he bore to learning was in fault.

'The Village Schoolmaster',
OLIVER GOLDSMITH

I didn't like the look of the place. St Joseph's National School
was a grim, grey edifice built in 1913 on the banks of the
River Lee about a mile from Cork city centre. Directly opposite, on the far bank of the river, were the suburbs of
Sundays Well and Shanakiel, terraced and grand with the
mansions of the merchant princes. But St Joseph's drew the
bulk of its pupils from an area known as the Marsh. Poor
and neglected, it was a mix of old tenements and new council
flats. Other boys travelled down from estates on the city's
north side or from farming areas to the west. I arrived at
St Joseph's fresh from a private school in Dublin, a place which
had its own swimming pool and rugby pitches and where
we wore uniforms and caps in the manner of English public
schoolboys.

My school career had been troubled. I'd started out in an
all-Irish speaking '*scoil*' and had been moved on because my
teacher was an old viper; after that I went to a prep school

73

called Miss Carr's, run by a genial old lady and filled with the children of the Dublin middle class. I thrived there but on reaching the age of seven I had to move up to a senior school. This was St Mary's in Rathmines, another citadel of the middle classes, where I struggled to settle. By now things at home were becoming more fraught and every raised voice from a teacher had me jumping.

I was taken out of St Mary's and sent to the more easygoing Terenure College where I was a happy pupil until my parents' separation forced another move. By the time my primary education was complete I had been to five different schools. A child who was not so frightened and troubled might have fared better, been more resilient in the face of aggressive teachers. I was simply scared.

Yet until I reached Cork my education had been exceptionally privileged. All private schools and middle-class children. At St Joseph's I was immersed in the reality of Irish primary education for the majority. On my first day at St Joseph's we were lined up in the yard and marched up a steel staircase into the school building. Ahead of us was a long, dark corridor that smelt of polish and chalk, and at the very end of that, on the left-hand side, was the Brother's class.

The Brother belonged to the 'hard-but-fair' variety of headmaster. In his younger days he'd been a promising Gaelic footballer, and he was still fitter and tougher than the largest of his pupils. His school was not one of the hell-holes, similar to some run by the Christian Brothers and other religious orders, where the leather strap ruled. This was also the early 1970s and the nationalistic element of our education was receding. Ireland joined the EU in 1973, a year after I started school at St Joseph's. The word was out that we needed to be more European, if we were going to benefit from all the jobs and money on offer from Brussels. The Brother belonged to the Presentation Brothers, who were always seen as one of the more politically moderate outfits, certainly by comparison with the ardent nationalism of the Christian Brothers.

To a little Dublin boy fresh from a broken home and with a strange accent, St Joseph's was a mighty challenge. My first encounter was with a farmer's son whom I will call Lonergan. The boy looked like a mountain man with broad shoulders and big shovels of hands. Lonergan came to school each day with his hair standing on end as if he had only that moment rolled out of bed; he had buck teeth which advanced with each month and he smelled of fried food. On my first day in class Lonergan turned around and asked if I was 'handy'. Not knowing what the word meant, I said yes. *Yes. Yes, always anxious to please. Whatever you want me to be, I will say* 'Yes'.

No sooner had the teacher left the room to get some books than Lonergan turned around and punched me hard in the chest. I was thrown backwards. There was laughter around the class. The others waited to see what I would do. Tears came to my eyes. I did nothing. There was more laughter. 'Handy my hole,' said Lonergan.

In this way I discovered that 'handy' meant hard, tough, able to fight your corner, and I was about as tough as butter. The atmosphere was feral. Every weakness was noted. Our teachers were good men and women. But physical violence was often the preferred method of control and chastisement. Hardly a day went by when somebody wasn't given a few lashes of the cane. You stood at the top of the class, watched by eyes that were both fearful and relieved that it wasn't happening to them.

The Brother would produce his bamboo cane and tell you to hold out your hand. Sometimes boys were so frightened they pulled their hand back at the last minute. He waited until their hands were steady and then brought the cane thrashing down on the open palm. All at once you were assaulted by

75

sharp stinging agony. Your hands were hot as if someone had poured molten metal on them. Blood rushed to your cheeks and you blushed with shame. After the first couple of strokes your hand started to go numb from the pain. You tried hard not to cry. But I saw some of the hardest boys in the class with tears in their eyes after being beaten.

When it was done you clasped your hands under your armpits and went back to your seat. It was impossible to write after that. I remember that there were always a few minutes of strange quiet after a beating. Everybody felt the shame and the shock of that sudden eruption of violence. We were beaten for not doing our homework. We were beaten for mitching. We were beaten for making a nuisance in the class (i.e. talking or trying to attract attention).

Yet the Brother was a moderate. His violence was never gratuitous and never tinged with sadism. He genuinely liked us and did his best for every kid in the class. In beating us he was simply exerting control in a manner that was widely accepted by society, and sanctioned by the state.

On that first day in school I was introduced to a daily ritual. The Brother instructed us to walk quietly across the corridor to a tiny room. 'No messing or there'll be hell to pay,' he warned. I asked the boy sitting next to me what was happening. 'We're gettin' soup,' he said. After a few minutes the Brother returned with a huge steaming vat and several loaves of bread. The smell of soup filled the little room. Boys pushed against each other, elbowing to get to the front of the line. Plastic cups were handed around, and then one by one we dipped them into the vat of soup. An older boy handed out a chunk of bread. In my previous school, boys were packed off by their parents with nice lunches. There was a tuck shop that sold buns and soft drinks. There was none of that at St Joseph's. I suspect that for quite a few boys in that room the Brother's soup was the only guaranteed hot meal of the day. It was devoured rapidly, and the leftovers mopped up from the pot with bread.

The class was fairly evenly split between those who were studying to go on to secondary school and those counting the days to when they could escape and get work. Of the latter nearly all came from poor families with no history of educational achievement. The bright kids would pass the entrance exams for secondary and probably go on to university. Those who were designated as 'thick', or who could not be bothered working, would either leave for a factory job, or idle away another few years in a technical college, where you could learn a trade or at least convince your parents you were learning a trade.

After a few more hidings from the likes of Lonergan I began to develop my own way of dealing with bullies. I wouldn't run away. Since I couldn't beat them I would talk my way out of trouble. Make a joke; use my brain, relishing it when they were trapped in their English comprehension and came to me for help. It worked for the most part. To most of those boys I must have seemed very strange. I was scared of them. I kept myself apart from them. I did not seek to make friends. At break times I asked permission to stay inside and read. When forced to go outside I would wander around the edge of the schoolyard, ignoring the scrum of football-playing, fighting boys, and dream of escape. After a while the bullies ignored me. I made my own world. I kept filling my head with stories and lived there among the characters. In these stories I was always a hero.

I joined Cork children's library and read book after book about history. There were books on my old hero Napoleon, but also Bismarck, Julius Caesar, Alexander the Great. My mind ranged back over centuries, following Alexander over the wind-blasted plains of the Oxus, crossing into Gaul with Caesar's legions, turning back the invaders at the gates of

Rome, dying gloriously at Waterloo. Around this time, my twelfth birthday, my mother gave me a copy of a book about South Africa. She knew I still dreamed of Africa as my place of escape. But Cork library had only a limited selection of books about explorers. This new book was different. It wasn't about the white men bringing civilisation to the natives. It was about the natives themselves. It would help to set me on a path to Africa.

The book was *Cry the Beloved Country* by Alan Paton. It told the story of a rural preacher from a place called Zululand and his quest for his son in the distant city of Johannesburg. The preacher was a different kind of hero to those I had wanted to emulate before. He was a humble man and confronted violent injustice in a peaceful way. The book introduced me to a concept called 'apartheid' where people were separated from each other on the basis of their skin colour. We did not see many black or coloured people in Cork. Perhaps one or two in the entire course of my childhood. Through Alan Paton I learned about the cruelties of segregation and the struggle of those who were voiceless. There were lines towards the end of the book which I read and re-read, lines I would commit to memory and cherish: *But when that dawn will come, of our emancipation, from the fear of bondage and the bondage of fear, why, that is a secret.*

~

On the last day at St Joseph's, the Brother let us out early. It was June 1974, and the sky was a rare, perfect blue. We galloped cheering down the wrought-iron stairs to the playground. The Brother told me to take care of myself and to stop in and see him any time I wanted. He was a decent man and had done his best for me but the experience at St Joseph's had felt like a long grey winter. The experience did, however, make me streetwise. I had gone there as a timorous middle-class boy and emerged with enough cunning to negotiate my way around the bullies. In later life, in distant places I would use the skills I'd developed in the playground to deal with characters far more threatening than Lonergan. I learned the important rules: talk them down. Outwit them. But don't ever run away from them.

On my last day I could relish the fact that I had survived. And I had three months of the summer ahead before starting secondary school at Presentation College, a hundred yards or so away on the other side of the street. 'Pres' drew its pupils from a different social world to that of St Joseph's. Only a handful of boys in my year at St Joseph's would cross the road to Pres. It was a private school and most of the parents could never have afforded the fees. Besides, there was a first-class academic education on offer in other schools around the city. What Pres or its rival, Christians, offered was social cachet, the promise that boys would be turned out as young gentlemen ready to take their place among the city's business elite. In the old days Pres had taken a less voluble line than other schools on the national question. This probably reflected the class origins of many of the pupils whose parents formed the Cork establishment and who would have shivered nervously had the teachers in Pres begun to denounce imperial Britain, though this didn't stop the writer Seán O'Faoláin from leaving school and joining the ranks of the IRA.

There was also a strong hereditary element to Pres. Like many of the other boys who entered Pres that year, I had had uncles and cousins who went to the school. Although my grand-father, Paddy Hassett, had been a revolutionary gunman, he sent his sons to a school that was modelled in many respects on the elitism of the English public school. Unlike in most of the other Cork schools, in Pres they played rugby and cricket. The Gaelic games of hurling and football, which my grandfather loved, were banned. Paddy wanted to give his boys every advantage and his decision to send them to Pres reflected the prestige of the school among the newly emergent Irish middle classes. Heading for a job interview on the South Mall, home to the main banks and insurance companies, there was always the likelihood that the candidate would be facing an old Pres boy on the other side of the desk. If the candidate happened to have played rugby for the Pres first XV his path was virtually assured. And to those who won a Munster Schools Senior Cup medal there was no end of employment possibilities. In this way some less than bright sparks found their passage eased into bountiful jobs.

In the rest of Ireland, Cork city had a reputation for being cliquey and snobbish, a place where your family background and the jobs your parents held were critical markers of social status. Those wearing the Pres school uniform occasionally attracted hostility because of its reputation as a bastion of privilege. One man fought to change that.

~

The following September I started at Pres and met a man who would change my life. Brother Jerome Kelly terrified the life out of me the first time I saw him. He was stout, balding and wore severe dark-rimmed glasses, of a kind that had gone out of fashion in the late 1960s, but which was still *de rigueur* among the Irish religious orders. Jerome looked a great deal more frightening than the Brother at St Joseph's; his black robes flapped as he strode across the playground past the waiting lines of boys, like an immense bird of prey marshalling its victims.

Brother Jerome had grown up on a small farm in the bleak fastnesses of the Beara Peninsula, one of the poorest areas of the country, and he had joined the Brothers immediately after leaving school. The religious life was a traditional route of escape for many boys in the poorer parts of the country. There was a large amount of snobbery attached to urban impressions of religious brothers. The popular belief was that they were all reared in smoky, dark cottages, gorged on bacon and potatoes, regularly beaten senseless by their mountain-man fathers, until such time as they could escape to the city and get good jobs beating the daylights out of us.

Jerome was different. He wasn't escaping anything, so much as racing to embrace the world. After teacher training he left Ireland to become a missionary in the West Indies. The ignorant chatter among schoolboys was that the brothers were free to beat as much as they wanted on the missions, so that when they came back home they were half savage. In fact mission service had a radicalising effect on the Irish religious orders. Men like Jerome arrived in the West Indies and Africa as the colonial era was coming to an end and nationalist movements were on the rise. Those who came home often found themselves at odds with the stifling conservatism of Ireland. Jerome's response to the country he found on his return was to try and change the children who entered his school: fill them up with ideas about justice; make them want to change their world.

The initial impression created by his formidable appearance was unfounded. When we filed into the big hall to be welcomed by Jerome he *asked* rather than *told* us to sit down, and when he spoke it wasn't with the declamatory bellow of the staffroom autocrat but with calm assurance. He started to use words like 'responsibility' and 'potential'. I remember being a little shocked. I'd expected nothing more than a list of do's and don'ts. School was about rules and punishments. Jerome did list the rules – neat uniform, hair an inch above the collar, expulsion for bullying – but most of the talk was about how we should use school to get the best out of ourselves.

I did not immediately distinguish myself. Within a couple of weeks I was in trouble for talking repeatedly in class. In Pres you weren't beaten by the headmaster for breaking the rules. Jerome did not approve of corporal punishment. He had his own sliding scale of punishments. You might be given detention or extra homework. If the offence was sufficiently serious, parents would be called in or you could be suspended. At the end of the line there was expulsion which good middle-class boys dreaded, for in Cork it was the kind of stain which might tarnish a reputation for ever.

A fortnight after arriving I found myself arraigned before Jerome. My co-accused was the future Ireland and British Lions rugby star, Michael Kiernan. We were thrown out of class and sent to Jerome's office for talking despite repeated warnings. Jerome was sitting with his arms folded, shaking his head and looking at us as if we'd committed murder. After a few seconds of that baleful glare you not only believed that you'd killed someone but would've willingly signed a confession attesting to the fact. Jerome had big presence.

'Right, gentlemen,' said Jerome, 'what have you got to say for yourselves?'

We snivelled something about being sorry and not getting into trouble again.

'I am sure that's true,' he said, 'but first I have a job for you both.'

It was dark by the time we'd finished cleaning a long section of the Mardyke Walk. Immortalised by Joyce in *A Portrait of the Artist as a Young Man* and Seán O'Faoláin as the haunt of lovers in his story *The Talking Trees*, the mile-long thorough-fare ran from the school gates towards the west of the city and parallel to the River Lee, the rugby pitches of Pres and the grounds of the Cork Cricket Club, forming a green band between the river and the road.

With a faint rain falling we stood under the yellow street

lights waiting for Jerome. So intimidated were we by his presence that by the time we'd finished, the Mardyke was, in the words of my grandmother, clean enough to eat your dinner from. Jerome smiled at us when he arrived: 'Now, lads, you've made a very useful contribution to society. Off home with ye!'

The clean-up operation was tedious and exhausting but it did not seek to humiliate. And to anybody who'd been on the receiving end of a cane or a leather strap that was a revolutionary concept.

But I kept on getting into trouble, always for mouthing off in class or playing the fool. I engaged with those subjects I found interesting such as English and history but switched off when it came to maths and science. I refused to apply myself to things which bored me and would either retreat into my old habit of daydreaming or seek to entertain my colleagues with impressions of the teachers. I had inherited some of the Keanes' love of mischief-making; I was also very desperate for notice. I was perpetually late and an inventor of some genius when it came to explaining missing homework. After a few months of determined attention seeking I received my first suspension from school. This was serious. Three strikes and you were out altogether.

Jerome called me in. He was shaking his head as I walked through the door. 'You are in a bad position, boy. You need to make some choices,' he said. He went on to describe the options. They were few but emphatic: I could stop messing and work hard, or leave and go to some far less gentlemanly establishment, in other words back to the world of Lonergan and his cohorts. I pictured in my mind's eye the logical consequence of expulsion from Pres. There would be family disgrace, the loss of my new friends in Pres, the prospect of a different school most likely under the rule of the cane, and the firm belief that expulsion would lead eventually, but inevitably, to either the unemployment queue or jail. I was nothing if not prone to dramatic visualisations. So I changed.

Jerome kept a close eye on my progress. He recruited me into the school debating society, a good outlet for my performing instinct, and would call me in every few weeks to see how I was getting on in class. They were fatherly chats sprinkled with little nuggets of Jerome wisdom, chief among them the imprecation: 'To thine own self be true.' Jerome knew I came from a broken home. He knew I was adrift. But where other headmasters might have seen a troublesome idiot who should have been booted out of school, Jerome went out of his way to help me grow up.

He was a revolutionary figure in Irish education. I cannot imagine another school run by a religious order where the headmaster, a devout Catholic, would institute philosophy classes alongside religious instruction, or where he was happy to allow one of his teachers to ask us to prove to him the evidence for the existence of God. It was done to make us think. Jerome abhorred the idea of faith and belief being taken for granted, as much as he opposed the notion of a society with no spiritual values at all: 'Think for yourselves, boys.'

In the mid-1970s he decided to build a radio and television studio in the school, a move prompted by his conviction that if we were to succeed in our careers we needed to know how the mass media worked. I had my first broadcasting training in the Pres studio and went from there to appearing with classmates on a local radio schools' programme. The experience was priceless. I could feel my confidence growing. For the debating matches Jerome would pack a team of four of us, occasionally accompanied by a girlfriend or two, and head off into the distant recesses of the Irish countryside to speak in bleak convents or cavernous boarding schools. Debating taught me to think on my feet and gave me the self-confidence to speak in front of large groups.

It also exposed a chronic lifelong weakness, a tendency to leave everything to the last possible minute (a sure sign I was made for a life in journalism). Time and again I would find myself hiding in the toilet before the debate, frantically scribbling down my notes while my team-mates waited impatiently. I lacked the self-discipline to focus until the clock forced me into action. When time caught up with me I usually managed a creditable performance, occasionally even winning a medal.

~

Jerome was acutely aware of the school's image as a place of privilege. He had been raised in poor circumstances himself, and had served in the West Indies at a time when the anti-colonial struggle was reaching its crescendo. When he taught us religion Jerome emphasised social justice. At the heart of his message was a simple code: talk without action is meaningless. He became an activist. In 1972 he set up an organisation called SHARE – Schoolboys Harness Aid for Relief of the Elderly – to attack the housing crisis among Cork city's elderly poor.

When he arrived in Cork, fresh from the missions, Jerome was immediately struck by the wretched living conditions of many residents of the Marsh area. This was just a few hundred yards from the gates of Pres. There were damp and crumbling buildings. Rat-infested tenements. Here the elderly poor cooked on primus stoves and kept warm under coats, blankets and piles of newspapers. Many were social outcasts. Perhaps they had a drink problem, or depression, or maybe they had no living relatives or had lost contact with their families – they were all Jerome's people. Through his example he made them ours. Jerome visited them and listened to their problems. Then he asked the schoolboys if they would volunteer for a visiting roster. At the very least the elderly poor would have someone to talk with.

Once the visits were running he suggested an annual collection to raise money for the elderly. Jerome's idea was that he would raise a large sum of money and then challenge the city corporation to match it. Between them they would build new homes for the elderly poor. He used a mixture of flattery and relentless pressure to get his way. Jerome was a force of nature. He worked the phones, went to endless meetings at City Hall and used the local media to highlight the crisis of the elderly. City officials who helped were sure of generous praise when Jerome outlined his plans to the *Cork Examiner*. As for those who didn't help him? Nobody dared refuse. 'You just keep at them, boy,' he would say.

By the time I arrived at Pres the annual collection was an established success. New housing projects went up all over the city. But there was another success for Jerome. By using schoolboys to manage the project he gave us an early taste of responsibility and, just as important, a sense of social justice. I came to love the man for his bustling energy and because he cared about me. Jerome Kelly ensured I didn't become an educational casualty. I look back at secondary school and feel blessed. Jerome and I stayed friends after I left school. He would occasionally call and ask me to do something in relation to SHARE or Pres – as astute a manipulator of the old boy network as always. I could never refuse him.

~

Jerome was ahead of his time. But the country was starting to catch up with him. We were exploding out of the concrete overcoat lovingly tailored for us by Éamonn de Valera. Despite the best efforts of the bishops and the politicians we were having fun. On television we had brave current affairs programmes where we could watch our politicians being grilled by tough interviewers; a journalist called Vincent Browne had emerged as the scourge of a lying, swindling political class; Senator Mary Robinson, a future President, emerged as a powerful advocate of women's rights; government ministers were ruthlessly satirised on television on a programme called *Hall's Pictorial Weekly.*

The Ireland of myth and reverence was being dismantled in front of our eyes. There were also the first stirrings of a sexual revolution. Ireland being Ireland it was pretty tentative. But there was enough happening to provoke parish priests into apoplectic sermons on a weekly basis. The Capitol cinema on Patrick Street introduced jumbo seats for courting couples; on the weekends it screened films like *Virgins on the Verge* and *Rosie Dixon Night Nurse* as late shows.

Contraceptives were still officially banned, however. Our Prime Minister even voted against legislation being introduced by his own Minister for Health. But an Irish schoolboy could get a supply of 'rubber Johnnies' if he was determined enough. Most of the condoms bought on the black market by teenage boys were never used. They were blown up as balloons, furtively shown to friends at the back of the class, sold on to other boys, occasionally shown to girls in the hope they'd get the hint.

Pornography was also starting to appear in Ireland. I went to England with the Catholic Boy Scouts once in the mid-1970s. A gang of the older boys went from the campsite in Chingford into Soho and came back with 'dirty' magazines. 'Dirty' was the word given to anything which had a sexual content, however vague. There was a troop leader whom we called 'Stab the Rasher' because of his skinny frame and sneaky nature.

'Come here and look at this, Keane,' he shouted from the tent door.

I was eager to be wanted and ran over. He showed me a photograph. There was a woman and a man doing something, but I wasn't sure what. The man was standing over the woman holding his *langer* (the Cork word) and she was looking up at him smiling. I felt ill and started to walk backwards. This caused Stab to explode with laughter. 'Come here, lads,' he shouted to his friends. 'Come here and look at the fucking face on Keane, will ye!'

I ran off but when I came back an hour or so later they gathered around me laughing.

I hadn't even the vaguest clue about girls. My mother taught in a Protestant school in Cork. The Protestant girls of Cork had names like Bronwyn, Paula, Penny, Susan, Stella. They were children from the outlying farms and old Cork businesses, the remnants of a much larger Protestant population driven from the country after the Troubles of 1921–2.

I thought those girls exotic. It was widely said among my counterparts that Protestant girls were the best because they let you go all the way. That turned out to be nonsense. But they were different. They had not endured the grim piety of the nuns, and so they were more at ease around boys, they could joke and laugh with us, they treated us as humans rather than some predatory species sent by the Devil to torment them. And then a girl named Penny took the initiative and kissed me at the Cork Grammar School disco in the spring of 1975. I walked around on air for days. Not because I loved the girl, but because I had discovered I was not a toad. On the other side of the world Saigon was falling. Cambodia was succumbing to the Khmer Rouge. A few hours up the road hundreds of people were dying in the Troubles. None of it touched us.

In the summer of 1976 I fell in love with a girl whose brothers went to Pres. I first met her in a café where schoolboys and girls spent hours sitting over a single Coke. But it took me months to become bold enough to ask her out. And then at the end of a warm July night she found my courage for me, and drew me into a spearminty kiss.

My girl. The pride I felt in walking with her. My girl had fair hair and green eyes, she smelled of shampoo and fresh clothes, and she was not afraid; this I remember about her best, the energy and hope in her, the laughter which drew me out of the long mourning for my absent father.

Those evenings of summer lingered forever, a deep blue that held its breath before the dark. My girl was the daughter of a sea captain and this added to her mystery; he had travelled to the places I dreamed of and she, by association, carried their exotic promise with her. Our love affair was intimately tied to the city we both loved.

We walked all over Cork together, up its steep hills and out to the Lee Fields, across the 'Shaky Bridge' over the river and all the way south to the marina where ships glided past, ludicrously large on the narrow waterway. Outside the city, on the coast, we cycled to the seaside villages dotted along the harbour mouth – Crosshaven, Myrtleville and Fountainstown, Roches Point – the last of the Irish mainland seen by hundreds of thousands of emigrants taking the boat to America. We would set our bikes down on the sand and swim. Even at a distance of nearly thirty years I remember the clear lines she cut through the water, the emphatic expression on her face as she headed out from shore, the water beads on her shoulders as she sat on the sand afterwards, and later the two of us stopping to catch our breath at the top of the hill leading back into the city and seeing all the twinkling lights of evening strung out like stars across the valley.

In winter I remember walking past the Lough on the way

to her house, past the moorhens and swans, and stopping to look at my reflection in the water, wondering if I would ever feel so happy again. I had come to that love affair as a boy without confidence, who believed himself ugly and unworthy, and was pining for a father in a distant city. The girl and her family welcomed me into their hearts and home. And though the love affair ended, I remember those days as among the most precious I've ever known.

~

A former classmate recently reminded me of something Jerome had said in our last few weeks at school. He had taken us for our regular religious instruction class. 'You'll be heading out into the world soon,' he said. How much would we take with us of what we had learned in Pres? he asked. 'The thing to remember, boys, is that the world out there seems to operate on the principle of people walking all over each other. That is not the way you learned here. Don't walk over people.'

I met Jerome for the last time shortly before the new millennium. By then I was a well-established journalist. He was already seriously ill with leukaemia but still busy with building houses for the elderly poor. It was an August afternoon in the garden of my cottage in Ardmore, a few yards from the sea on one of those rare Irish summer days when the action of the world seems suspended. In the drowsy stillness my son Daniel played around us on the lawn. Jerome asked if I had put his name down for Pres. 'Of course, but only if you go back to being headmaster,' I said.

We laughed and spoke about old times. He was still the headmaster at heart, still with an eye for the telling observation. While my wife was in the house he whispered to me. 'Make sure you give time to your marriage. Don't become too wrapped up in your work. All that work will go in the end but your family won't, if you work at it.' His instinct for getting to the heart of my world was as acute as ever.

I asked him why he had worked so hard to keep me at Pres. 'That Fergal was a troubled boy,' he said. And that was that. It was the only explanation needed. A few months later I had a call from Cork. It was a colleague of Jerome's. He was dying. The leukaemia had attacked again. This time there was no hope of remission. The end was only days away.

I booked a flight to Cork for the following morning and arrived at the Bon Secours Hospital around lunchtime. Walking up the hallway I saw members of his family standing around crying. He had passed away a few hours earlier. I was late. I had been late for him all my life. I think he would have smiled at that, shaken his head and told me to do better next time.

CHAPTER SEVEN

The Junior

When adventure came to me first it was in a form I was not expecting.

'Adventure', FRANK O'CONNOR

'If I couldn't write,' he said, 'I'd go stone fucking mad.'

We were walking across the bog near Listowel a few days after mid-summer. The turf had been harvested and was drying in ricks. The sun shone and the salty wind from the Atlantic made for good drying. John B was holding forth about writing and writers. He was now Ireland's most successful playwright; his novels and short stories sold in huge quantities, there had been expressions of interest from Hollywood in several of his plays and he was writing columns for national daily and regional newspapers. Every morning he vanished upstairs to a room overlooking the marketplace. From there you could hear the tattoo of the old manual typewriter rattling all morning. I was able to observe his routine because I had a summer job as a barman in the public house he owned with his wife Mary. For John B there was no question of not writing.

'Do you see in here?' he asked that day in the bog, pointing to his temple. 'Inside in this head they'd be jumping up and down. Words. I'd be stone mad, boy. That's what I'd be!'

The Junior

Our walk to the bog had a purpose. The night before I'd mentioned to John B's wife Mary that I wanted to talk to him about my future. I was eighteen years old and had just left school. Mary guarded the gates to John B. She protected him from the tourists, scroungers and chancers who would take all of his time. His old, real, friends knew when to call and when to leave him to his writing. Even with Mary's protective shield the list of supplicants was impressive. People came to be photographed with him, to ask for autographs, to know if he could do this or that to help a son or daughter get a job. A man as generous as John B needed protection.

I knew that to get his mind focused on my particular problem would need the intercession of Mary. That evening at tea he suggested a walk. 'We'll go out to Lyre,' he said.

We walked for about twenty minutes. John B pointed out various landmarks: the townland of Lyre where one of the last of the great matchmakers – a vanished breed in modern Ireland – had run his dancehall in defiance of the local clergy, and far off on the road to the coast he pointed to Lisselton, my Kerry grandmother's country. John B did all the talking. That was the way with him. Although many would probably disagree, I think he was a very shy man. He used laughter to keep people from staring too deeply into the private world of his heart. On television and radio he was loquacious and funny. He carried that persona into his private life, and it could be hard to penetrate beyond the stories and jokes and reminiscences. It is a habit of the Keanes. We use laughter and stories to weave a protective wall around us; my father did it and I do it too.

Yet when a family member faced real trouble or needed a favour John B's attention was absolute. He could sense distress immediately and was protective of those he loved. I knew that at some point on this walk he would indicate when we might discuss the real subject at hand. We reached his stretch of bog. John B turned to me. 'What do you want to do?' he asked.

I explained that I wanted to be a journalist. I told him about school and Brother Jerome's radio and television studios, about the debating team, and how I'd developed an obsessive interest in what was happening in faraway places. The previous year a film called *All the President's Men* had played in Cork with Dustin Hoffman and Robert Redford as two crusading journalists on the trail of a crooked president. I came out of that movie with a new form of hero in my mind. He carried a notebook and pen and didn't take no for an answer.

I'd always loved English and history but I'd also become an avid reader of newspapers and magazines. The conflict in Northern Ireland, which had previously existed on the margins of my consciousness, I now followed closely. That summer of 1979, the tenth anniversary of the outbreak of the Troubles, saw a dramatic escalation. In August, while I was working in John B's bar, the South experienced one of the periodic overspills of violence. At the start of the month the IRA shot dead a customer in a bank in Tramore, about half an hour's drive from the village where my family usually spent their summer holidays. But the big shock came a few weeks later with the assassination of Lord Louis Mountbatten in County Sligo. The former Viceroy of India and cousin of the Queen died along with three other people, including two teenage boys. On the same day the IRA attacked the Paratroop Regiment at Warrenpoint, near the border with the Republic. Eighteen soldiers were killed in two bombings. When I heard the news I wanted to be there with a notebook recording the story. I didn't mention my dreams of Africa to John B at this stage. Even though he was a man who had achieved his own dream it seemed like too much of a leap of belief at that stage.

'So you want to learn to be a writer,' said John B. 'How badly do you want it? Do you want to do anything else?'

I said there was nothing else that interested me.

'Then I know the man for you,' he said.

That was the end of the conversation. John B always set the limits on a conversation. You might begin it but he always drew the curtains.

A few days later I was pulling pints for a group of farmers when my Aunt Mary called me into the kitchen. 'You have an appointment tonight. You're going to Ballybunnion with John B. Neily Buckley will see you.'

Neily Buckley owned the biggest regional newspaper in the area, the *Limerick Leader and Chronicle*. It was also the oldest paper in Ireland, founded in 1766 to advance the voice of the Catholic merchant classes. By the time of our meeting Neily was in his seventies and suffering from ill-health. John B was a columnist on the paper and a very old friend of Neily. The rendezvous was at the Railway Bar, overlooking the magnificent surf of the Atlantic.

On the way in John whispered to me: 'Don't drink more than one pint. They'll be watching to see if you can hold your drink.'

I promised moderation. My uncle had not been given any special insight into my drinking habits. I think he assumed that I, along with my cousins and most of the teenage boys of Ireland, would swallow free drink wherever it was available. This was not such an occasion, he made that clear.

Inside, an elderly couple sat at the bar drinking. They did not look like powerful newspaper proprietors. The old man smiled a lot but I have no memory of the conversation. I was as good as my word and kept to the one pint. John B did most of the talking.

Afterwards he took me for a drink in a pub on the way back to Listowel. 'They wanted to get the measure of you,' he explained.

Given that I had hardly opened my mouth I thought this might be difficult. 'Not at all. You can tell a lot about a fella by looking into his eyes,' he replied.

The following day a call came through for John B. It was

Neily Buckley. I stood near the door and heard John B thanking him: 'I am sure he'll be good. He won't let you down.'

I was in! I was going to be a reporter. With the help of the John B Keane employment agency for mendicant nephews, I had climbed onto the first rung of the ladder. John B came into the kitchen smiling:

'Well, 'tis up to you now, my lovely boy!'

~

Up to that point my life had been a series of departures over which I had no control. I had left schools and houses; I had followed my mother out of her marriage. Now I was leaving of my own choice. Although Limerick was only two hours away by road I sensed that this journey was the beginning of something much longer. I loved Cork but in my heart I doubted that I would be coming back. I left with two suits, bought for me by my mother, a pair of black and a pair of brown shoes and a wallet full of money sent to me by my Aunt Mary in Listowel. 'That will keep you going until the first pay packet arrives,' she had said.

My grandmother May H gave me a small bottle of Holy Water on the night before I left and told me I was doing the best thing I'd ever done: 'John B has given you the finest start you could ask for. Go and make a success of it, love.'

Both my parents were enthusiastic about the idea of my becoming a reporter. Although I had seen little of my father in the previous year, he continued to write and he sent me a card wishing me well in the new job. At a distance of nearly thirty years it is difficult to convey what a note like that could mean; although his communications could be sporadic – I never knew when the weather would close in around him – I cherished every letter, birthday or Christmas card. They were an argument against the aching loss, the anger.

I asked my mother not to take me to the train. I couldn't bear a leave-taking in that station where I had known so many sad scenes waiting for my father. We embraced and made light of the leaving. I would be home at weekends. Maybe I would get a job on the *Cork Examiner*. But my mother knew the truth. She knew I wanted to go to foreign places and cover wars. My mother understood my dreams of Africa better than anyone, for she had introduced me to the continent.

It was a sunny September morning – 17 September 1979 – and I took a taxi down to the station, bought myself a copy of the *Cork Examiner* and settled myself into a seat on the train. The train was carrying me away from Cork and the world of my childhood on a journey that would take me to the ends of the earth. I could not have imagined then quite how far I would travel. I was ambitious and wanted to roam the world, but I knew that the prospects of graduating from a local paper in Ireland to being the foreign correspondent of my dreams were slim. I remember now – with some shame at my presumptuousness – how I wrote down a career plan that would make me a famous foreign correspondent. I would start on a local paper, graduate to a national daily and somehow end up working for ITN. That was in the golden age of people like Sandy Gall and Mike Nicholson – swashbuckling journo heroes who reported from places like Afghanistan and Uganda, and whose voices I would mimic, cutting what I imagined was a dashing pose in front of the bedroom mirror. But Limerick had to be conquered first.

The city had a bad reputation among Cork people. Convinced of our own immutable superiority, we regarded Limerick as rough and ugly. When my school played rugby matches in Limerick the supporters travelled in fear of assault from the city's voracious hooligan element. Once a large crowd of simpering Pres boys had to be escorted to the train by the police past a crowd of stone-throwing louts. The city would later earn notoriety as 'Stab City', the haunt of some of the country's most vicious criminal gangs.

Limerick was also regarded as a citadel of conservative Catholic Ireland. Back in 1904 there had been a pogrom against Jews in the city, inspired by a Catholic priest who denounced the Jews as 'bloodsuckers'. They were beaten and harassed and subjected to a two-year trade boycott. Most of the 150-strong Jewish community departed. As late as 1970 the Labour Mayor of Limerick, Stevie Coughlan, thought it proper to publicly praise the priest involved. Coughlan referred to 'the Jewish extortionists', and indicated that they had only got what they deserved. There was uproar but the Mayor was unrepentant. To be fair though, Limerick's attitude to the Jews was in tune with a national lack of sympathy – as evidenced by the de Valera government's refusal to allow large numbers of Jewish refugees from the Nazis to seek asylum in Ireland.

The Bishop of Limerick, Jeremiah Newman, was arguably the most conservative figure in the Irish hierarchy and was quick to clip the wings of any liberal-minded priests. A shy man at heart, he was fond of a drink, and prone to unfortunate public pronouncements, once even admonishing charities which sent money abroad instead of spending it on the poor of Ireland. I saw him make that remark and was convinced he was drunk at the time.

But though conservative, even reactionary, voices were loud in Limerick they were by no means enjoying unchallenged dominance by the time I arrived in the city. There was a radical, socialist movement challenging for representation in the Dáil in the form of a charismatic councillor, Jim Kemmy. Kemmy was elected and quickly became a prominent thorn in the side of the Catholic Church and its conservative allies. Even among the religious orders there was evidence of dissent. There were priests who'd returned from mission work abroad, and others who worked on the huge council estates that ringed the city, who could see that the dream of a holy Ireland had ended up in drink and drugs and unwanted pregnancies.

But what gave Limerick its defining personality was a cutting sense of humour. The phrase: 'Go away outa dat, you ould bollix,' was a frequent response to any sign of pretension. Limerick scared me at first, but I left loving the place.

~

'What time do you want your dinner, mister?'

Mister! Nobody had called me that before. I was halfway up the stairs of my digs when I heard the words. I felt a pang of loneliness. With one word the old woman had wrenched me into the world of the grown-up. My landlady, 'Mrs C', was kindly and pious, with the martyred expression familiar to all students of Irish womanhood.

Question: *How many Irish mothers does it take to change a light bulb?*

Answer: *None. I'll just sit here in the dark.*

'What time do you want your dinner? Every day, like. When do you want it?' she repeated.

I said that I would be home from work around 6 p.m. – usually, though that 'usually' would take on a flexible quality as time and the effects of socialising wore on. Mrs C had a special devotion to St Jude, the patron saint of lost causes. I think she often had recourse to him during our association. Mrs C had a son who visited occasionally. He claimed to believe all journalists were liars. This was a view he expressed loudly at any opportunity, usually with a guffaw and punch on the arm. When I ran into him twenty years later he was still adamant on this point.

There was another *mister* in the house, a lad I will call Joe, from somewhere out in the country. Joe had a large moustache, somewhat overstated for a boy in his late teens, and he wore a wooden cross around his neck, of the kind fashionable among fans of folk masses and singing priests. Over the course of the first few dinners it became clear that we had very little in common. Joe was always ready with a wistful stare when I arrived down late to breakfast, or arrived in for dinner smelling of an after-work visit to the pub with my colleagues. Such was to be the atmosphere of my home for much of the next year.

~

My heart pounded as I climbed the stairs. The girl at reception had told me to go on up. I was expected, she said. The editorial room was the first door on the right, halfway up the stairs. I could hear typewriters clattering furiously and smell cigar smoke. I knocked on the door. There was no answer. I knocked again. Still no reply. Shaking with nerves I opened the door and walked in.

The room was crowded with middle-aged men. They were either typing or talking on the phone. At the end of the room there was an elderly, dignified-looking figure who sat behind a larger desk, sucking extravagantly on a sweet and making notes in a large diary. On the walls there were black-and-white photographs of older reporters, men who wore old-fashioned suits and, I presumed, were long deceased. Also on the walls, the effects of cigar smoke could be seen in a vague brown shading that covered the original paint.

I had only ever seen one other newsroom, the vast and bristling acre across which Dustin Hoffman and Robert Redford strode in *All the President's Men*. By contrast this little room looked like the back room of a bookie's office. One of the typists paused from his work and looked up at me. He was balding, portly, wore thick glasses and was smoking a cigar. He took the cigar out of his mouth in order to address me. 'Yes? What do you want?' he barked.

I stepped backwards. 'I'm here to see the editor. My name is Fergal Keane. I'm the new reporter.'

'Keane?'

The cigar smoker smiled. Then he addressed his companions: 'Well, lads, he's here! The junior. At last we get to see the cut of him.'

The others raised their heads to take me in.

The cigar man stood up and came forward to shake my hand. 'The name is Cormac Liddy,' he said. 'Mr Liddy to you.'

One or two of the others smirked as he said this.

'What are you laughing at, Phelan, you fucking ape?' he shouted.

A fair-haired youth sitting near the door burst out laughing.

'Mister my arse,' said Phelan in reply, leaning back with his hands behind his head.

Liddy turned to me smiling: 'You needn't take any lessons in manners from that customer.'

Liddy knocked on the editor's door and then ushered me in ahead of him. Sitting behind the desk was a silver-haired, pipe-smoking man who was busy laying out the front page of that day's paper. 'That's Mr Halligan. He's the editor.'

Liddy then slipped discreetly out of the room, trailing a cloud of cigar smoke. Halligan stood up and shook my hand. 'Good to have you with us. I'm sure Cormac and the rest of them will make you welcome.'

Brendan Halligan was a brilliant newspaperman. He was also, as I would soon find out, the toughest of editors. Halligan had been born of Irish parents and brought up in the north of England. He had worked on local papers in England before becoming the *Daily Mail* correspondent in Dublin. Halligan was passionate about Ireland. It is often said that the children of Irish parents growing up in England tend to view Ireland in one of two ways: they either want to shed their parents' identity and be British or, feeling like exiles in the country of their birth, they embrace the land over the water. Halligan was definitely in the latter category. He quit the *Mail* to edit a newly established local paper in Ireland, and then moved to the job in Limerick.

Brendan Halligan liked me, which was just as well for I would've hated to have him for an enemy. Sharp, rigorous, a man of emphatic views, when Halligan turned his questioning eye on you, you prayed to heaven you'd got the facts. I came to fear his red pen slicing through copy, pointing out errors of grammar and spelling or demanding that I check the accuracy of some point of fact. He once threatened to throw me out of his office window when I mis-attributed a quote. To this day I cannot be sure if he was joking.

After a few words of welcome Brendan Halligan introduced me to the newsroom. My daily boss would be the elderly man in the corner, nicknamed 'Chum'. He was the news editor. When the atmosphere in the newsroom became especially raucous – a not infrequent occurrence – Chum would gently rap on his table and call out: 'Settle, lads, settle for the love of God.' This would be followed by a long muttering. It never had any great effect. Chum was a gentleman journalist, a man from a different age when lunches were long and deadlines more elastic. He enjoyed regular refreshment and we could set our watches by his morning visits to the pub behind the building. When he returned he would interrogate each of us on the progress of whatever story we were working on.

The great terror for the junior reporter was the Chum 'special'. This usually arose after a call from a source who would have overheard a rumour in the pub. On the basis of this the junior would be expected to produce a front page lead. Too often the trail proved false. I was once sent off in search of a secret NATO radar station in County Limerick on the basis of a rumour picked up in the pub. Ireland was not a member of NATO. To erect a secret radar station under the noses of the preternaturally suspicious County Limerick peasantry would have required stealth well beyond the combined abilities of the CIA, MI6 or anybody else. I was laughed out of every shop, pub and house I visited. By the time I returned Chum had forgotten he'd even sent me on the story.

He was a kind-hearted man though. On my first day at the *Leader* Chum sent me to the annual general meeting of the Limerick Harbour Commissioners, knowing that, as a junior reporter with no money, I would appreciate the free lunch. I was to shadow one of the other reporters – a long-haired, bearded, denim-wearing character called Billy Kelly. Billy had made a name for himself with a series exposing police brutality in the city, and also penned a weekly satirical column. He was a tough reporter and quickly became my hero.

The Harbour Commissioners' meeting was stupefyingly dull. But its aftermath was a delight. A local councillor got to his feet, and simpering in our direction, asked that the 'gentlemen of the press join us for lunch in Hanratty's Hotel'. I followed Kelly and we were soon joined by the cigar-smoking Liddy. Having been assured by Kelly that it was permissible, I ordered a pint of stout. A waiter and menu arrived.

'I'll have Duck à l'Orange,' I said.

'You will in your arse have duck. You'll have steak,' interjected Liddy. 'On your wages you'll never pay for steak yourself.'

Like so many of my countrymen Liddy put great faith in the power of steak. It was food for the 'quality'. Steak suggested abundance and prestige. So I ordered the fillet steak.

Walking back to the office I offered the opinion that journalism was a grand job. Liddy and Kelly simply nodded, too stuffed to disagree. To a young man earning around £40 a week, after tax, such receptions were a godsend. As the months wore on I was regularly glutted with the good meat of Limerick's hotels.

~

On my first afternoon at the *Leader* I was taken on a tour of the 'stone' – the lair of the printers which sat at the back of the building, up rickety stairs and down several narrow corridors. Along with the typing and shorthand lessons I was expected to take, the time spent on the stone was geared to teaching me the nuts and bolts of the newspaper trade. The paper was in its last days under the regime of hot metal. Stories and headlines were still made up in lead, then hammered into place on the page, before being placed on the ancient printing machines.

The stone was the preserve of the printers. They were tough, suspicious Limerick men who would have regarded the arrival of a Corkman in their midst with moderate alarm, fearing perhaps that I was the advance guard of an invasion from the south. But when it was mentioned that I was John B. Keane's nephew they softened. Throughout Ireland his name acted as a passport to welcome.

The age of lead was noisy, dirty, time-consuming and glorious. But it would be gone in a few years. I had entered newspapers at a time of rapid change. In Britain the great printing unions would soon be humbled by Murdoch; the cold wind blew across the Irish Sea and their Irish counterparts were forced to accept radically altered working conditions and redundancies. Computers would simplify printing and accelerate the process of newsgathering and production. I didn't know it then but I was witnessing the end of the industrial age in newspapers.

My first writings were modest. They were little stories based on press conferences: a junior minister's pronouncements on road safety; a row over licensing hours; a new route from Shannon airport to New York. When my first by-line appeared I proudly sent a copy to my mother and grandmother. John B called me from Listowel with congratulations. I loved turning up at press conferences and announcing myself as the *Leader* man: the paper was well respected and influential; whatever you wrote was watched and commented on. Frequently if you were late for an event it would be delayed until your arrival.

Some time in my first year I went to Halligan with a bright idea for boosting the circulation of our Tuesday evening tabloid edition.

'Why not have a Bonny Baby competition?' I asked.

'As long as you run it and make sure none of the pictures get lost. Baby pictures are important to the women of Limerick,' the editor replied.

The competition was a success. Circulation rose moderately and there were slaps on the back for me, even from the normally acerbic Liddy. I cannot remember which ham-fed cherub from the city of Limerick won the prize, but I do know that misfortune soon followed. I had placed the pictures of the finalists in a shoebox and given them to the photographer working with me on the competition. He later claimed that he had given the box back to me, which may well have been true. But somewhere between us both the box was lost. Soon the switchboard screamed with the aural assaults of furious mothers. The girls in the front office were tormented. Worse still, one of the mothers was a paper seller with a stall directly in front of the *Leader* office. For several months I slunk in and out of the office by the back door, a skulking figure hurrying along the Limerick backstreets.

In the editorial office I was frequently reminded of my place. Wind-ups were part of my initiation. I was sent to find a rubber mallet, a glass hammer, the 'eye-kit' for photographs in which people squinted at the camera flash. 'That allows the boys back on the stone to open the eyes,' was the helpful explanation. I asked for this device at one of Limerick's leading photographic agencies, only to be laughed onto the street. 'Was it Liddy sent you?' the proprietor asked. In this case Liddy was innocent.

Another reporter was rumoured to have been sent to a City Council meeting with an important letter for the City Manager. It was the week before St Patrick's Day, an important fact in the entertainment that followed. My colleague raced breathlessly into the chamber and approached the Manager's secretary. The Manager was a powerful figure. He allowed the politicians to think they ran the city but he drew up the plans and signed the cheques.

The secretary passed the letter to the Manager who paused in the outrolling of some councillor's speech to read the contents. He smiled. The Manager wasn't given to public smiling. He began to heave with laughter then passed the letter back to his secretary who gave it back to the reporter. I will spare him embarrassment and substitute a different name. The message read as follows:

'My name is John Breen and I want my arse painted green for St Patrick's Day.'

The reporter quickly made his excuses and left.

CHAPTER EIGHT

Local Lessons

If it fulfilled the one and only condition, truth, the journalist's duty was to publish it whatever the pleasure, pain, satisfaction or annoyance it might cause.
        Publish and Be Damned, HUGH CUDLIPP

Mrs C's desire to run an orderly house was starting to restrict my social life. One incident in particular threatened to blight my reputation permanently in the good woman's eyes. One evening I was sent to shadow the West Limerick correspondent, a man from my father's home town who was the paper's hottest reporter.

Jimmy Woulfe had also come to the *Leader* via my uncle's recommendation. Jimmy was assigned to go to Tournafulla, a hamlet in the hills between Limerick and Kerry, where the local senior hurling team had just won themselves a place in the Limerick county final. Woulfe took me to a bar where we'd been invited to meet the team and coach. They were all farmers or rural labourers, big-boned men who said little but who smiled enthusiastically whenever Jimmy asked a question. He took copious notes of what little they did say. I noticed early on in the proceedings that numerous pints of Guinness were flowing my way. Unwilling to upset my hosts I quaffed them quietly.

At some point the door of the bar was locked. A lock-in. The barman instructed us to keep our voices down, lest a passing guard be embarrassed into having to raid the place. The pints kept coming. The big men became more talkative. When they discovered I was John B. Keane's nephew the Guinness flow became a flood. Large hands slapped my back, bringing me to the edge of intestinal upheaval on several occasions. I struggled. I knew it wouldn't do to be seen vomiting up my porter in such company.

I lasted until I reached the car and then exploded, speckling Jimmy Woulfe – in the immortal phrase of Flann O'Brien – with 'buff-coloured puke'. He was kind about it, perhaps due to his own mellowness. The photographer near whose car the upheaval had taken place drove me back to Limerick with a broad smile. 'You are some fucking tulip,' he said.

I woke to the screaming of the alarm clock and a smell of vomit. Nervously I raised my pounding head. There was a trail of sick from the bedroom door to the bed. I then realised that I was lying on the floor, in my clothes.

I looked out the window and saw a horse standing in the front garden. Frightened that this was a hallucination, I quickly closed the curtains and ran to the toilet, noticing on the way that flecks of vomit extended along the landing. I staggered to the bathroom and retched until there was nothing left. Then, grabbing lumps of toilet paper, I began to clean the stairs and bedroom floor. I looked out the window once more, squinting at the bright light. The horse was still there. In fact there was also a horse in the next-door neighbour's garden. I decided I would ask Mrs C about this once matters had calmed. (She later explained that Limerick had a resident population of wandering horses.)

At breakfast my fellow lodger gave me a 'you-wouldn't-catch-me-carrying-on-like-that-in-a-hundred-years' look. 'A hard night, was it?' asked Joe, smiling.

'Moderately so,' I replied.

Then Mrs C entered the room, bearing a large tray on which sat a threatening mound of greasy rashers, sausages and eggs.

'Oh Jesus,' I groaned, under my breath.

'What was that?' snapped the devout Mrs C.

'Grace,' I replied. 'Just saying grace to myself.'

She gave the appearance of being satisfied with this, but as she left the room Joe leaned across.

'You shouldn't be taking the Lord's name in vain. It'll upset the poor woman.'

I wanted to tell him to fuck off but I hadn't the strength. He had the better of me and knew it.

'Sorry,' I said, and then faced into the greasy horror of breakfast. Mrs C returned to the room.

'That's an awful queer smell upstairs, boys,' she said.

I said nothing. Joe said nothing. She turned to me, her expression a mix of pity and also, I thought, some fear. She was wondering what kind of creature had descended on her good clean home.

'It was a bad burger,' I explained. 'It caught me off the hop in the middle of the night. I was looking for the toilet but got lost in the dark.'

Only a fool or a kind human being would have accepted the excuse. Mrs C was a kind human being.

Some weeks later I had a chance to redeem myself. The Pope was about to arrive in Ireland, the first visit by a pontiff to the land of St Patrick, most Catholic of nations and exporter of missionaries to the heathen millions for centuries. As a local reporter I would have privileged access to Limerick racecourse where the Pope would say Mass on the last day of his visit.

This lifted my standing in Mrs C's eyes considerably. When I further revealed that my Aunt Kathleen, my father's sister, would actually be meeting his Holiness my stock went through the roof. (Kathleen was a Reverend Mother at one of

Limerick's biggest convent schools, a big-hearted, wonderful woman who was loved by the children she taught and represented what was best in the Irish Catholic Church.) It was as if, knowing me, Mrs C felt she was in direct personal contact with the Pope. I adopted an expression of conspicuous piety for the days leading up to the visit. The Kathleen connection gave me one of my first scoops at the *Leader*, something along the lines of: 'We talk to Listowel nun who will meet Pope'. In those days the secular revolution was in its infancy. We were still a pious people, at least in our public demonstrations of faith.

~

Pope John Paul's visit gave us our first taste of international celebrity. It was also a landmark in the history of the modern Irish state. For those who imagined that the changes of the sixties and seventies had laid the foundations of a modern, secular republic the public response to John Paul was a surprise. From the moment *Il Papa* arrived at Dublin airport on 29 September 1979 the country erupted in an ecstasy of faith. Not since Kennedy came nearly twenty years before had we been so flattered. Twenty thousand people turned out at Dublin airport to greet him while television carried live coverage of every holy minute. More than a million people – one third of the population – attended the first papal mass in Dublin's Phoenix Park, the same place where my grandparents had witnessed the Eucharistic Congress in 1932.

The Pope travelled on to Drogheda and publicly appealed to the IRA to end its violence. On bended knees he beseeched the gunmen: '. . . to all of you who are listening, I say: do not believe in violence, do not support violence. It is not the Christian way.' But the papal appeal had the same effect as the denunciations of an earlier generation of religious appellants during the War of Independence – that is to say it didn't make a blind bit of difference. A few days later the IRA gave their answer by killing a Protestant father of three. That atrocity seemed to pass us all by in the excitement of the moment.

By the time the Pope reached Limerick the city was vibrating with anticipation. Yet to me the mood was not triumphalist. The atmosphere resembled a giant picnic rather than an assertion of Church power. People thronged to the Limerick racecourse to hear the Pontiff speak but I remember above all the brightness and good humour of the crowd.

On the day of the Limerick appearance I got up at around three in the morning to find Mrs C already in the kitchen making sandwiches. I showed her my laminated press pass which she touched gently as if it were some sort of precious relic.

People were on the move across the city. More than a quarter of a million flooded into the racecourse. The majority spent the night camped out to get the best view of the Pope. They sang hymns and said prayers. The *Limerick Leader* would later report that 300 children had been separated from and then re-united with their parents. For the first time I watched the international media in action. There were brash, loud people from a foreign television network, setting up cameras and lights. A car drove past crowded with reporters and photographers from the Associated Press: they looked rough, tough, travelled, everything I wanted to be. I felt like a hick with my brown three-piece suit and notebook. Then my determination to do the best job I could took over. The *Limerick Leader* had despatched its entire editorial staff to cover the visit and was producing a special commemorative edition.

Our opposition, a much smaller paper called the *Limerick Echo*, had gone to great lengths to produce exclusives, one of its reporters even promising a priest that she would join the Legion of Mary if he would give an exclusive account of his own meeting with the Pope. (I would later marry this pious journalist.) My own part in *Leader*'s grand operation was relatively small. I'd only been in the job a couple of weeks and Halligan was still taking my measure. The cigar-smoking Liddy was despatched to Rome to travel on the papal plane back to Ireland. His account of the journey caused some mirth in the editorial room.

> Never in all these years have I found a story so hard to write as I try to describe my feelings of intense joy that I had been privileged to meet this saintly man, or perhaps more appropriately this saint of a man. It has taken me nineteen attempts to write these few paragraphs.

Nobody doubted Liddy's genuine joy and emotion. But various other disrespectful suggestions were offered as to why Liddy, a talented writer, took so long to compose his epic.

The Pope came to earth in a helicopter, the first of those machines I had ever seen. My memory is of a white-clad figure emerging surrounded by priests, beyond them a cordon of Irish police, and then a vast, unending crowd which erupted into sustained cheering. All around me people were weeping. Until I began research for this chapter I had no memory of what the Pope actually said. After everything that had happened in the previous few days, not least the passionate appeal to the IRA in Drogheda, the media were in thrall to this most charismatic of men. When he met the press after Drogheda the assembled journalists burst into a spontaneous rendition of 'For He's a Jolly Good Fellow'. Swept away by the excitement we missed the real import of his words in Limerick, and the marker he was laying down for the future direction of the Catholic Church.

In Limerick John Paul II revealed his conservative self. It was the voice that had rung out from pulpits in Ireland for decades, but diverted by the magic of his evident kindness, we barely heard his message to the Irish faithful. The Pope used Limerick to denounce the evils of abortion, contraception, divorce and working motherhood. 'Ireland must choose,' he declared. Whoever advised him was well out of touch with the changing social mores of the Republic.

But in the enthusiasm of the moment nobody in the press thought of shouting: 'Hold on a minute! It's not that simple here any more.' It would have been the equivalent of farting loudly in Mass. For the forces of revanchism in Ireland the papal speech in Limerick acted as a rallying cry. In the wake of the visit the Catholic right set out to change the Constitution so that it would include a ban on abortion, above and beyond the existing strict legal ban on termination.

It led to the bitterest public debate in the history of the modern state. Nobody took up arms but the (ultimately successful) attempt to have a Pro-Life amendment inserted into the Constitution set liberal and conservative Ireland at each other's throats in the early 1980s, and prepared the ground for future divisive struggles over contraception and divorce.

~

The Pope's visit was the only really huge story of my time in Limerick. Most of my work as a junior reporter revolved around covering the district courts, local health, education and City Council meetings. I spent much time recording the guff and blather of local politics. Councillor X said this and Alderman Z said that; the City Manager replied that he would look into the problem, the Lord Mayor asked the member to withdraw the allegation, and so on. Some of the councillors worked long hours for their constituents; others were party hacks who did what they were told and collected their expenses; some behaved like bored schoolboys, heckling the opposition and guffawing oafishly whenever one of their own side scored some tedious point. I hated council meetings but they produced reams of copy to fill the paper, and councillors would regularly harangue reporters who failed to mention them in the newspaper.

'That was a great speech I gave about the rat problem. Why didn't you put it in?'

I wanted to say: 'I didn't put it in because you are a bore and very likely a cretin and I am only here because it is an expected part of my apprenticeship and soon I will take leave of you and your grubbing for publicity so will you now please fuck off and leave me alone.'

Instead I said: 'Sorry about that. I'll get you in next week.'

Covering the courts was different. Real life was on display here, not mediated by any blathering politician. To someone who had spent his secondary school years in middle-class Ireland – as Louis MacNeice wrote: '. . . banned forever from the candles of the Irish poor' – the experience was shocking, an intensive immersion in the social collapse of large swaths of one Irish city.

The defendants were almost exclusively drawn from the city's council estates. Their crimes ranged from theft of a church poor box to hideous gang rape. They were whey-faced and thin, coughing from cigarettes; they smirked at the police and waved to friends, shuffling into court and into the maw of a criminal justice system which processed them as indifferently as it had processed their fathers and uncles and cousins.

They were destined for jail, followed by unemployment and jail again. The system regarded these young men with contempt and they returned the compliment. Everybody in the little courtroom understood that there wasn't going to be any attempt at rehabilitation: the judges, lawyers, the defendants most of all. It wasn't going to happen. The criminal poor were written off as irredeemable, a nuisance and occasional source of horror but never enough of a critical mass to disturb the dreary calm of the Republic. The system was designed to keep criminals out of circulation, not transform them into useful citizens.

So they travelled across the city to the Victorian misery of Limerick jail, or up to one of the state reformatories to be brutalised until their sentence was done and they were thrown back into the world from which they'd come. They came from estates like Southill and St Mary's Park and Ballynanty, grey and ugly, like Finglas where I'd spent my early childhood. You knew as you sat there, hunched under the pink-faced little judge, crammed in beside the solicitors, that you would very rarely, if ever, hear a defendant give an address from one of the wealthier areas of the city.

Meanwhile anybody who suggested that the city's crime problem might be getting a little out of control was roundly condemned. It was in Limerick that I first heard that favourite phrase of the politician: 'You're after blowing that way out of proportion.' A journalist who hears that should realise he is onto something good. The reckoning in Limerick would come long after I left the city.

~

In my time in Limerick a gun-related crime was a rarity. But by the early part of the new century shootings were no longer unusual. Twenty years after I left Limerick, the city exploded in gang warfare. Rival families murdered each other and anybody unlucky enough to stand in their way. The social problems that created the crime had been centuries in the making: tenements had existed in all the Irish cities since the collapse of agriculture during the Famine; successive British and Irish governments had made either half-hearted efforts or no effort at all in dealing with the problem. Those who didn't get out to England or America scrabbled for jobs in factories. When the factories closed they joined the people who had never had jobs and became our long-term unemployed.

They were given dole money and offered places on training schemes that trained them for non-existent jobs. The worst cases washed up at the offices of the St Vincent de Paul in search of charity. In Ireland's cities nobody ever entertained any serious thought that this order might change, or that there might spring from these desolate estates a violent breed of criminal whose activities would give Limerick the reputation as the home of the country's most violent armed gangs.

I was appalled by the idea that the poor would fester away for ever on their estates. But along with the rest of the city's comfortable classes I never really believed they could pose a major threat to anybody but themselves. The arrival of drugs on Ireland's big council estates changed the equation. Heroin began flooding into Ireland in the 1980s. With drugs came the opportunity to make big money. Then guns came in and local Al Capones emerged. The police force were regarded with contempt by the gangs. Suddenly politicians began talking about a breakdown of the social order. By that they meant *their* order – the order that had existed since the foundation of the state, a country where the poor were encouraged to be happy with their lot and offer up any suffering for the repose of the Holy Souls.

Words like alienation and social justice sprang into the vernacular. The poor had arrived. They could hardly walk out their front doors without finding an earnest young person with a clipboard anxious to canvas their views, or go to the shops without stumbling into a journalist eager to expose the wretchedness of their lives. Those early years on the crime-beat taught me an important lesson, one I would carry with me to the most conflict-ridden regions of the earth: the poor and downtrodden will stay poor and downtrodden; they will always be unseen, people who are talked about rather than talked to, until they do something terrible. Then we pay attention.

~

Besides covering courts and running copy back to the stone, the junior was responsible for dealing with the army of complainers, cranks and outright lunatics who came to the front office. The local newspaper is a target for many and various bores. Some are relatively genial. They want nothing more than to hand their letter or manifesto to a human being. But there are others who believe that only you can avenge their tragedy or fix their lives.

A new, terrible phrase entered my life: 'There's someone in the front office wants to see a reporter.' I learned to fear men who came armed with large bundles of correspondence, claiming corruption and conspiracy on the part of higher officials. Long hours were spent politely taking notes while the girls from the ad-sales department grinned in the background. But it was one of these calls that gave me my first lead story, introduced me to my first African friends and plunged the *Limerick Leader* into a national controversy.

Gabi Okeh Oparah was studying politics at the National Institute for Higher Education in Limerick. He was one of a small group of black students, mostly Nigerian, who'd been coming to the city since the mid-1970s. One night Gabi and a few of his Nigerian friends decided they would go to a disco at one of the city's most popular venues, the Limerick Savoy. They got to the door only to be told by the bouncer that blacks were not welcome. There was a minor argument but it was made clear that Gabi and his friends weren't getting in. Humiliated, they left without making a fuss. This wasn't some rural backwater but a night club in the centre of the third biggest city in Ireland at the beginning of the 1980s.

117

A few days afterwards, Gabi arrived at the *Limerick Leader* front office with his story of racism. Halligan called me into his office. It sounded like a good story, he said, but we would need proof. I was sent down to meet Gabi and get the details. Gabi was in his thirties and had grown up in Biafra, a place with enormous resonance for Irish people because of the part played by Irish missionaries during the rebellion of the late 1960s. He had a gentle sense of humour and described the events of the previous weekend in a slow, deliberate fashion.

I arranged to meet him after work for a drink. Black faces were still an unusual sight outside Dublin. I felt self-conscious as I walked into the bar with Gabi, aware that several of the other drinkers were watching me closely, curious about my appointment with the dark stranger. Over a beer I made a plan with Gabi. He would gather up his friends and go to the Savoy on the following Friday night. But this time I would be standing directly behind him, along with a photographer carrying a concealed camera. Halligan gave the plan his immediate blessing but warned me to say nothing to anybody else. The Savoy was a big advertiser and he didn't want anybody tipping off the disco management.

That Friday afternoon he called me into his office. My heart sank. I feared the Savoy had somehow found out what we were planning. 'Don't tell me . . . it's off?' I said.

'No, it's not off. I just wanted to give you a few words of advice.' He was as calm as ever. 'What you need here is only one thing,' he said. 'Make sure you can hear whatever the doorman says and make sure you get a good note of it. I will want to see the note. Make sure South [the photographer] gets the picture, but above all concentrate on hearing the doorman. Don't get involved. You are there to report whatever happens, not to draw attention to yourself.'

By the time I reached the Savoy that night there were already crowds queuing to get into the disco. Gabi and the other black students lined up, I slipped in behind them with the photographer. By the time we reached the front of the queue the bouncer, a brawny man in his fifties, was whispering to a colleague inside. He'd spotted Gabi but must have assumed I was just another customer. Gabi walked forward and presented himself. I shuffled closely behind him. Then the doorman spoke:

'There are no blacks allowed in here.'

Gabi feigned surprise and asked him why.

No explanation was forthcoming, just a repeat of the rule. 'No blacks allowed.' I heard the words and immediately pulled out my notebook and committed them to paper. The photographer whipped out his camera and captured the scene: a bemused doorman caught in the glare of the flashlight, the students milling around him. With the evidence secured we retreated.

Halligan ran the story as the front page lead with pictures the following weekend. There was immediate outrage, not all of it directed at the management of the Savoy Theatre. Some in Limerick felt that the newspaper was dishonouring a fine venue. A narrow xenophobic streak in Irish life manifested itself. A printer at the *Leader* taunted me with the words 'nigger lover'. One of my editorial colleagues started whispering about the danger to our advertising revenue, as if we should have looked the other way when the students came complaining. The proprietor of the Savoy also owned a huge car dealership which spent tens of thousands on promotions. For the first time in my career I understood that the excitement of getting a good story isn't always matched by popular appreciation.

I am sure Brendan Halligan came under pressure after the story appeared but he never flinched. It was a thrilling and scary few weeks. The story made it to the national papers and a television crew arrived to interview me. As the controversy escalated one of Ireland's top bands pulled out of a concert at the Savoy and the Students Union began a boycott of the premises. Then the Nigerian ambassador to Ireland waded in and condemned the exclusion of black students. The Irish Department of Foreign Affairs, horrified at the potential damage to the country's image, put pressure on the Savoy management. The Savoy caved in and apologised, even offering to put on a special evening for Limerick's black students.

Halligan didn't crow over the apology. 'Always resist the temptation to rub people's noses in it. It's not the point of what we do. We publish the story, let them do what they think is right,' he said.

The Savoy story had made a splash. It convinced Halligan that I had the makings of a reporter, and it showed me that for a reporter to take on powerful interests he needed the backing of a brave editor. That was what made the *Limerick Leader* such a brilliant place to start my journalistic career. My boss was a man who looked beyond the timid horizons of so many of his contemporaries. Halligan was a great editor with a strong sense of social justice, a delight in making mischief for the powerful and an exacting insistence on accuracy. I would never have become a journalist without him.

~

Brendan Halligan was also the first person in journalism who spotted that drink might become a problem for me. In Limerick back then there was a plentiful supply of free drink for the thirsty young journalist. At receptions we were plied with as much as we could hold, and often more than we could hold. I drank pretty much like every other junior reporter in town: we guzzled what we could once the day's work was done. I felt again the rush of ease I had found with my first drink years before and I loved the conviviality of the pub, the sense of time suspended and the banishing of any worries I might have carried with me through the door.

On Fridays, after being paid, we sometimes drank at the bar of the Railway Hotel and Halligan would hold court at the centre of a group which included the resident correspondents of the national press. They were big fish to me, men who dealt in daily deadlines, who had their own expense accounts, who talked fast and laughed and swore a lot. My editor-hero sat in the middle, the smoke from his pipe curling around the flushed faces of the drinkers, mostly listening to the conversation and occasionally interposing a thoughtful observation.

But I often drank too quickly, as if the liquid in my glass might be taken from me at any moment, and after four or five drinks I was overtaken by melancholy, sitting amid the group but not with them. Halligan said to me once as we were leaving the pub: 'You'll go far if you can keep your head on your shoulders. You know what I mean?'

Halligan knew my father's history and he'd been around newsrooms long enough to see many good men and women taken by drink. But that comment was as far as it went with him; he believed a reporter could drink what he liked as long as he got the story done first. I always managed on that score. Even up to the end, years away, I would always deliver.

~

I saw my father only occasionally in those years. I don't really know why; I don't have a ready explanation that makes sense, except perhaps that I was avoiding him and the pain of what was happening to him. Maybe also I didn't want his warning shadow getting in the way of my own affair with alcohol. We communicated mostly by letter and phone.

Once I went to see him, in mid-summer, a hot day when I escaped to Dublin to cover some story with a Limerick connection. I had a few hours to spare and decided to seek out my father. I went to RTE where he normally recorded in the afternoons. There was no sign of him. I tried the usual pubs in Donnybrook: Kiely's and McCloskey's.

'No, we haven't seen him today.'

Then I went to his flat on Marlboro Road. It is the place with which I associate him most. He spent years in the red-brick Georgian terraced house with the overgrown gardens at the back. The first time I visited there was a note pinned to the front door. It was written in red biro on a piece of brown cardboard. It said callers should knock once for the tenant on the ground floor, twice for Mr Keane and three times for the remaining tenant.

I knocked twice on the door and when there was no response I paused and knocked once. An Indian man came to the door. He was soft spoken and asked me who I was. I explained and he showed me upstairs to my father's room. I knocked again but there was no answer. I went into the room but my father was out. Nothing of what I saw there – the detritus of a life being consumed by alcohol – mattered so much as the book that lay open on his bedside table. It was a copy of the Bible. I picked it up and saw that my father had underlined some words. It was a sentence from the *Psalms*: 'Lord let me feel thy mercy in the morning, for I have hoped in thee.'

I was taken aback. In one line my father had given me a glimpse into the heart of his suffering. *Lord let me feel thy mercy in the morning.*

How many regretful, shivering mornings had my father endured? I ran down the stairs, out the front door and into the crowds. I searched for my father among their faces. I wanted to find him then and hold him, take him somewhere safe. I could not find him. I still cherished the illusion of rescue but he was beyond me, as elusive then as he had always been.

~

Later that year I went to see a doctor in Cork. I had become depressed. When I drank I felt worse. I didn't drink any more or less than colleagues of the same age. It was just that the booze took me down when it raised them up. The doctor asked for my family history. After listening and taking some notes he looked me directly in the eye. I imagined it was the manner he adopted when telling people they were suffering from a terminal illness.

'What you need to realise is that you can't ever drink again. Do you understand me? It's not an option for you.'

I nodded and agreed with him. That would be a speciality of mine. I agreed with whatever any doctor told me. But this time I did stop drinking. I used the power of my will, because in those days it was still a powerful tool. I quit and started to work even harder. Work became my substitute.

CHAPTER NINE

Short Takes

Our intention is to be the voice of the people, to speak for them, to give utterance to their ideals, to defend them against slander and false witness.

First leading article of the *Irish Press*, 5 September 1931

My father said Dev was so crooked if he swallowed a six inch nail he'd shit a corkscrew. He hated Dev because of Michael Collins. I saw him weep for 'poor, murdered Mick Collins' and call Dev a 'backstabbing murdering bastard'. Éamonn said that Dev had not only ordered the killing but that his own wife knew it and wouldn't speak to him for years afterwards. He called Dev the 'bastard son of a Spanish ukulele player from the Bronx', a scurrilous reference to the late President's Iberian father.

There is no proof that Dev ordered the murder of Michael Collins or that Sinead de Valera stopped speaking to him, or indeed that he was illegitimate. But it didn't stop my father repeating the story frequently. In 1982 I phoned my father from Limerick with the news that I was taking up a job on the newspaper Dev founded. I was breathless with excitement: 'I've got a job on the *Irish Press*. A national job, Da!'

He was happy for me and himself and set aside any atavistic

political impulse. 'Sure we'll see more of each other. We can thank Dev for that,' he said.

Every job you take changes your life in some way. But joining the *Irish Press* would entirely alter its course. In the space of a year I went from being an unknown provincial reporter into someone who had a shouting chance of becoming a foreign correspondent. It also introduced me to the person who would become my wife and travel with me around the world.

I was twenty-one years old when I joined the paper's staff in Dublin. Yet had a Keane been offered the job a few decades earlier they would have thought hard about accepting it. In Ireland you could tell political affiliation by which newspaper was taken at home. A house which took the *Irish Press* newspaper was making a statement of support for de Valera and Fianna Fáil. The Keanes most definitely did not take the *Press*. In the old days taking a job with Dev's paper would have been similar to the scion of a Tory family switching his allegiance to the *Morning Star*.

But Ireland and its politics were changing. My father's view of the *Irish Press* had also altered over the years. He knew the editor, Tim Pat Coogan, and respected the paper's literary output: it was the only daily newspaper in Europe which ran a weekly page for new fiction and poetry. It was also a strong supporter of the Irish language, a factor which weighed strongly with my bi-lingual father.

I was surprised to get the job. The interview hadn't gone well. Halfway through the phone rang. Tim Pat Coogan picked it up and, turning away from me, began a long conversation, a conversation that continued until he was called away from the interview. I sat there while the two other executives, sitting on either side of him, continued to ask questions. They did not seem embarrassed, indeed they acted as if this was entirely normal practice during interviews for Irish Press Newspapers Ltd.

The editor was still on the phone when I left the room. I wondered if he even knew who I was or why I was there. I learned later that Tim Pat Coogan rarely came to the newsroom from his office on one of the upper floors. But he had seen enough of me to make up his mind. Tim Pat was a man who tended to polarise opinion. Arguably the best-known journalist in the country, and certainly Ireland's first journalistic 'celebrity', he was also an historian and television pundit. He was admired in Republican and Irish-American circles for his writings on the Troubles, but those who took a more revisionist, anti-Republican line on Irish history tended to dislike, even loathe him.

To a young lad, fresh off the train from Limerick, Coogan was a near mythical figure – one of a handful of journalistic superstars in the country. When he turned away from me during the interview I was shattered. Convinced that I'd come across as a rustic buffoon and had no chance of getting the job, I loped back to the railway station. Ahead of me, I was sure, lay a lifetime on provincial newspapers, trudging up and down to the District Court, faithfully recording the blather of the county councillors, my soul shrivelling under the daily assault of the mundane.

'Maybe you'll get the job because he didn't have to listen to you,' my old friend Liddy said. Two weeks later a letter arrived bearing the imprint of the *Irish Press*. The letter offered me the position of 'general reporter'. I was going to Dublin!

The boys on the *Limerick Leader* were enthusiastic. They crowded about me in the editorial room, passing the letter around. On my last night in Limerick the editorial staff threw a party. There were nice speeches and promises to stay in touch. The following morning as I sat in my car to drive away I noticed the stub of a cigar stuck in the windscreen wiper. It was Liddy's farewell. The man who had so scared me when I arrived had become the best of friends.

Halligan came out of his office to say goodbye. He smiled and patted me on the back. 'I would have liked you to stay but I know you have a plan,' he said.

~

The prospect of moving to Dublin excited and intimidated me. I hadn't lived in the city for a decade, not since we'd left my father at the beginning of the 1970s. Once on the way to work I saw him from the bus, walking down Donnybrook towards Herbert Park where he would sit and read the papers, pick out his best from the racing pages and chat with passers-by.

He could not see me and there was something unselfconscious about the way he wandered along, unobserved (he thought) and chatting to himself. It reminded me of Patrick Kavanagh's lines:

> *On Pembroke Road look out for my ghost*
> *Dishevelled with shoes untied,*
> *Playing through the railings with little children*
> *Whose children have long since died.*
> *O he was a nice man*
> *Fol dol the di do,*
> *He was a nice man*
> *I tell you.*

Dublin was *his* city. I still cannot go there and walk its streets without thinking of him. To that extent it will always be a haunted city for me. He had lived there longer than any other place and though he often cursed it, damning its 'bowsies' and 'gurriers', Éamonn was at home among the grey stone, the fanlights and the shadows of Georgian Dublin. Though the property developers had destroyed much of its heritage, Dublin retained a spectral elegance. It was still the city of MacNeice's

'Grey brick upon brick/declamatory bronze' in which the shades of conqueror and rebel flitted along the backstreets; it was also a place which could be harshly real, where the laughter heard through the open door of its pubs carried with it the faintest undertone of mockery.

My father would always be a *culchie*, a country boy, in Dublin, however much its citizens came to know him and, in the case of many, to love him. At the heart of the city the Liffey meandered past the windows of the *Irish Press* on the way to Dublin Bay, malodorous at low tide but enchanting on the flood, when the street lights along the quays played on the water.

Éamonn arrived there as a teenager without a penny in his pockets, the most impractical man in Ireland, a man who could hardly boil an egg, but who won over the cynical souls of literary Dublin with his passion for words and his enthusiasm for life. His drinking companions were men like Paddy Kavanagh, Brendan Behan and Flann O'Brien; they were quick-witted and sharp tongued and would cut a man down to size in very quick time. My father once told me they gave him a fool's pardon. I don't believe it was that. The poet Brendan Kennelly, another native of North Kerry, wrote once of my father's 'fierce fidelity' to his art. I think that's what Kavanagh and Behan recognised, a core of something genuine. It was why they indulged this boy from Listowel and took him to their hearts.

Behan was especially good to my father, bringing him to his home for Christmas and advising the country boy about the traps of Dublin life. My Uncle John B recalled for his biographers how Behan instructed neophytes like my father in the art of drinking:

Brendan's idea was to buy a pound of brawn and put it in his pocket, and when hungry, take out a slice and eat

My first newspaper appearance – London, January 1961 – with my parents and my godmother, the actress Siobhan McKenna.

On the beach in Ardmore with my maternal grandmother, May Hassett. Throughout childhood she was a port of shelter.

In Ardmore, aged around two years. I am still returning to that village by the west Waterford coast.

ABOVE: My Kerry grandparents, Bill and Hanna Keane. He was a village schoolmaster who instilled in his children a love of books. Hanna fought with the IRA in the War of Independence.

LEFT: My father's greatest hero, Michael Collins.

RIGHT: Fr Davey O'Connor, principal of St Michael's College, Listowel. My father regarded him as a monster.

BELOW: My father, Éamonn Keane. This photograph captures the romantic dreamer in him.

BELOW RIGHT: My mother, Maura Hassett, in the back garden of St Declans, the house in Cork where I spent some of my happiest hours.

LEFT: A photograph taken on my first Holy Communion, sometime in the late 1960s.

BELOW: With Brother Jerome Kelly, headmaster and visionary. He kept faith with me where many others might have despaired.

With my uncle John B. Keane,
playwright and novelist. It was he who
'got me a start' in journalism. He was
the most decent man I ever knew.

As a young reporter in Ireland interviewing the legendary,
and now infamous, Charles Haughey.

LEFT: Anne Flaherty, fellow reporter on the Irish Press, whom I would later marry.

RIGHT: Clowning in the bush in the unlikely company of then Tory MEP, Paul Howell. This photograph was taken on my first trip to Africa in the early 1980s.

ABOVE: With my father in Belfast. It was one of our last meetings.

BELOW: My grandmother, May Hassett, and mother, Maura. This photograph was taken towards the end of my grandmother's life. She died shortly after I moved to South Africa.

it, washed down, of course, with Guinness. He was serious about it. In those days people like Brendan thought lunching impinged on their drinking. It was the advice of a lovable man.

Behan's wife Beatrice recalled why her husband had welcomed my father: 'Brendan used to tell me he found the Keanes great company. I think he admired their imaginations and wit.'

By then Behan was a celebrated international playwright. His play *The Hostage* had been a huge success in London and New York and his autobiography *Borstal Boy* had received critical acclaim. But Behan's descent into alcoholism was well under way. He ran up debts, owed large sums to the taxman, was arrested for fighting and was hospitalised. My Uncle John B told his biographer about meeting Brendan in a bar opposite the radio studios where my father worked. It was the day of an all-Ireland Gaelic football final in which Kerry and Dublin were playing. Behan drank one double gin after another and was soon very drunk. Later that day, while my uncle was away at the match, Behan was badly beaten up. Within six months he was dead from alcoholism. Paddy Kavanagh would also die from drink and Flann O'Brien too. My father saw them go but their decline did nothing to restrain him.

I always found that strange. 'How can you watch that happen and not give up the drink?' Now I understand the naivety of that view. It assumes a power over alcohol which the chronic alcoholic cannot find.

~

Dev had been dead for nearly twenty years when I joined the *Irish Press*. His son, Major Vivion de Valera, had died the previous year. The newspaper was now being run by the major's son, Éamonn de Valera Jnr, known to staff as 'Major Minor'. He had something of the physical appearance of his grandfather – the narrow face, the austere expression, but with little of his vision or strength. 'Major Minor' presided over the collapse of the newspaper amid industrial action and considerable bitterness.

Dev had established the *Irish Press* in 1931 to counter the propaganda of his various political enemies who had enjoyed, until then, a monopoly of broadcasting and print media. The *Irish Independent* was staunchly supportive of business and the big farmers, never friends of de Valera, while the *Irish Times* in those days represented the voice of a dwindling Protestant minority and a small Dublin intelligentsia. De Valera understood that if he was to have a realistic chance of coming to power he needed his own propaganda outlet. The *Irish Press* slogan was: *The Truth in the News* – which was true except where the news and de Valera's interests came into conflict. In those days the paper faithfully articulated the Fianna Fáil line and even when I arrived, fifty years after its founding, the paper was expected to be broadly supportive of the party.

Despite Éamonn de Valera's innate conservatism, the newspaper had radical roots. When it was first published it acted, like the Fianna Fáil party itself, as the voice of 'the men of no property'. These were the small farmers, rural labourers and those sections of the urban working class who weren't allied to the labour movement. But as Ireland stagnated under de Valera's rule so did the *Irish Press*. The newspaper became more inward looking and conservative, genuflecting to the alliance of Church and state, a mouthpiece of the ruling establishment rather than a watchdog. Ironically it was a row over his financial control of the newspaper that eventually ushered Dev from parliament to the sinecure of the presidency, ending the age of stagnation and pie-in-the-sky dreams of a self-sufficient, Irish-speaking republic. The paper that had helped him to power now helped to ease him out of it.

The arrival of Tim Pat Coogan as editor in the 1970s signalled a change in direction. Coogan was the first editor from the post-revolutionary generation; he was faithful to the Republican ideal but wanted to disentangle it from conservative Catholicism and the more reactionary elements of Fianna Fáil. The days of slavish obedience to Dev's party were over.

It was a measure of how much things had changed that by the early 1980s the paper wrote the political obituary of the Fianna Fáil leader Charles Haughey during a vicious leadership struggle, when the bitterness within the party surpassed anything that occurred between it and the opposition. Unfortunately Coogan had misjudged the moment. Haughey would survive the challenge. The obituary was printed before Haughey resigned: many months before he resigned. I was one of its co-authors.

~

The newspaper's address was Burgh Quay, named after one of the De Burghs – the powerful Anglo-Norman earls – but it was popularly known as 'Purge Quay' because of the level of suspicion, intrigue and general instability which surrounded the newspaper. The newsroom was deep and wide and to my eyes as big a football field. It was divided into two main sections with the reporting staff close to the windows overlooking the river, and the subs and editors occupying the area closest to the printing presses. A thin cloud of cigarette smoke floated above the heads of the journalists, like the evening smog over a great city. There were ten or so reporters at the main desk in the centre of the room, a few of them typing, another on the phone and others chatting. Watching over them were the group chief news editor and the news editors of the evening and morning papers. Behind them sat the chief sub-editor and his team.

The chief sub on the *Irish Press* was the soon-to-be famous novelist John Banville. He was a courteous, civilised man who was largely responsible for making the *Press* the most literate paper in the country. But I suspect he looked down the room towards the reporters' table with a feeling of unease. It may of course simply have been his ascetic expression, but I never spoke to him without feeling like the janitor's son approaching the headmaster at a public school. Our reporters' table was littered with notebooks, mugs of tea, overflowing ashtrays, half-eaten bags of chips, rolls of carbon-backed copy paper and early editions of the evening paper.

Descending through the fug of smoke were several strands of wire, patched through from the ceiling, and connected to some battered-looking telephones. I would learn that access to a telephone could often be regarded as a luxury on the *Irish Press*, which was then experiencing an outbreak of financial trouble that would lead to its closure a decade later. Along one wall, as you entered the room, was a series of booths with telephones and typewriters. A huge clattering noise reverberated from this area punctuated by calls of 'Copy!'. A shiftless-looking youth would then amble from the news-desk to one of the booths and collect a piece of freshly typed paper. This was the domain of the copytakers, a formidable group of women led by 'Miss' Maureen Craddock, a veteran of the War of Independence, whose bird-like, demure appearance belied a heart of steel. Having faced down the Black and Tans, Miss Craddock was ready to make mincemeat of any reporter foolish enough to treat her with anything less than due deference.

Among her associates was a rather deaf, elderly woman whose voice at the end of the line inspired terror in the hearts of the reporters. They were never quite sure how their copy would translate after being typed up by her. Shouts of 'What?', 'Will ya repeat that?', 'I didn't get that. Go again' constantly erupted from her booth.

To hear her voice when you were dictating a sensitive story where the subjects might be in listening range was terrifying. On one occasion I was sent to cover a visit by a controversial police band from New York who'd come to march at a Republican parade. They had taken refuge in a Republican bar in the north inner city where I managed to track them down and extract a few quotes. The only phone was in the bar so I called in to copy only to be greeted by the fearful tones of our partially deaf copytaker.

The story included several strong quotes from a politician opposed to the march. I remember the words 'terrorism' and 'condemn' featured large. By the time I'd repeated this several times I could detect a rather unhealthy silence in the bar. Hanging up the phone I turned around to find several of New York's finest ranged around me in a circle. 'What was that about terrorism?' demanded a very large cop.

I was saved by the intervention of the *Press* photographer, a man with impeccable Republican credentials, who explained that whatever my personal feelings I had to report what the other side was saying. Once we were safely outside he upbraided me:

'Will ye for fuck's sake learn to keep your voice down.'

I explained who the copytaker had been. A sympathetic smile then appeared on his face.

'In that case,' he said, 'it's lucky we both weren't lynched.'

~

The heart of the *Press* operation was the newsdesk. From here the news editor could bark orders at the reporters and receive abuse from the chief sub and the editor of the evening paper.

The system could best be described as 'adversarial'. Through-out the morning reporters would be despatched on stories or given clippings from the morning papers to follow up. The younger staff, or those held in contempt by the news editor, would be remorselessly interrogated on the details of their copy. 'Did ya ask him?' or 'Did ya check?' were the mantras.

Getting beaten by the opposition paper the *Evening Herald,* even on the most minor detail, could unleash a storm of abuse from the editor, pouring downward onto the heads of the news editors and from them to you. The pressure worked. The news section was generally regarded as the sharpest in the country, certainly the best on a big breaking story, with every reporter in the building despatched to cover all conceivable angles. It was a brilliant training ground for a neophyte. By the time I left the *Irish Press* I would feel ready to take on any story.

As edition time for the evening paper approached the news editor, and not infrequently the editor, would come and stand behind the reporter typing the lead story. The copy boy would be roused from his habitual state of semi-awakening and made to stand beside the news editor, waiting until the first para-graph of copy was complete. This would then be ripped from the typewriter by the reporter, handed to the news editor for quick perusal, and then thrust at the copy boy, who would run it to the sub's desk for a headline, and race from them to the printers. This process, known as 'short takes', was repeated with every paragraph. I loved it. I loved the minute-by-minute tension, the sense of a great enterprise which hung on the reporter's speed and skill and which, when completed, might be rewarded with a gruff bark of 'that wasn't bad'. It was the journalism I had imagined myself doing when I set off to meet the owners of the *Limerick Leader* four years previously.

The *Irish Press* was an extraordinary place to work, popu-lated by eccentrics, dreamers, drunks, left-wing revolution-aries, ultra-conservatives, poets, mystics, wholly engaging chancers and some of the best journalists I have ever encountered. One of them was a Kerryman, Con Houlihan, who wrote a sports column but refused to countenance using a typewriter. He wrote in beautiful flowing script, a paragraph to every page. The writing was magnificent and he never missed a deadline. Another was a combative sports reporter named John O'Shea, who could have led an Irish Olympic swearing team. O'Shea revelled in controversy and went on to found the hugely successful developing world charity GOAL. In later years I would meet him in places like Congo and Sudan as he employed the same robust techniques of the *Irish Press* newsroom on reluctant governments and corrupt officials.

Unlike the *Limerick Leader*, which had switched to computerised printing before I left, the *Irish Press* still depended on hot metal. The rear of the building reverberated to the clanking and wrenching of the printer's mallets and shook like a rocket preparing for take off when the presses rolled. The offices were permeated with the odour of ink, newsprint, cigarettes and fried food. By the standards of today's airconditioned, plant-filled offices, the working conditions were wretched. Our opposition at the Independent Group, on the other side of the river, had a canteen into which we would occasionally sneak, to be met with pitying stares from our well-fed rivals. The only 'facility' at Burgh Quay was a tap with boiling water for making tea. The pay was the lowest of any national paper and expenses were a luxury – doled out with extreme bad grace by a management that seemed to regard its journalistic staff as at best a collection of ungrateful children, and at worst a bunch of thieving scoundrels. The contempt was mutual.

On my first day at the *Press* an old reporter approached me – he was actually retiring that day – and insisted that I follow him to Mulligan's pub, directly behind the office. This shabby, smoke-filled hostelry was more like an extension of the newsroom, and was the scene of more intrigue than the court of Cesare Borgia, all of it directed at management.

The retiring reporter ordered a small Powers whiskey. I asked for a Coke.

'A Coke?' he said. 'Will ye not have a proper drink?'

I said that I never drank during working hours. (This was during my extended period off the booze after the doctor's warning in Cork.)

'*Jaysus*, aren't you the fine man. Well, let me tell you something. If you think you can work for those bastards up there without a stiff drink or two every day forget it.'

It was barely lunchtime and the old reporter was half-drunk already. He told me he was going to live by the sea in County Wicklow.

'Isn't that a long way out from town? Won't you miss your friends here?' I said.

'I don't give a shite if I never see the place again. Let me give you one word of advice. Don't ever let the fuckers grind you down, because they will in that place if you let them.'

I drank my Coke and mentally swore that if I found myself drunk and disillusioned at the end of my career I would jump into the nearest river.

~

One of the first people to welcome me at the *Irish Press* was another *Limerick Leader* man who, years before, had made the journey to Burgh Quay. Michael O'Toole was a gentle, sad-eyed man with a marvellous wit who wrote the social diary for the evening paper.

The job of the social diarist was probably the most punishing on the newspaper. Each evening he sallied forth to tour the various receptions, press launches and opening nights. Returning to the office late at night he would have to write

1,300 words of copy. This was left for the early sub-editing shift which would come on duty at around six in the morning. The routine, followed five nights a week, could reduce talented men to alcoholic decrepitude. O'Toole survived through a combination of self-discipline and shyness – he could flit in and out of rooms without being drawn into rounds of social drinking with people he did not know or care about. Before his untimely death in April 2000, O'Toole produced a brilliant memoir of his days on the *Irish Press*.

Among other incidents, he recalled the arrival of the feminist revolution at Burgh Quay, when a soon-to-be-famous journalist rushed into the office of the gossip columnist and bared her breasts in a show of defiance:

'Absolutely splendid,' he replied, 'now please put them away, my dear, because there's a thousand words to go and the deadline approaches.'

Even in the early 1980s, when most newspapers had begun their migration from the conviviality of the pub to the blandness of the water cooler, a culture of hard drinking survived around the *Irish Press*. This is O'Toole's description of the atmosphere in the 1970s drinking heyday at Burgh Quay:

When I drifted into journalism at the ripe old age of twenty-three the bohemians and eccentrics were still thick on the ground. There was a man who rode a bicycle to which he had attached a rather large sail. Another when drunk, made a habit of prostrating himself like a mediaeval monk before the night news editor chanting and begging pardon . . . Even though Flann O'Brien was taking satiric licence when he wrote that any piece of *Irish Press* copy which didn't bear the imprint of the bottom of a porter bottle from Mulligan's or the White Horse would automatically be held suspect and spiked by the chief sub, there was a fearsome amount of hard drinking.

O'Toole described how the 1973 productivity agreement between management and the National Union of Journalists
'stated blandly that there would be "full co-operation in the
observance of proper standards of conduct in this regard and it
is recognised that there is a certain problem concerning drink".'

A certain problem concerning drink. That was as glorious
an Irish euphemism as was ever spoken. At one stage an American time-and-motion specialist was brought in. Among the
measures he tried to enforce was a re-design of the newsroom
so that visitors would not be assailed by the smell of drink
when they entered.

By the time I came on the scene the drinking had eased a
lot, but there were still memorable outbursts of alcohol-related
eccentricity and insanity. One night-town reporter was a man
of violent instincts when he had taken drink. His job was one
of the loneliest in journalism. Long after everybody else had
gone home, the night-town man and the night sub-editor
would wait until the final edition had rolled before trudging
home. There is something unnatural about an empty newsroom. I did a few night-town shifts and could never accustom
myself to the air of quiet.

The routine was stultifying. You spent the hours in a little
booth making check calls to the police and fire brigade. From
Donegal to Bantry Bay, the entire length of the country, you
disturbed dozing policemen to be told, more often than not,
that nothing was happening. But you always had to bear in
mind the possibility of a 'monster' story breaking. When I
whined one day about the tedium of night-town, an older
reporter reminded me that two of the biggest stories of the
1970s – the Stardust disco fire and the explosion on the ship
Betelgeuse – had happened in the early hours. There had been
massive casualties in each. But the biggest story to come my
way was an occasional gangland murder, the result of Dublin's
spiralling heroin epidemic.

For the regular night-town man the torment of ringing police stations at two in the morning eventually became too great. I remember being on duty on a late shift when he punched the night news editor, hurled a typewriter at one of the duty reporters and then screamed abuse at all who approached him, before vanishing into the night, a vapour trail of whiskey fumes following in his wake. He left the country soon afterwards. Nobody on the paper expressed much surprise.

The Saturday night shift for the *Sunday Press* enjoyed a reputation of special horror. One of the news editors was an enthusiastic fellow whose return from the pub invariably saw reporters diving for the phones and pretending to be involved in elaborate interrogations. I soon learned why. The journey to the pub brought about a dramatic change in our man. While enjoying his Guinness he became inspired. Listening to the suggestions of other drinkers and adding a few of his own, he would return to the office and fire off orders in every direction, all of them involving telephone calls to people who were either enjoying the sacred pleasures of the *Late Late Show* or were tucked up in bed.

Early on I was told to telephone a Reverend Mother late at night and demand her comment on a highly controversial story that had appeared on the front page of a rival paper. An old hand would have pretended to make the call, shouting his questions loudly for the news editor to hear and adding finally that he was sorry to have woken up the housekeeper and would call again tomorrow to get a comment. Unhappily I made the call, rousted the Reverend Mother out of her holy bed and was bitterly harangued. 'This would never have happened in the Chief's [de Valera's] day,' she screamed.

For reasons to do with its Republican antecedents, and the editor's sympathies, the *Press* sometimes provided a berth for men who were once described to me as 'retired Republican activists'. Among these was the tourism correspondent, a man called Gerry O'Hare, who had joined the IRA in Belfast when the Troubles erupted in 1969, and who had served time in prison both north and south of the border. By the time I arrived on the scene Gerry was no longer involved with the Republican movement. He was a gregarious and warm-hearted man who enjoyed the Dublin social scene. But for many years Gerry faced a major difficulty as tourism corre-spondent. He knew that Britain was a big destination for Irish holidaymakers but he was unable to set foot in the country because of fears of arrest. He made up for this exclusion by travelling enthusiastically to as many other places as possible.

On a typical shift day I could find myself sitting opposite O'Hare the former gunman; beside him Greg Ryan, reporter and trainee Protestant minister; Larry Kildea, a Glaswegian with the quickest mind in the building; George Douglas, a northern Protestant who was the industrial correspondent; possibly making up the morning shift would be Anne Flaherty, who, like me, had trained on local newspapers in Limerick, and who had only recently arrived Dublin. She was petite, pretty and radiated calm.

I was shy around women. I struggled to strike up a conver-sation with a girl, much less ask her out. With Anne this didn't arise. We came to know each other as working colleagues long before there was any romantic involvement. We were both involved in long-term relationships with other people.

As these relationships came to an end we grew closer as friends and then, over the course of a long summer, began to fall in love, though with neither quite sure what the other was feeling. We shared a passion for books. Anne was studying Anglo-Irish writing at Trinity College. The poetry of Yeats became my romantic semaphore. Whenever possible I would work the conversation around to his poems for Maud Gonne:

Had I the heavens' embroidered cloths,/Enwrought with golden and silver light, . . ./I would spread the cloths under your feet: . . ./Tread softly for you tread upon my dreams.

I also produced some risible poems of my own. Memory has been kind enough to obliterate them. It must all have been sadly obvious and I doubt that my literary pretensions made much of an impression.

Then some of the *Irish Press* staff decided to strike over pay. I was a young militant. Those with families to support and who understood the paper's precarious finances better than I were reluctant to join the strike. If the *Irish Press* closed they would struggle to get a job anywhere else. Wrongly, and full of the unthinking passion of youth, I condemned them as lickspittles. Anne was more measured. She argued with me, forced me to think. 'You can go and get another job. What are they going to do?'

I did picket duty and queued to collect the dole. The experience of waiting in line with Dublin's unemployed in those pre-Celtic-Tiger days took some of the edge off my militancy. Unemployment in Ireland had risen from 7 to 17 percent between the year I left school, 1979, and the mid-1980s. Growing up in Cork I had seen the after-effects of industrial closures, the men hanging around on street corners, the long queues at the Labour Exchange, but becoming, however briefly, one of those unemployed was unnerving.

On days when we had no picket duty I would arrange to meet Anne. We took trains to the seaside or went for long walks in the city, talking about the strike or books and films. I felt more at ease in her company than I'd imagined was possible with any human being. Yet it took me many months to tell her what I really felt. It only happened after a friend on the newspaper took me aside.

'Look, it's as obvious as anything that you are mad about the girl. Just ask her out,' he said.

'What if she says no?'

'She won't. I guarantee.'

'But we are friends at the moment. It could ruin the friendship if I try to move it up a gear.'

My friend said that nobody who knew us believed it was a simple question of 'friendship' any longer. So I wrote a letter to Anne. I wrote because I was afraid to speak. I can't remember exactly what I wrote; there was a certain amount of perambulation, but at the end I said that I found her *lovable*. I cringe now at my awkwardness.

I kept this letter in my pocket for several weeks until my friend asked if I had spoken with her. We were walking down O'Connell Street near the General Post Office at the time.

'I haven't spoken to her but I have written a letter,' I said.

'I don't believe you. Did you post it?'

I admitted that I hadn't.

'Prove you wrote it. I don't believe you.'

I produced the letter. He immediately grabbed it and ran, dodging his way through the traffic until he reached the GPO. He raced into the GPO, the building where Pearse and his comrades had gone to glorious defeat in 1916, and despatched my missive of love. A few days later I arrived in the office to begin my afternoon shift. There was a note waiting. It was from Anne suggesting tea in Bewleys that evening.

We sat there among the evening crowds smiling at each other, not saying very much. When the time came for me to go back to the office, she suggested making a detour and walking as far as Trinity College. Most of the day's lectures were over. There were students rambling across the quadrangle, a few American tourists were snapping holiday shots. We walked in comfortable silence. When it was time for me to return to work Anne leaned forward to kiss me goodbye. It was something I had so often imagined yet could not quite believe was happening. We embraced. The surrounding world folded away.

I got married on a warm, misty day in July in a country churchyard halfway between Anne's home and mine. Looking at the photographs now I can't really believe how young we looked. I was twenty-six years old, Anne not much older. Speaking strictly for myself I can say that I wasn't remotely mature enough to make promises to anyone. But I am lucky I did. Glad beyond telling for the friendship and love that have endured.

I proposed to Anne the year before, during the state visit to Ireland of President Ronald Reagan when I'd been despatched by the *Irish Press* to live for several weeks in a small County Tipperary village. Ronald Reagan's ancestors came from Ballyporeen – 'the place of the small potatoes' – at the foot of the Galtee mountains, and the village was to be one of the main photo opportunities during the visit. Reagan was an unpopular figure in Ireland owing to his support for the Contra rebels in Nicaragua (there was a vocal pro-Sandinista lobby in Ireland) and because, as an ageing right-wing Republican, he could never measure up to the golden charm of the lost Jack Kennedy.

I had a lot of time on my hands in Ballyporeen. Within a few days I'd covered every imaginable connection between the Tipperary village and the American President. Gazing into the vast empty tundra of the second weekend, I struggled to come up with a story idea. Happily the native curiosity of the Irish and the lamentable state of the local roads combined to get me out of trouble: so big were the visiting crowds that part of the road leading into Ballyporeen collapsed, leaving a small but – in the eyes of the press at least – significant crater in the road.

This produced a suitably melodramatic, if somewhat tongue-in-cheek response from the local Fianna Fáil county councillor, a portly and wonderfully good-natured man by the name of Con O'Donovan. Over the preceding week we had become friends. His irreverence and capacity for gentle mischief-making reminded me of my Kerry relatives. Over tea and apple tart on the night of the Great Road Collapse, Con asked me if I'd thought any more about the matter we'd discussed earlier in the week, i.e. my single status. Like many countrymen of his generation Con O'Donovan believed a man who stayed single heading into his thirties faced the danger of a life of lonely bachelorhood.

'A boy like yourself should be settling down by now,' he said.

I said that I'd been thinking a lot of marriage. In fact I was very keen. But I wasn't sure about the response. Several hints had been made but not picked up on.

'You can hint away till the cows come home and you'll get nowhere. Just ask the question. What's stopping you?'

There and then I made up my mind to desert my post – for the night – and race across country to Ennis where Anne was staying with her family. At one o'clock in the morning, by the side of a County Clare lake, she said yes.

~

Anne was kind to my father. When I would come and complain about him, threatening to sever ties because he wasn't the person I wanted him to be, she urged me not to make judgements. 'Stay in touch with him. You'll only regret it later on if you don't.'

I struggled to take that advice. Sometimes I sought him out through instinct: I needed to find him, see how he was, to try and rescue him, or, if he was in a sober phase, to sit and drink coffee with him and reassure myself. Other times it was because Anne's words echoed around in my head. *You'll regret it later.*

By the mid-1980s the damage to his health was acute, and though we did not know it, his heart was becoming vulnerable to major failure. Yet though he could suffer from the blackest depressions, my father managed to remain, at heart, an optimist. Each time he came out of hospital after treatment for alcoholism he believed that this time life would surely be better. He had lost much in his life. But he always believed in the possibility of a better future. I never saw him emerge from a stay in hospital without a head full of new ideas for poems and stories. The carelessness about his appearance which characterised the bad days would be replaced by an almost adolescent zest for fine clothes. The first stop when he came out of hospital was always a men's clothes store. He bought suits and shirts, and a colourful tie or two, and when I called to see him he would announce, in an English upper-class accent: 'Lord Chaos is pleased to receive you.'

If he had money he was generous to the point of recklessness. I never saw him pass a beggar without giving a large handful of change. When he was broke he borrowed from me but he always paid me back when he came into funds. The weeks after hospital were always hopeful weeks; he bustled along, writing all day and calling me to go out for supper in the evenings. 'What do you think of this?' he would ask, pushing a fresh hand-written manuscript across the table. Mostly he wrote about Kerry and the people of his childhood.

My father had a countryman's appetite and his taste in food was simple. We would go to a small café in Rathmines called the Pronto Grill and he would order a huge mixed grill, eating as much as he could, as if to make up for all those days and nights that had passed without any food.

I remember those days as the happiest in all the time I knew him. He acted as if he had been given his life back, and though his disease returned, and would eventually kill him, I am glad for those hours in the Pronto Grill or the Slowboat Chinese, or the café near Rathmines Bridge where I sat with Anne and my father listening to the rush of his enthusiasms.

He had some loyal friends who loved him to the end and would always call me when he was unwell. One of them, a young Dubliner called Nicky Wilson, was a human being of quite rare kindness and generosity. I think he saw the humanity in my father long after others had given up on him. Now I believe it was because Nick knew that if the situation were reversed my father would have done the same for him.

CHAPTER TEN

Into Africa

My people are walking
always walking.

AGOSTINHO NETO

I am here. I am stepping into Africa.

I had visualised this moment so often when I was a boy back in Dublin, or later as a teenager in Cork, hunched over history books in the city library. I had constructed my dreams around this continent, a place to bury memories of rain and weakness. I expected wide-open plains and thorn trees, the red spray of bougainvillea, perhaps some animals grazing on the edge of the runway and crowds of people swarming around the plane as I descended the steps. I expected noise.

But at midnight in Khartoum, there was silence. White-clad figures flitted across the tarmac – customs officials and security men in their djellebas – and sitting outside the terminal were a few porters, listless and bored in the heat. Some soldiers began walking towards the aircraft as we walked down the steps. Their leader ushered us towards passport control. A man in sunglasses stamped my passport. *Sunglasses at midnight?*

I set out for Africa with many warnings. *Don't drink the*

water. Don't trust anybody. Be prepared to pay lots of bribes. Never criticise the government if you're talking to a local. In Sudan: *avoid any offer of alcohol like the plague.* An Italian priest had just been given many lashes for making altar wine. It wasn't an issue: since my encounter with the doctor in Cork – a year before – I was still off alcohol. It wasn't difficult. It would be years before booze got the kind of grip which made abstinence a struggle.

I came to Sudan in the time of the dictator Jaafar Nimeiri. He fulfilled many of the requirements of the African 'Big Man'. He was greedy, cruel and paranoid and sat brooding in his palace by the Nile, surrounded by courtier-conspirators waiting their hour. Nimeiri came to power in a Soviet-backed coup and then switched sides, staying in power with US support until he was driven from power in the mid-1980s. Although he introduced Sharia law in the south he was more of a cunning pragmatist than an absolute Islamist. He kept a close eye on the fundamentalists. This was my first foreign assignment. Earlier that year I'd left the *Irish Press* to take up a job with RTE. Another journalist had dropped out of the trip and I was asked at the last minute if I would mind going to Sudan. I nearly screamed my reply:

'Do I mind? No, no I don't mind at all.'

Sudan was to be the starting point of a long journey. I was to accompany a delegation of European politicians who were travelling to the front line where Eritrean guerrillas were fighting Ethiopian soldiers. The Eritrean struggle with the Marxist regime in Addis Ababa had been going on for more than a decade and had killed thousands. The Europeans were being sent to assess the need for food aid on the Eritrean side. Among the party were an Irish Republican, a Tory and a good-natured but fearfully ponderous Belgian. I was twenty-three years old with several thousand dollars in my pocket, a return air ticket and a camera jacket of the kind I believed all genuine foreign correspondents wore. I wince now at the memory of the callow boy who boarded the Sudan Airways flight from Brussels.

~

The Europe from which I'd travelled saw Africa through two prisms: it was either a place of wild and dangerous people who were to be avoided at all costs, or a place of wild and delightful animals to be viewed from the safety of an air-conditioned minibus. One Africa was safaris and gin and tonic and Meryl Streep croaking about a farm at the foot of the Ngong Hills; another was a slightly guilty feeling once or twice a year when some fly-speckled, emaciated child appeared on the nightly news. Africa was also the last wild frontier of plunder where small numbers of Westerners went to work on the oil, diamond or gold fields.

However we saw Africa we did not connect with the continent except in ways that were sentimental, idealised or ruthlessly self-interested. It was a place of competing stereotypes. The natives were quirky and entertaining, all beaming smiles and dancing, and funny ways of speaking English. Or they were crazed, drunken, sexually rapacious, machete-wielding mass murderers.

I liked to believe that I was free of such prejudice. After all, I'd read so much about Africa. In Limerick I'd made my first African friends with Gabi Oparah and his students, and in Dublin I'd pestered African stories onto radio news programmes as often as I could. But now, standing on African soil for the first time, I was assailed by a sense of surprise. Nothing in all my reading had prepared me for this first collision with the difference of the place.

Along the road from the airport we passed roadblocks manned by sleepy soldiers. Nothing, nobody else, moved.

Sleepless that night, I lay awake listening to the endless barking of dogs and, somewhere far off in the city, heard the sound of a woman ululating, the high-pitched wail floating across the streets. I was excited and tense, knowing that my first encounter with an African war was only a few days away. And it struck me with some force that I was consciously risking my life.

In Africa – everybody said it – life was cheap. Sudan was in the grip of hunger. Neighbouring Ethiopia was in the middle of a civil war with the peoples of Eritrea and Tigre. I was sent to the region to cover both of these miseries. Back then, almost everywhere you wanted to travel in Africa was experiencing some kind of upheaval. The Four Horsemen were wearing out their mounts galloping back and forth, up and down across the continent.

Eritrea had been more or less permanently at war for the last century. Eritreans had fought the Italians, had been occupied by the British and from 1962 had fought a guerrilla war with Ethiopia, and were now battling the Dergue regime of Mengistu Hailie Mariam. The Dergue was slaughtering Eritrean civilians in bombing raids. In fact the Ethiopians bombed everything that moved in Eritrea. We'd heard rumours they were using napalm. The Eritrean liaison people had sent word from the border that we would only travel by night. We were told that the MiG jets supplied by Moscow didn't have night-vision equipment. They would only get lucky if you were stupid enough to leave the headlights on.

Shortly after dawn, I rose and went to the window. Placing my hand against the glass I felt the heat of the day rising, pressing in against my air-conditioned cocoon. Already the sun hammered down on the dusty street. I saw men leading packs of donkeys and camels along the road. They shouted to one another in Arabic while small boys darted in between the animals, playing hide-and-seek. This was a caravan just in from the desert on its way to the camel market at Omdurman on the other side of the city. It was noisy and chaotic. When I opened the window the smell of animals, diesel, human waste, swept into the room. I saw a man cuff one of the boys about the head. The blow looked harsh to me, but the boy laughed and then screamed something at the man before running away. Watching the press of men, boys and animals, I felt a surge of joy.

Every morning a weasel-faced secret policeman would turn up at our hotel to announce that we were not to go anywhere without his permission. After several days of filing in and out of government offices, waiting for our permits to enter the interior, I was starting to tire of Khartoum. We decided to ignore the secret policeman and went to Omdurman where Kitchener had butchered the Mahdi's army; we were entertained to gin and tonics and lunch by the British ambassador, an ascetic man who seemed to genuinely love the place; we went walking along the Nile and saw the hulk of an airliner which had crashed there some years before and I annoyed the secret policeman by jumping out from behind pillars in the hotel. He was not a good spook. He was too nervous, too easily surprised.

The Sudanese eventually gave us our permit and we set off into the desert, but not before passing what seemed like a hundred roadblocks around Khartoum. I remember the brutal quality of the light, screaming harsh and white in the mid-morning, and the heat which turned our ancient mini van into a travelling oven. We had also seriously underestimated the amount of water we would need. After just an hour of driving a third of the water supply had been consumed. We had hours more to travel before we would find a settlement of any kind.

The road passed through an endless tableau of desolation. It varied only in degrees of bleakness, a desert of sand here, an ocean of rock and scrub there. In the heat and lack of water we lapsed into bickering. The Belgian politician claimed that the desert was full of 'Huge mooses!'

I burst out laughing.

His secretary – pale, thin, neurotic – rounded on me:

'He means mice. Which you should have known! How clever are you to be laughing at how he pronounces things?'

I shut up.

Then the two other politicians began to argue. The Irishman, Niall Andrews, was telling the Tory, Paul Howell, that the British would eventually negotiate with the IRA.

'Never. Never. We will not negotiate with terrorists,' replied Howell.

'Oh, you mean like you didn't negotiate with Jomo Kenyatta? Or you didn't give in to terrorism in Palestine? Come off it, for God's sake.'

This is the way with long journeys in the heat, a replay of every dreadful trip you made with your parents as a child, only magnified a thousand times.

Matters threatened to get even more passionate when we spotted the first refugees. They were a family of five, a mother and father and three small children, one a baby just a few months old. They emerged out of a sun-blasted wilderness and held out their hands for food. The Sudanese driver would not allow us to stop. The family vanished in our rear-view mirror, swallowed up by the immense landscape and the heat which twisted the shapes of every figure or tree or mountain.

We passed more nomads. Some of them had made camp in the desert, the women with long black hair and striking cotton robes – green, red, black – and their hands covered in intricate patterns of henna; the men wore long robes and carried swords strapped to their backs, while the children ran to the roadside to shout at us and beg for food. The bigger groups had a few camels and donkeys with them, but none seemed to have any substantial supply of food. I do not know how they survived in that place. There was no water, no visible supply of food, and the climate was intolerably fierce. In such places the weak – mostly the very young and the old – died quickly. They were buried in the sand, a few prayers were said, the women ululated, and once the cool of the evening descended, the tribe moved on.

The South African singer Johnny Clegg wrote a song called 'Scatterlings of Africa' about the endless migrations across the continent. *They are the scatterlings of Africa/ Each uprooted one . . .* It would become my emblematic image of Africa: people constantly on the move on roads, desert tracks, mountain paths, jungle trails. They moved from the village to the city, from the front lines to the refugee camps; they easily carried what they owned because they owned almost nothing: women with giant stacks of firewood on their heads, men pushing carts loaded with bundles of bedding and clothes, children carrying water, or people carrying people, the wounded and diseased.

We reached a village. A few soldiers sat dozing next to a roadblock made of two wooden chairs and an empty oil drum. It was here, in the middle of God-knows-where, that I had my first encounter with an Africa I would come to know intimately in the years ahead: the Africa of the small man afraid of the Big Man who is afraid of the even Bigger Man. The soldier looked us over, inspected our passports, studied the travel permit and shook his head. He was worried, he told our Sudanese driver. If he allowed us to go through there could be trouble.

'Does he want a bribe?' I asked loudly.

'Don't be foolish,' the driver snapped.

'Don't bet on our friend not speaking any English,' Andrews said. 'Offer him a bribe and we could be locked up for months.'

The driver started talking to the soldier again: Why trouble? Trouble from whom? he asked, knowing the answer. From the government, the soldier said.

We were told to follow the soldier. He trudged across the road to a walled compound and waved us through. Inside about twenty people sat around in the dust. They looked exhausted, hungry and dirty and were apparently waiting to see the soldier's boss. He went ahead of us, deferentially, barely tapping the door. A voice barked from inside. The soldier peeked his head around the door and said something, explaining our presence and, I suspect, making sure his boss didn't blame him for our arrival.

For the arrival of foreigners was an important matter, a potential source of trouble with Khartoum. What if they got lost and died of thirst? Or suppose they were really spies, despite their permit. Could permits not be forged? And if they were spies and destabilised the country and, heaven forbid, were about to overthrow the government, and you were the official who let them slip through . . . the possibilities were too terrible to imagine: torture, death, or at the very best a lifetime exile to somewhere even more remote and godforsaken than this.

The Boss came out. He wore a cleaner uniform than the guard. And he was definitely fatter. He looked bored and was not happy to see us. Niall Andrews, an amiable and roguish figure, stepped forward and sprayed the man in Celtic mist, unleashing a salvo of blather about us being representatives of the European Union, great friends of the Sudanese people, and the disbursers of vast amounts of aid to the government in Khartoum, aid which, in the fullness of time, would reach this very village and improve life for everybody. He would have asked 'the Boss' to share a whiskey and sing a song if it were any other country than Islamic Sudan. Andrews was an old chum of Charles Haughey and had learned the art of political flattery at the master's side. His travelling companion, the Tory, Paul Howell, chipped in with various supporting comments. It was an entertaining double act from the political rivals. All of this was listened to without making much of an impression.

'You will wait,' said the Boss. He motioned for us to follow him into his room.

You will wait. If I had a dollar for every time I heard those words I would be a rich man indeed. We did wait. And wait. Hours passed. The murderous heat of the day yielded to something marginally more bearable. Eventually the Boss returned.

'You may go,' he said.

It was getting dark now. We couldn't travel after dark without being shot by jittery soldiers. Howell was annoyed: 'Go! Where can we go at this hour of the night?' he exploded.

It was a fair question. On every side of us lay a desert bristling with scorpions, poisonous snakes and, for all we knew, the 'huge mooses' described by our Belgian friend.

The Boss shrugged his shoulders. It was none of his concern. 'Go now. Please. Go,' he said. Andrews motioned for the rest of us to leave the room. He stayed behind with the Boss. Through the window I could see him smiling and laughing and dreaded to think what promises were being made on the EU's behalf.

After ten minutes or so he came out: 'The best that fucker will do is to let us sleep outside the police station. Still, it's better than nothing. At least we'll have concrete instead of sand and spiders.'

That first night under African skies passed restlessly. We met some long-distance truck drivers. They were travelling from Port Sudan in the east with container loads of goods for Khartoum. We were a pronounced curiosity – dirty, pale, nervous, hungry, not what they expected of Westerners. The truckers crossed this great emptiness hundreds of times a year: from the coast to the city and back to the coast again. They shared their tea with us and asked us to sit by their fire. And they sang for us, a song about a flower of the desert – it went *siera lai, siera lai* – a plaintive, sweet song of the eternal distances. We shared no language with them, and we had nothing to offer in return for their hospitality. But it did not matter. It was my first experience of a central truth of Africa: for every grasping border guard there would be ten more people who would give you food and shelter, never with the expectation of payment.

The night was memorable for one other occurrence. As we bedded down outside the police station, Niall Andrews rambled off to go to the toilet. A few minutes later I heard furious snarling, followed by the sound of snapping jaws and full-throated barking. A human voice rose above these, bellowing: 'Oh, holy Jesus.'

I jumped up and saw a figure galloping towards me out of the darkness. It was Andrews, fleeing with his hands in front of his crotch and an expression of terror on his face. In the darkness he had pissed on the village mongrels as they slept, and now they were chasing him. I hurled stones. Our driver followed suit and we drove them away.

'Vicious bastards,' shouted Andrews. Then he burst into loud laughter.

~

In the coming days I would travel to places so remote and strange that it would feel as if I'd crossed into a parallel universe. I swam in the Red Sea with limbless soldiers from an Eritrean war hospital who hurled themselves from their wheelchairs into the water and played water polo as if the stumps of their arms and legs were merely scratches; we travelled on and the desert became rocky and we entered the mountains where it was cold by night and the stars were more numerous and brilliant than the books of my childhood could ever have conveyed. I drove hundreds of kilometres by night down a twisting sliver of road with the lights out so that we wouldn't make a target for a passing aircraft – our driver an old guerrilla, toothless and taciturn, a respected killer among his peers, who kept one hand on the steering wheel while another cradled his assault rifle.

By day I rested in shelters made of dry bushes or in caves while the Ethiopian fighters flew overhead scouring for targets. I ate porcupine and pasta and felt an endless tormenting thirst – if you travel with rebels you eat and drink what they eat. I visited a war hospital that had been carved into the mountains by human hands and interviewed the menacing Stalinist who ran the Eritrean People's Liberation Front (EPLF) and who would later become the first leader of an independent and internationally recognised state.

I also nearly came to blows with a Tory MEP. The almost-fisticuffs happened in a prisoner of war camp. We had been taken there by the Eritreans to see how wonderfully well they treated their enemies. The EPLF were master propagandists and realised they had an ace card in the Western media. Journalists as a whole love a David versus Goliath narrative. So the EPLF gave them plucky little Eritrea standing up against the vile Marxist monolith of Addis Ababa. Very few reporters bothered to look at the EPLF's own attitude to democratic freedoms. It was roughly the same as that of their Ethiopian counterparts, though, it has to be acknowledged, without the mass-murdering ruthlessness of the Dergue.

The Ethiopian prisoners were kept in a narrow valley. There were several thousand men and only a handful of guards. But the camp was hundreds of miles away from the Ethiopian lines, across the most atrocious terrain in Africa. An escapee would either be recaptured by Eritrean civilians or die of thirst amid the rocky valleys. After a day listening to Ethiopian prisoners telling us how well they were being treated, I turned to one of them and asked if he ever thought about escaping. Before he could answer Howell was on top of me.

'Are you a complete fucking idiot? I mean really . . . what do you expect him to say? All of these guys are listening to every word he says. Suppose he'd made a mistake and said he did think of escaping. Think of the shit he'd be in because of you.'

At this the red cloud swam in front of my eyes. Some old Irish instinct kicked in. The posh English voice shouting down at me in this fashion unleashed an atavistic tirade:

'Who do you think you're talking to? You don't rule me. Do you understand? You don't give me orders,' I roared.

We each lunged towards the other. Between the heat, tiredness and hunger we were both operating at the far ends of our emotional range. Luckily Niall Andrews was on hand to step between us.

'Dear God, lads, you're letting the side down. Calm down now,' he said.

And then we became instantaneously aware of an immense silence. We stood still. Howell looked behind my shoulder. Then I turned and looked. On the hillside, thousands of prisoners were standing, transfixed by our performance. Nothing as entertaining as this had happened in years.

Howell looked at me and smiled. I smiled back, and we shook hands. Of course he was right. My question was crass. It had popped into my inexperienced, exhausted mind and out of my mouth before I realised that there could only be one answer. I tell the story now to illustrate how little I knew then of the complications of war.

~

A day later we were getting ready to make our way out of Eritrea when we stopped at a small military post in the mountains. The guerrillas wanted us to see another of their innovations. This time it was a printing press which produced school books. I leafed through a few. There were pictures of a very evil looking Uncle Sam figure on the cover and long chapters on Marxist economic theory inside. The EPLF was disciplined and, so far as we could see, free of the corruption rampant elsewhere in Africa. But it had a cartoon view of international politics and a fierce intolerance of opposition.

The leader of the EPLF did not see himself coming to power in a democratic election. This was, after all, 1983 and talk of democracy in Africa was a long way off. Power was won and lost through the barrel of the gun and the distribution of patronage. It was less than two decades since the end of the colonial era in most of Africa – Zimbabwe was barely three years free – and the continent was mired in corruption and brutality. In the former British colonies like Zambia, Uganda and Kenya the state had set about robbing its people virtually from the moment of liberation. French Africa had given us the delights of the Central African Republic and its child-murdering 'Emperor' Bokassa, not to mention the dictatorships of Chad, Gabon and Congo Brazzaville; the Portuguese had abandoned their African colonies in a rush less than a decade earlier after centuries of brutal exploitation, and both Angola and Mozambique were now being dismembered by civil war; in the former Belgian territories of Congo, Rwanda and Burundi, state power operated without law or any semblance of natural justice. Down south of the Limpopo River apartheid South Africa seemed to be heading for a violent uprising.

No honest observer could have looked at Africa then and felt hopeful. The colonial powers were gone but a new set of meddlers and exploiters had replaced them. They were American and Russian, spies and diplomats, military advisers and arms suppliers, who all fought the Cold War by proxy. They sent the guns. The Africans did the dying. The Americans sent Peace Corps volunteers on one plane and CIA agents on another; the plump Soviet and East German advisers who lounged around the pool in Addis Ababa and Angola were a new breed of colonist. They mouthed the language of internationalism while rummaging deep in Africa's pockets. What they were – all of them – was white men who thought they knew better than the blacks.

There were others too, a new kind of carpetbagger who saw in the chaos and corruption the opportunity for great wealth. They were representatives of mining corporations and oil companies. From the great mines of the Rand to the remotest fringes of Zaire they took the wealth of Africa and exported it overseas. They would never be personally touched by Africa's wars, except in the most positive way: war was good for business. War meant chaos, unstable regimes and men who were susceptible to bribery. This in turn meant planes that could land empty and take off fully laden in the middle of the night, glutted with diamonds and gold, and it meant lucrative contracts to sell arms to countries sinking under the weight of debt.

The wealth of Africa would have been great enough to build glistening cities, schools to educate every child on the continent, hospitals that were well equipped and clean. Instead it vanished to Europe and North America. In return a few dictators got Swiss bank accounts and all the guns and caviar they could buy. The conditions of war had another plus. They made it much easier to ensure that troublesome human rights activists, the people who might have asked awkward questions, were silenced. In times of 'national emergency' the enemies of the state had no protection. So the one thing that might have laid the foundation for change – a vibrant civil society – was never allowed to take root across most of Africa. I had come to Africa in an age without hope.

~

Despite being in Eritrea a week, we hadn't yet found the war. The jets were there above us, but as we hid during daylight they had nothing to bomb. We heard the roar of their flight and watched the snail trail of their vapour on the afternoon skies. The war was thousands of feet above us and I was getting impatient, beset by more than the usual insecurity. The trip had cost – by the standards of RTE – a lot of money. At this rate there wouldn't be much to report when I got home.

Then a tall, thin, bespectacled man approached me. He introduced himself as a doctor. He had worked in Europe for some years but had come home to join the struggle. I thought there was something different about him. He was much less strident than the other EPLF people I'd met. We chatted about the working conditions – very dusty, not enough medicine, the constant danger of attack – and then I asked him about napalm. Was it true the Ethiopians had dropped the burning jelly on villages?

Sure it was true, he said. The Dergue sent planes loaded with napalm and phosphorus bombs. Napalm is a jellied petrol which sticks to the skin and burns terribly, sucking the oxygen out of the air when it hits. The phosphorus also sticks and burns through the bone at a temperature of 5,000 degrees Fahrenheit. The doctor said the Dergue hit people on market days. The idea was to terrorise the population out of support-ing the EPLF.

'But that's a breach of the Geneva Conventions,' I said.

At this he laughed. A short, bitter laugh.

'Come with me and I'll show you the Geneva Conventions.' I followed him up the valley. He pointed to a small tent about two hundred yards further on. We climbed over some rocks until we reached the entrance to the tent. A light breeze was blowing the dust up around us.

'There is a wounded boy here,' the doctor said. 'Please wait until I have seen him. When I call you can come in. He comes from a remote village and he has not seen a white man before. I don't want you to frighten him.'

The doctor wanted to explain to the boy that there was a stranger outside, and that this stranger had white skin and a machine which would take the sound of his voice and play it to people who lived thousands of miles away. After I'd waited for about ten minutes the doctor called me. He opened the flap of the tent and ushered me in.

What I saw knocked me backwards. In Ireland on television you rarely glimpsed the reality of violence on the news. We saw reports from Belfast but the police and military cordoned off the area and the scenes-of-crime people moved in. The body was usually gone or too far away to see by the time the cameras arrived. The wounded were occasionally seen but always in the context of a clean, modern hospital ward and surrounded by the best care possible.

On this Eritrean hillside there were no nurses, only an exhausted doctor with a tent in which to care for a ten-year-old boy who'd been caught in the open when the MiGs swooped down.

His name was Ande Mikail. At first I could see only his face. The doctor had placed a foil blanket on him to conserve his body heat (the irony of terrible burn injuries is that patients can die of hypothermia). Ande Mikail had sallow skin and dark eyes. They looked straight into mine with an expression of pure terror. How must I have looked to him? How strange?

The doctor wanted to show me the wound. He lifted the blanket. Underneath, on Ande's stomach and groin, was a large dressing. As he lifted the dressing, revealing the raw meat of the wound, the blackness and yellow of infection, the child cried out. There was a terrible smell, rotting flesh and chemicals.

I asked the doctor to replace the blanket. 'Please. I've seen enough.'

The doctor translated the boy's story. It came in short sentences. A Morse code of agony. Ande had been visiting the market with his sister when the Ethiopian planes attacked. There was a booming noise and then everything was on fire. Ande was on fire. He screamed and screamed. Then somebody put the fire out. He was taken to hospital and the doctors gave him medicine. They cleaned his wounds every day. Ande didn't know what happened to his sister.

The wind pushed through the tent again. Ande cried out. It was a sharp, penetrating cry. Even the breeze caused him agony. The doctor explained that the big problem was keeping dust out of the wounds. But on a mountain side in one of the most arid parts of Africa, the chances were small. Particles of the yellow earth floated around us.

The doctor would do his best for Ande Mikail, but his best was probably not going to save the child. I couldn't take looking at him any more. I tried to smile at the child, the doctor, and I left the tent. Outside I sat on a rock and smoked a cigarette. My hands were shaking. I felt sad first. Then I realised I wasn't so much sad as furious.

I didn't know much about the international order. Living in Ireland and reporting on Irish news most of the time, the Cold War was largely an abstraction. Africa was known to us through the annual collections for 'Black Babies' held by religious orders, or the appeals for the starving that cropped up three or four times a year on television. A man called Bunny Carr came on the radio and said we, the Irish who had experienced famine ourselves, should help the starving in

Africa. We heard sermons delivered by missionaries home on leave from Nigeria or Kenya. They told us about the dignity of the people and how much they struggled. But those returned white men with their strange sallow skins and old-fashioned clothes had been so long away from us that we regarded them as half-foreign.

They touched our sympathy though. The Irish gave huge sums of money to charities operating in Africa. We sent our UN troops to do peacekeeping duty in Congo where several of them were brutally killed. But you could sum up our collective understanding of what was happening in Africa with the phrase 'Sure isn't it desperate' followed by a shrug of the shoulders and the steering of the conversation back to more familiar territory.

Now I had seen the mess up close. It could never be an abstraction for me again. I knew that the maiming of Ande Mikail would pass unpunished by the world. The dictator who sent the pilot to bomb the village would not be called to account, nor would the Soviets who'd sold him the jets, or the international arms manufacturers who supplied the napalm, or the international community which did nothing to enforce the humanitarian laws that were meant to outlaw such attacks. Nothing would happen.

That moment on the Eritrean hillside was a point of departure for me. I had seen news photographs of war victims and I'd watched documentaries. But they didn't smell the way that tent did, and the eyes of the dying on the screen had never caught me the way Ande Mikail's had. Having looked into the eyes of this child of war I could not look away again.

Years later, when I came out of Congo, a producer in London said to me over the phone: 'I don't know how you tell those stories.' I know what I wanted to say. I wanted to say the question really is: how could one not tell those stories.

But I knew how sanctimonious that would sound down an international telephone line, and so I just muttered something about it being the job. I still believe the unspoken answer was the right one.

CHAPTER ELEVEN

The Land That Happened Inside Us

> *For the land that happened inside us;*
> *that nobody can take away,*
> *not even ourselves.*
>   *An Instant in the Wind,* ANDRÉ BRINK

My first sight was not land but sky, a red line that appeared far off to my left. It spread slowly through the blue. Sunrise over southern Africa. I was half awake when the captain announced that we had just flown over the Limpopo River. Anne reached across and squeezed my hand. We would be landing in Johannesburg in just over an hour.

This was the southern spring of 1984, six years before I would get the job of BBC Africa correspondent. It was my first visit to South Africa, still the country of apartheid, a place I knew only from books. Reform was a dream. So too was any prospect that I might ever be based there as a foreign correspondent. I knew that if I was to have any chance I'd need some experience. So Anne and I had decided to take our tape recorders and notebooks and travel around the country. I would do stories for RTE, she would sell them to the news-papers.

We happily lied and told the South Africans we were tourists, and were welcomed in by the all-white immigration officials. Driving in from the airport to Johannesburg I saw a group of black workers huddled on the back of a small pick-up truck. The white driver sat in the cabin on his own. An every-day picture of South Africa to anybody who knew the place, but to me it was the first emblem of division.

We travelled around the country by train and car for over a month, stopping in big cities and tiny villages, visiting town-ships which were on the brink of rebellion and getting lost in the impoverished Bantustan of Transkei, where black South Africans were being dumped in their tens of thousands, victims of forced removals from urban areas. At Port Elizabeth, the same city where they'd tortured the black leader Steve Biko less than a decade before, we walked beside the Indian Ocean, with the surf thundering onto sands the colour of gold, and looked up to see a crowd of black children looking down at us. Nearby there was a sign: Europeans Only.

So many memories come back. I went into black townships for the first time and felt white in a way I'd never done before. The small streets, hemmed in on every side by shacks, immense oceans of corrugated iron and plastic, were terrifying to a newcomer. I was seeing what most white South Africans never experienced. In New Brighton township, outside Port Eliza-beth, our car was confronted by stone-throwing youths but they stopped immediately when they recognised the driver, Father Teddy Molyneaux, champion of the poor, friend of Steve Biko and of Donald Woods, and native of my father's home town, Listowel, County Kerry.

Ted came out to South Africa as a missionary just as grand apartheid was being enforced. By the time I met him he'd been under security police surveillance for many years. The police knew he'd given his passport to Donald Woods to help him escape from the country. (A friendly official in the Irish Department of Foreign Affairs smuggled a new one to Ted soon afterwards.) They were also aware that Ted was well loved in the townships. He wasn't bothered by the surveillance and routine harassment. He was the first to tell me that liberation might come within a decade; I remember scoffing at the time.

From New Brighton we drove to Cape Town and saw Robben Island in the distance. Mandela was still a prisoner but would be free in six years, something the white shopkeeper I met on Long Street could never have anticipated. We had a furious row.

'They are like children. You're not going to get up and give the keys of your house and car, the keys of your safe to your kids, are you?'

It was a familiar theme of white rationalisations – the black man as child. *They're not like you and me. Look what's happened to the rest of Africa. They have different standards. We are a First World people, they are Third World.*

I called him a racist, and said there would be a bloodbath if the whites didn't change. He told me to get out of the shop. 'And don't ever come back!' he shouted after me.

In fact years later I did but the shopkeeper was gone, his premises amalgamated into a much bigger store. Perhaps the new black-ruled country was too much for him to take.

South Africa was fighting a war beyond its own borders in those days. There were soldiers in Angola and fighting against SWAPO (the South West Africa People's Organisation) in what is now Namibia. On a train to Cape Town we saw the 'troopies' – white conscripts – heading off for training, cannon fodder for apartheid in a losing war, while a group of older soldiers, the permanent force and probable veterans of Angola, got violently drunk in the carriage next to ours. All night they shouted at each other. Then there was a scuffle, screams, and after that quiet. I think they had been fighting among themselves.

A week later on the slopes of the Lebombo Mountains, close to the Mozambique border, we stopped to pick up a young hitchhiker. He was a teenage Afrikaner on his way home from boarding school to his parents' farm.

'What do you think of the situation?' Anne asked him. It was like Belfast in that respect. Everybody knew what 'situation' meant. Everybody had a view.

'We are being attacked by communists and terrorists. They going to take us over. When I leave school – just two years – I go in the army and fight them,' he said.

Every day on the news bulletins we heard short items about fighting between South African troops and 'terrorists' on the border, read out in the beautifully modulated tones of the announcers. The most grotesque atrocities seemed acceptable, desirable even, when delivered in those fruity 1950s voices.

Later that night we were caught in our first African thunderstorm. Lightning picked out the figures of black people standing under trees, lit up momentarily, huddled against the storm; it was mesmerising, beautiful, terrifying. The landscapes of that first journey live with me: the blue of the Outeniqua Mountains folding one into the other until we crossed down into the wheat lands of Swellendam, the camel thorns and mopane trees of the bushveld, the smells of dust on a farm track after rain, the southern ocean, its scent drifting up to meet us long before we saw it, and the light, always the memory of clear light, on an October evening as we crossed the Hottentots Holland Mountains towards Cape Town. It was the most beautiful, tormented country I had ever seen, and I could not wait to return.

As we were driving to the airport on our way home I spotted billboards for the late edition of the *Johannesburg Star*. It read something like 'Riots Rock East Rand Townships'. I didn't realise it then, hardly anybody predicted it, but these were the first eruptions of a mass protest movement that would usher in the last days of the apartheid state.

~

Two years later the escalating protests would bring me back. This time there was no breeze through immigration. The official at passport control looked directly into my eyes:

'What is the purpose of your visit?' he asked.

He was bald, mid-fifties I guessed, with water-blue eyes. The voice was soft, faintly camp, and almost uninterested. Not an Afrikaner, I thought, maybe even one of those English-speaking liberals. I felt relief.

'Oh, just a few weeks' holiday is all,' I replied. 'Go to the bush and to the coast.'

He raised his eyebrows, pursed his lips. My relief had been premature. 'You come here on your *own* for a holiday?'

Pause.

'In the middle of winter?'

Another pause.

'Really?'

One interrogative limped after the other. I was convinced he didn't believe me. My heart started to race. Sweat began to form on my temples and around my neck. I prayed he hadn't spotted my funk.

'A solo holiday, eh? I think I should share that with my boss.'

I mentally prepared myself for the inevitable: a quick consultation with his boss, a call to the airport police and back on the first flight to London. But then, after flicking through the pages of my passport, he smiled:

'Holiday, holiday. Surely you could have found a nice girl for yourself to keep you warm in this African winter.' He laughed and winked at me. The stamp crashed down on the open page and he waved me through.

The month was June in the fateful year of 1986. The year of the State of Emergency, disappearances, tortures, bannings. By its end every significant black organisation in the country had been outlawed, all major leaders were in detention, and hundreds of black South Africans had been killed by the white state.

I arrived on 15 June. The following day would be the tenth anniversary of the Soweto student uprising. It was a day of powerful significance for black and white, for it remembered the moment when black youth challenged the might of the apartheid state and watched it tremble. The generation of '76 had seen their parents humiliated under the white man's writ, corralled by an immense arrangement of laws. There was a law saying who you could have sex with (not with a white if you were black), a law saying where you could live (not anywhere near whites), and laws saying what jobs, schools, cinemas, toilets, buses, trains, restaurants, hotels you could enter. Eighty percent of the wealth was held by 10 percent of the population (white naturally). The state spent four times as much on the education of a white child as it did on a black. The South Africa of white rule was the Republic of Selfishness.

None of it would have been possible – it could certainly never have survived as long as it did — without the help of the West. Our governments, locked in their Cold War paranoia, kept up diplomatic relations with the racists, traded weapons technology with them, resisted attempts to impose sanctions on them, permitted their racially segregated sports teams to tour our countries. It remains one of the great moral questions of the latter half of the twentieth century. How did we cooperate for so long with a system that was so evil and de-humanising?

The geo-political explanation is that we went along because we didn't want the Reds to dip their toes in the icy waters of the Cape. But our assumptions about South Africa were underpinned by racism. We saw South Africa's potential through the prism of African failure. We predicted ineptitude, corruption and, yes, savagery; we remembered the Congo and the raped white women and crying blond children, the howling black mobs, and when P. W. Botha despatched silky spokesmen to London and Washington to warn of these very evils in South Africa, they were met by politicians who nodded with understanding.

We must judge governments not by their words but by their deeds. There was no shortage of rhetoric about apartheid. When the system was at its worst, when there was no glimmer of reform, our leaders sat on their hands. They called it 'constructive engagement'. This meant you kept talking to the racists. When they shot, tortured, 'disappeared' people, you did ... nothing. *Keep talking. In the end the regime might come around.* The implication of decades of Western policy was that blacks, coloureds and Indians couldn't be trusted to run their own country. It was the 'blacks are children' argument, but expressed in more subtle terms, and always with the pious assurance that we were acting with their best interests in mind. The blacks were ready for democracy. It was white South Africa that wasn't prepared.

When the government of Johannes Balthazar Vorster decided that all subjects would have to be taught through the despised medium of Afrikaans, black schoolchildren rebelled. The immediate rebellion was crushed like all the rebellions before. But the kids of Soweto, and countless other townships, achieved something no other generation had – they'd seen the fear in the eyes of the white state. And when the students were released from prison they began to organise themselves, rallying around new trade unions and civic groups, so that by the time I arrived in June 1986 the regime of P. W. Botha was facing the first serious threat to its continued existence. The new rising had started in the townships around Johannesburg.

Then it spread to Cape Town and the ANC strongholds of the Eastern Cape. Within the year the regime faced a countrywide uprising on an unprecedented scale.

A new tactic of school boycotts had pushed children to the fore of the protest movement. In cracking down, the state focused a lot of its force on children. By the end of 1985 more than 2,000 children under the age of fifteen were being detained under security laws. A study of 131 child detainees showed that 34 percent had experienced solitary confinement; 72 percent suffered physical abuse; 25 percent were subjected to attempted suffocation; and 14 percent were given electric shock treatment. Remember, we are talking about children *under fifteen*, having electrodes attached to their bodies – toes, fingers, testicles – so that they could be tormented with powerful jolts of electricity. All of this information was made public by human rights groups. It was known in Britain and America.

While torturing with one hand the 'Groot Krokodil', P. W. Botha, was promising reform with the other. His foreign minister, the garrulous Pik Botha (no relation), had even said he might see a black president in his lifetime. But instead of 'crossing the Rubicon' as he promised, the President reverted to the politics of his predecessors, drawing the wagons into a laager and opening fire.

The day I arrived back in Johannesburg it was bitterly cold, one of those beautiful high-veld rainless winter days, when the skies are the colour of lapis lazuli and the sun burns every patch of grass the colour of honey. Later it grew foggy as the smoke of countless coal-burning stoves was carried on the breeze from the black townships. With that acrid scent of smoke and the clouding of the sky the immense brooding presence of the majority declared itself. They were hemmed in now in the townships and squatter camps, waiting for their hour.

Beneath the bluster and bullying of President Botha, white South Africa was terrified. Johannesburg was an armed camp. There were soldiers posted at key intersections. Large squads of policemen, swinging whips as they walked, patrolled the main streets. The last voice of liberalism in the press, the *Weekly Mail*, carried a headline which read: 'The Rule of the Big Stick'. But its pages were decimated. Under the new security laws the paper couldn't mention any actions or criticism of the security forces. The government succeeded in stifling coverage by the foreign press as well. It relied on the journalists' fear of deportation.

Anybody who broke the laws would be expelled and swift examples had been made of Michael Buerk of the BBC and Peter Sharpe of ITN – Pretoria feared the impact of their television reporting on public and political opinion at home. Self-censorship became routine. Much of the brutality went unreported, emerging only years later at hearings of the Truth and Reconciliation Commission.

On my first night I visited the leader of the Black Sash, a human rights group run by middle-class white women, and had my interview constantly interrupted: 'I'm so sorry, darling,' said Sheena Duncan, as the phone rang for the umpteenth time, 'but they are arresting everybody. It's unbelievable what's happening.' She promised to get somebody from her network to call me the following day. The state-run radio was reporting calm across the country. The big crackdown had worked.

I had never experienced the awesome spectacle of total state power. I was starting to get nervous. My immediate concern was avoiding arrest. If they were harassing journalists who were working in the country legally, i.e. those with work permits, I didn't fancy my own chances if caught by the security police. At the best they would have interrogated and deported me. At worst I would have been given a beating followed by a spell in a South African prison, notorious for their toughness.

On 16 June I tried to get to Soweto with the help of a worker from a church group. The office in Dublin advised me against it. 'It's not worth it. Monitor it from the TV and radio,' an editor said.

He was right. I was foolish to even try. We set out along the highway that leads south of the city, and were approaching the off-ramp for Soweto when I saw the police checkpoints. They were *everywhere*. Police and soldiers, armoured vehicles, unmarked cars, helicopters prowling overhead. The driver looked at me as if to say 'no way'. I nodded my head and we carried on past the off-ramp and found our way back to the city centre.

Journalism is nine-tenths luck. And after a dispiriting start mine was about to change. Back at the hotel there was a message. It was from a social worker I'd met on the earlier trip. I was told to head downtown to a building called Khotso House. It was the headquarters of the South African Council of Churches and would soon be bombed by apartheid agents. Right then it was the last place of sanctuary for the victims of state terror.

Looking anxiously over my shoulder – convinced that every security policeman in Johannesburg wanted to catch the RTE reporter – I did my best to saunter nonchalantly up the steps into Khotso House. Inside there was an atmosphere of crisis. People were moving quickly from office to office. I saw a group of young boys talking to a woman – she looked like a lawyer – in a corner. I asked if I could interview them. 'Okay,' she said. 'But no names, no mention of where they were arrested.'

The boys were terrified. One had a badly swollen face, and his left eye had closed up. I saw flecks of blood on his T-shirt. They described how they'd been taken to a police station and beaten up. One described how an Alsatian dog had been set on his friend. The police had stood around smoking cigarettes and laughing during this. I also remember a boy in his early teens saying he would leave the country now and join the ANC's military wing to fight the regime. I felt sorry for him. The ANC's Umkhonto We Sizwe – Spear of the Nation – was possibly the least effective guerrilla army in Africa. Its ranks were heavily infiltrated by government spies. If he wasn't killed he would be betrayed and imprisoned.

I rushed from office to office, aware that it was late in the afternoon and the black church workers would be trying to get back to their embattled townships. A man came out and introduced himself as Joe Seremane, a worker with the South African Council of Churches. Joe was of small height and very softly spoken. He wore a plaid shirt and blue jeans, looking more like a folk singer or poet than a political activist. He said he had been a political prisoner on Robben Island, and he was lying low now, trying to avoid being arrested again.

'What is it like when they raid your home?' I asked.

He answered quickly.

'We have a conservative culture in our homes and families. So can I ask you to imagine what it's like if you are a black child and the whole house is woken up in the middle of the night. There are police shouting in Afrikaans and torches shining. And these guys they knock the door down when they come for you. Then this black child sees his father dragged out of bed and paraded naked on the floor in front of him. You can't describe the shock for that child.'

I wanted to ask whether he had been talking about what he'd seen as a child himself, or what his own child had seen. Mind you, in South Africa it was perfectly plausible that he was speaking in both contexts. Police raids had been a fact of black life for over a century.

But Joe was called away before we could talk further. Then somebody made a phone call on my behalf. I was given another address. This time it was a Church-owned house in the suburbs. Again more children who had been beaten with whips. One had his leg stippled with shotgun pellets. A few days later I was in Cape Town at a nursery school in a 'coloured' district listening to the teacher talk about how plain-clothes police had turned up and thrown what looked like sweets into the playground. They turned out to be pellets for lighting fires. Some of the children had eaten them and become ill.

In the Crossroads squatter camp behind Table Mountain, an ocean of plastic and corrugated iron, swamped by rain, I disguised myself as a priest and in the company of a local Irish clergyman drove through the checkpoints, smiling as piously as I could at the soldiers and policemen. Driving around the rutted streets we passed small groups of youths on the corners, but every so often they would scatter as we approached.

At first I thought they'd mistaken us for Special Branch, in spite of the priestly garb. But then the priest pointed towards the mirror and I looked and saw we were being shadowed by an armoured car, from which poked the rifles of a platoon of soldiers. The priest had lived in the township for many years.

Unlike Father Teddy Molyneaux in New Brighton, this priest didn't strike me as one of nature's radicals. But in his quiet way he undermined the apartheid state; certainly smuggling a journalist into the camps was taking a big risk. If caught he would have been thrown out of the country. I knew that he had also helped people who were on the run from the police, hiding them, helping them to get out from one safe house to another. He lived in a single room behind the church. There was a bed, a table, some books. They were thrillers, a James Bond book and something by an American writer I'd never heard of. More to calm my own nerves than anything else – the army was still trailing behind – I asked him what he did when the pressure really mounted.

'If there is nothing I can usefully do, or if it looks like they might be able to catch me at something and throw me out, I go back to the church and go to bed. Doesn't matter if it's day or night, I wrap myself up in the blanket and read a thriller. I stay there until it blows over.'

South Africa was full of people like that. They took chances every day. For blacks of course the risks were a lot greater. Generally speaking a white priest wasn't going to be killed (though the Anglican Father Michael Lapsley was attacked and maimed by a letter bomb). There were thousands of people challenging the state every day. Sooner rather than later it had to make a genuine difference.

～

Towards the end of my trip I went to a meeting of the main white liberal party – the Progressive Federalists – in an upmarket suburb of Johannesburg. The meeting was held in a church hall and was wrapping up by the time I arrived. Everybody in the hall was white, and everybody spoke English and believed apartheid was a dreadful thing. But this political party was allowed to organise. None of its members was under threat of arrest, torture or disappearance. I approached one man with my microphone and asked for an interview.

'I don't think so,' he said. 'I'll tell you what, let's talk the whole thing through over lunch tomorrow. But we talk off the record. I don't know that it would be helpful for me to go on the record. Let's have lunch.'

I passed on the opportunity. I felt confused by his response. These were Alan Paton's descendants, the representatives of the white liberal tradition in South Africa, the party of Helen Suzman, who had badgered P. W. Botha in parliament over the plight of detainees, the only people now who could open their mouths and not get thrown into jail. And this man wanted to talk about it over lunch? Why wouldn't he comment now?

Then and there I realised what had been evident to black South Africans for some time: the white liberals were a torn entity, caught between the fear of the white electorate and the impatience of the black majority. The parliamentary white liberals had played an important role in keeping some semblance of opposition alive. But by virtue of their skin colour and the protections afforded by their money and parliamentary seats, they would never understand how it felt to be non-people, or experience the denial of simple humanity that was at the heart of the black experience.

Now the liberals were being eclipsed as the political opposition by a black generation that did not need whites to speak for them. The children of '76 had become the young radicals of the 1980s and wouldn't settle for the long go-slow to federalised majority rule favoured by the parliamentary liberals. They wanted the future *now*. And thousands would give their lives to get there.

~

But the South Africa of those years was not, if you will forgive the exhausted but necessary cliché, a simple issue of black and white. There were militant whites who had been central figures in the struggle. People like Bram Fischer, who was the son of a leading Afrikaner judge, Joe Slovo, the ANC's military leader, and Neil Agget, a young trade union official, would become heroes to the black majority. Fischer was sent to jail for life and allowed out only when he was dying of cancer; Slovo's wife, the activist Ruth First, was killed by a booby trap bomb; Neil Agget died in the custody of the security police.

For the Afrikaans-speaking whites like Bram Fischer it took a special kind of courage to denounce apartheid. Speaking out meant exile from a close-knit community with a powerful sense of identity. The declaration: 'I am an Afrikaner' burned with a desire for belonging and the defiance of the embattled. But it also contained a plea for understanding; for the Afrikaners I met were never as sure of their ideology as they pretended to be. Many were insecure, guilt-nagged, and the bullying rhetoric was often a cover for fear. In spite of apartheid, they were a hard people to hate.

These extraordinary people had sailed from Europe, from Holland and France, to escape the religious persecution of the seventeenth century, and found they had new battles to fight, and enemies they could persecute. They fought the tribes of the African interior, and they fought the British Empire when it sought to constrain them. In the years to come I would spend many hours on remote farms drinking coffee with farmers and their families.

They were the most hospitable people I'd ever come across, and their love of the land of Africa was always palpable. They reminded me of my father's people. The land was everything. In Kerry they had a saying: 'What you have you hold. Let no man take it away from you.' The Afrikaner farmers spoke in the same direct way as my Kerry relatives; they shared a folk memory of oppression by Britain and, though the specific conditions were markedly different, they had created a dour, repressive state once they'd achieved freedom. The dead hand of the Church, the sanctification of dead heroes, the elevation of the pieties of nationalism in place of independent thought, the censorship . . . we had more in common than we thought.

Like the Irish, they could be a fiercely sentimental people. Listen to their folk songs. The sad melodies, the melancholy accordion, and the same themes always: land, family, God. They regarded the blacks as children, yet their view of the world was that of a people who remained trapped in a kind of endless childhood, one where God would always stand with them, and where earth had indeed become a kind of heaven. After the anguish of their grandparents in the Boer War, the suffering of their parents in the Great Depression, the Afrikaners of the 1980s and '90s had entered the promised land. Apartheid gave them everything. Land, jobs, houses. In such an earthly paradise who would want to grow up?

It is a hallmark of childhood that we need not confront too many painful realities. And for Afrikaners the reality, if they ever decided to contemplate it, was very painful.

The system which kept them in their place of privilege was already unravelling by the time I arrived in South Africa. The idea of dumping blacks into rural homelands was a failure. The numbers fleeing to the cities easily outnumbered the exiles. Despite the pressure of security legislation, blacks continued to organise. They now had their own powerful trade unions. The Afrikaner monolith was starting to crack. Increasing numbers of the Boer were questioning the morality of apartheid and, if they weren't too bothered about that, at least the political wisdom of continuing with a system they saw as doomed to failure.

Hardly any of the farmers I met would have accepted that. Most promised to become *bitter einders* and fight the blacks if majority rule were introduced. I used to listen to them ranting on about the blacks, but in the end I understood that they spoke loudly to drown the sound of their own fear. They were easy to caricature, and easy to laugh at. What other possible response can there be to a farmer who tells you that a black lives in a round hut because 'his brain is not made to understand any other shapes'.

When they weren't denouncing the Afrikaners' racism, liberal white South Africa and the Western media sniggered at them endlessly. There was much less mockery of the great mining houses who'd profited so much from the apartheid system, and who earned their vast fortunes from exploiting blacks. With their educated guile and slick PR men, the likes of Anglo American – the giant mining corporation – re-invented themselves as pillars of liberalism. But if the main charge of apartheid was profiting from the ruthless exploitation of others, then the mining bosses were as guilty as any farmer with his underpaid and abused labourers. And for the majority of Afrikaners there was no second passport if they wanted to escape a future black government.

The English-speaking business elite had connections in the motherland; the Boere had a contemptuous expression for them: *sout piel*. It means 'salt dicks' – with one foot in Africa and another in Europe, their genitals dipped in the ocean. Afrikaners on the other hand never tired of telling me they had nowhere else to go. There was truth in that. What was more striking was that they had no desire to leave. Although capable of extraordinary self-delusion in many other ways, in that crucial understanding of belonging they had the measure of themselves. I tried to imagine Afrikaners settling in London or Manchester. It was impossible. The Afrikaans writer W. A. De Klerk describes them well in his novel *The Thirstland*:

This at least had to be admitted: Africa was part of them; and they were part of Africa. Such was God's will for them. Such was his purpose. They were part of Africa.

The rebels within Afrikanerdom were still only a small group back in the mid-1980s, but they were having an impact on Afrikaner thought more profound than their numbers. On my third day in Johannesburg and after endless phone calls, I tracked down one of the heroes of Afrikaner dissent.

The Reverend Beyers Naude was thin and stooped and wore thick glasses. When I met him he was in the middle of talking to some township kids who were looking for somewhere to hide from the police. He spoke to them gently, making them feel at ease. The accent was rural Afrikaans. I picked up the tail end of the conversation: 'And you will be all right, I can tell you that. You will be all right,' he said. One of the boys stood up to shake his hand. Naude took the hand and then embraced the youth.

It was the kind of sight to make P. W. Botha choke on his *boerewors* sausages. Beyers Naude was an anti-apartheid legend. While a young minister with the *Nederduitse Gereformeerde Kerk* (Dutch Reformed Church), the body which had given apartheid its theological justification, he had proclaimed racial separation a sin against God. As a *Dominee* of the NGK, Beyers Naude had done the unthinkable. To be able to live with the transparent cruelties of apartheid, the Afrikaner elite needed to find justifications in faith. No more than any other race, they were not instinctually cruel. It was only by selectively deconstructing the Old Testament they found the words they needed. Naude had demolished the pretence with powerful sermons. Worse still, he'd been a member of the Broederbond – the Afrikaner secret society which dominated the state – when he made his declaration. Naude was kicked out of the Church and placed under a banning order. Being banned meant you stayed in one place. You couldn't talk to anybody but your family. It was house arrest whose prime goal was to silence those whom the state could not easily kill. Bumping off an Afrikaner church minister, however much a heretic, would have been unacceptable.

For Naude the banning was the best thing that could have happened to him, at least that was how he explained it to me. He felt he could look blacks in the eye, they could see he was something more than a liberal trying to salve his conscience while making sure he didn't take any risks. 'By far the most painful thing was the effect on my family,' he said.

For them it was really hard. When people have known you to be a certain way, think in a usual way, and then for you to change all of that and put yourself outside them . . . it's very hard for them to understand. But once I had understood that apartheid was so wrong, I could not have lived with myself . . . as a Christian and as a human being if I stayed silent. Look at the evil that is being done in the townships and across this country right now . . . how can one be silent in the face of this?

Naude spoke with what the Russian poet Osip Mandelstam, victim of Stalin's Gulag, called 'the muttering lips' of dissent. Sometimes such people seem possessed. Mandelstam taunted the dictator in what must have been the sure knowledge that it would lead to his own destruction; in South Africa Steve Biko could have withdrawn from public life. Beyers Naude could have had a comfortable parish in a nice suburb.

People like Naude and Steve Biko became the heroes of my adult life. I have met many such people in the intervening twenty-five years. Some of them were public figures, the leaders of campaigns, putative leaders of countries. Many others were everyday citizens – factory workers, peasant farmers, teachers, nurses.

Beyers Naude stands out because he was the first person I met who looked evil in the eye and decided that he could not avert his gaze. He went on to confront what seemed an all-powerful state, in a time when it used every weapon imaginable to destroy its enemies. In South Africa, the struggle against apartheid came down to a fundamental idea: the right of people to be recognised as human. No idea seems more self-evident, yet none is more dishonoured in the practice of international politics. The greatest crime of apartheid was its assault on the dignity that is the foundation of our humanity.

I left South Africa soon after my meeting with Beyers Naude.

The journey out was even more nerve shattering than the arrival. This time I had tapes, all of them filled with the voices of dissenters, every testimony a breach of the state security laws. If I was caught the consequences for the people I'd interviewed were serious. The police were hovering all around the airport. But there was no drama.

A quick stamp of the passport, no searching of my bags, and no questions from the security police who were waiting by the plane door. I made it out. As the plane banked over the city I saw Soweto to the south, covered by the fog of coal fires, the biggest city in Africa, its people entering the second week of the Emergency.

I was convinced South Africa was heading for a bloodbath. I thought the likes of Naude were isolated figures and that – as Alan Paton had written – 'by the time the whites have learned to love the blacks will have learned only to hate'. Had anybody told me, on the long flight back to Europe, that within five years the ANC would be unbanned, the exiles would come home and Nelson Mandela would walk through the gates of Victor Verster Prison, I would have thought they were mad.

CHAPTER TWELVE

Cute Hoors

'Where else,' you hear the muffled voice saying, 'Where else could that happen but in Ireland!'
The Best of Myles, FLANN O'BRIEN

Back in Dublin I realised there was much in our national political life to prepare me for the tribal battles and strangling corruption of Africa, and up north the bitter sectarian division seemed to offer all kinds of comparisons with the politics of fear in South Africa. Our southern politics were still, to a large extent, defined by the unreconciled differences of civil war; in the North the sectarian conflict was 'tribal' by another name; there was still a significant tendency in public debate to blame the old colonial power for our woes, *pace* so many African leaders, and we had a form of home-grown corruption that even the most ardent confidence tricksters in Nigeria would have admired.

My career at RTE was thriving. I was getting a reputation for strong 'actuality' reporting, getting close to the scene of the action and putting the voices of so-called 'ordinary' people on the air – in other words people who were not politicians or spokesmen for lobby groups. Soon after I arrived at RTE, riots erupted close to the council estate where I'd grown up. I claimed local knowledge and begged to be sent. There wasn't any particular rush on the part of my older colleagues, who remembered journalists being viciously beaten by the police at a Republican demonstration in Dublin a few years previously. The police force was still dominated by large and thick-set country boys with an innate mistrust of the metropolitan media whose tender backsides they would dearly love to kick. The trouble had been started by a gang of youths stealing cars and holding races along the main avenue. It developed into a confrontation with the police. By the standards of what I would witness later in South Africa this was small-scale trouble – flying bottles and rocks, a police baton charge.

The significant thing was my own reaction. I was at ease in the tumult. I felt no fear and focused on recording what was happening, making sure the little needle on my tape machine didn't soar too far into the red and distort the sound, pausing to deliver a running commentary on what I was seeing. It wasn't simply a question of being at ease. I thrived in the atmosphere of conflict. My senses had never been more wide awake. Instinct told me when to stand and when to run. I didn't get thumped by the police or the rioters and I managed to get the tape on air, the only rule that counts in broadcasting.

The editors started to pay attention and gave me a job as co-presenter of the main weekly current affairs programme, an hour-long mix of illustrated reports and set-piece studio interviews which included an annual face-to-face encounter with the Taoiseach.

In those days Irish politics was frustrating, corrupt and wildly entertaining, dominated by two figures who had known and disliked each other since university. Garret FitzGerald was the leader of Fine Gael. Known to the public, in terms that were at least partially ironic, as 'Garret the Good', he had cast himself as the standard-bearer for a more pluralistic Ireland. He spoke of a 'Constitutional Crusade' which would tempt the Northern Protestants into reunification by transforming the South into an open, secular society. But he seriously misread the Unionists if he thought a secular United Ireland was their ambition, and he eventually seemed to lose his own enthusiasm for the project after the Catholic right in the South gave the idea the same welcome as the Orangemen in the North.

Garret was an exceptionally ruthless politician, a trait he covered up by adopting the persona of a genial, absent-minded university professor. Though undoubtedly clever, and brave in his analysis of the problems in Irish society, I always felt there was something disingenuous about Garret the Good, a public sanctimony that sat badly on the face of a man who had risen to the top in the shark pool of Irish politics. You did not become Taoiseach in Ireland without knowing how to plunge and occasionally twist the knife, or without knowing people who would do the plunging for you. His party, Fine Gael, was the party my family supported. The Keanes had been in at the birth of Fine Gael and my grandmother had worn the blue shirt to defend the party's supporters from attack.

The connection would always make me slightly suspect in the eyes of Fianna Fáil politicians. After a few drinks in the Dáil bar I would very occasionally be assailed with the shout, from a close ally of Charles Haughey, of: '*Go way outa that, you fucking Blueshirt.*' It was said humorously but with a razor in the middle of the marshmallow. In Ireland everybody knew everybody's politics. You had to be slotted in somewhere. *Your man's a Blueshirt.* Or: *That crowd are black* [extreme] *Fine Gael.* Or: *Your man's savage Fianna Fáil.* Or: *His uncle was the head of the Fianna Fáil cumann in Castlebar.*

Sometimes the parties overlapped in families, revealing some unhealed wound from the Civil War, but more often than not fanatical loyalty was hereditary. Irish politics was made up of a million intimate connections. Government jobs, contracts, all doled out on the basis of someone knowing someone knowing someone. When a politician who, years later, became our Minister of Foreign Affairs was caught by the police drinking after hours in a pub he asked the policeman: 'Would you like a pint or a transfer?' And we all burst out laughing when we heard that one. *My God, what a character*. It would have been funny if cops weren't transferred or promoted on the whim of politicians, or if greed, ignorance and deviousness hadn't been elevated to national virtues.

~

Although the Keanes were *black Fine Gael* they were civil to and did business with people of all parties. A publican in a rural town couldn't afford political apartheid. Though it might seem strange, my Uncle John B always liked the Fianna Fáil boss Charlie Haughey. If Garret was cast as the face of goodness his opponent, Charlie Haughey, was regarded by the liberal media, and especially the British press, as malice incarnate. Charles J. Haughey, born in Swatragh, County Derry, the son of a man who'd fought for the IRA, saw himself as the one true ruler of Ireland and bestrode Irish politics like a Demon King. Long before his financial misdeeds were exposed, Charlie was the most controversial politician in the history of the state.

Known by his fawning supporters as 'the Boss', he was also one of the most charismatic public figures I've ever met. Now that various tribunals have revealed the astonishing venality of Haughey's Ireland, the fact that he took handouts from wealthy businessmen, denied allegations of diverting money meant for a liver transplant for a close friend into his son's business, evaded tax while urging the rest of us to pay our full share, among other things, it has become fashionable to say that we knew about it all along. We only knew a fraction. In those days, the clientelism, cronyism, greed, back-scratching, and Charlie's own extraordinary taste for high living – a private island, horses, helicopter travel – were merely muttered about.

All this he had achieved on the Taoiseach's humble salary of around £50,000 a year. Haughey made up the difference by taking cash handouts from big business and he used one of the country's biggest banks as a personal piggy bank, airily refusing to pay back the huge sums he ran up on overdraft. In the immortal Dublin phrase: *'He had a neck like a stonebreaker's balls.'* The bank deserved everything that happened to it. But the people of Ireland deserved better. With the notable exception of a fiercely dogged reporter named Vincent Browne, the press let Haughey off the hook. Browne persistently asked how Charlie could afford his lifestyle but the major newspaper groups and RTE were too afraid to confront him.

Haughey led a party that purported to be the staunch defender of public morality, holding out against the liberalisation of contraception and the introduction of divorce, steadfast in the defence of the rights of the Catholic Church, and keen to avoid a stand on any matter of principle if it could possibly be avoided. Back in 1960 when the bishops were busy screaming about immoral books coming into the country, the Archbishop of Dublin, John Charles McQuaid, gave Charlie a copy of Edna O'Brien's novel *The Country Girls,* a gentle and mildly sexual account of young girls moving from rural Ireland to the city. Charlie affected horror at the contents:

'Like so many decent Catholic men with growing families, he was just beaten by the outlook and descriptions,' said the Archbishop. One can but imagine the pious, wounded expression of the future Taoiseach as he returned the book to Archbishop McQuaid.

A year after he became Taoiseach, Charlie introduced one of the most bitterly hilarious laws in the history of a European state. The contraception legislation of 1980 stipulated that only married couples with a prescription, no less, could purchase condoms. The law said the condoms could be used 'only for bona fide family planning purposes'. So no slipping them to unmarried relatives or friends or gays or blowing them up as balloons.

The law came at a time when it was widely whispered that Charlie was having an extra-marital affair with a prominent Dublin journalist. Nobody printed a word. (Years later the journalist confirmed the story and publicly humiliated Haughey by taking to the airwaves with a detailed description of their romance.) I didn't give a damn about Charlie's private life; what I found hard to stomach was the way he was trying to legislate for mine. In those days the private lives of public figures were still largely out of bounds. That was partly to do with the long hang-over from the bitterness that attended the destruction of Parnell over his affair with Kitty O'Shea, and partly a commendable reticence about public shaming.

But there were other reasons. The Irish gossiped with great relish about who was doing what to whom but putting it in the papers might have forced us to confront our screwed up attitudes to sex, and might even lead in the direction of change.

There was another reason to avoid annoying Haughey. He exuded machismo power. When a satirical radio programme portrayed him as a Mafia don it was said that Haughey was privately flattered. Those who stood against him, like the Limerick TD and former Justice Minister Desmond O'Malley, were eventually driven from the party. The Civil War days when they might end up sucking mud in a Kerry bog-hole were gone, but there were all kinds of ways to cut a man down to size in a country where you held the power, and where decisions of all kinds, from land re-zoning to civil service jobs, were in the gift of party hacks.

Several attempts were made to unseat Haughey by members

of his own party in the early 1980s. I still have vivid memories of the vicious atmosphere when threats of physical violence were rife and some of his enemies had to be given protection by the police. Each night the press stood outside the Dáil surrounded by baying hordes of Haugheyites who loathed the media every bit as much as they did his political opponents. Not that you could have traced any of that to Charles Haughey. When his Justice Minister tapped the telephones of journalists, Charlie pleaded innocence and the minister was sacrificed. (He would later rise from the dead to tell the truth about the affair and bring Haughey's career to an end.)

Haughey and his supporters were a souped-up, spiv's version of the powerful party machine de Valera had created. It was in the field of planning that certain members of our political class thoroughly disgraced themselves. The shiny suited Ray Burke, a former foreign minister, and Frank Dunlop, former Government Press Secretary, were among those who found themselves in front of judicial tribunals having to explain the payments handed to politicians by property developers.

My grandparents may have disliked Dev's politics but they would have grudgingly admitted that he was motivated by high ideals. To Hanna Keane and Paddy Hassett, who'd risked their lives to help bring the state into being, the likes of Haughey would have been poison. It appears Dev was a good judge of character where Haughey was concerned. Charlie was selected to run de Valera's bid for the presidency in 1966, and his behaviour during the campaign left the older man deeply worried. 'That man will destroy Fianna Fáil,' he told a colleague.

The Fianna Fáil elite under Charlie Haughey dressed in sharp suits, collected fine art and generally affected the pretensions of a new Ascendancy class. Those further down the line had less sophisticated tastes: they guzzled chicken dinners and roared their support for 'the 'Boss', a political pygmy class grateful to be close to the smell of power and ready to abuse any who threatened their chieftain.

The Charlie I encountered was certainly smart enough to see this devotion for the tribal tub-thumping it really was; he enjoyed the applause but I suspect he nursed a private contempt for his army of sycophants. He was not unique in Irish history; rather, the ultimate incarnation of a creature that had developed over centuries: the '*Cute Hoor*'.

The word 'cute' in this context means sly; the word 'hoor' is a local corruption of 'whore', though not meant in any sexual sense and usually offered admiringly, e.g. 'By God, but isn't your man the *cute hoor* all right!' This might be uttered after said *hoor* had managed to get planning permission for an ugly new housing estate on one of the most beautiful headlands in the country, or after he had ushered some cousin or crony into a secure state job ahead of better-qualified applicants. The Cute Hoors were not whores; Ireland was the bagatelle. Haughey and his cronies were the pimps who flogged her honour to the highest bidders.

Cute Hoorism is the most expert form of opportunism known to man. Though Fianna Fáil were the arch exponents, elements of the trait exist in all spheres of Irish politics. The Cute Hoor is perpetually on the make. He has the cunning of the peasant and the greed of the landlord. For him nothing is more important than putting one over on the other side, pulling the stroke, and accumulating wealth and power for his own. The Cute Hoor knows when to make a show of defiance (for him all political acts are ultimately a 'show'), and when to genuflect. He pays ostentatious obeisance to the puritan founders of the state, but his behaviour represents a loud snigger at the ideal of sacrifice they embodied.

Not for him the bivouac in the cold Kerry hills, the hunger strike in Brixton prison or the firing squad at Kilmainham, though come closing-time he will sing a Republican ballad with a tear in one eye. In the memorable phrase of the great Irish satirist Brendan O'Heithir, Haughey and his entourage were a 'collection of over-dressed bookies' runners'. Yet, for all this, I didn't loathe Haughey. I never voted for him but I could not deny his charisma.

On a personal level Charlie could be an immensely attractive character. My Uncle John B and Charlie were on good terms – the Taoiseach always dropping in to John B's pub when he passed through North Kerry. One of his more inspired pieces of legislation was the abolition of income tax for artists, musicians and writers – a move that won him the lifelong gratitude of my uncle. Whenever I met Charlie he would ask after John B, before launching a humorous attack on my political heritage. 'All of you Keanes, sure you're all fuckin' Blueshirts!'

During one of the general election campaigns – there were many in the politically fervid 1980s – I was assigned to follow Haughey around the country. He could switch from charm to nastiness in a blink of his hooded eyes. 'If you come close with that again I'll shove it down your fuckin' throat' was a typical offering, spoken when my microphone drifted too close to his face.

Later that day I was riding into a rural town in his limousine when the cavalcade came to a halt. Haughey groaned. There had been many such impromptu stops and he was tired. 'What the fuck is it now?' he said. The two candidates for Dáil seats were dullards and hacks of the worst kind. I doubt if Haughey exchanged two words with them all day. The press officer bounded up to the window of the car: 'Boss, the candidates want to know if they can ride into town with you in the car?'

Whether it was the thrill of riding in a government Mercedes, or the glamour that might attach to their cause if they were seen riding into town with Charlie, the candidates hopped up and down like children desperate for the toilet.

Charlie glared at his spokesman, and then looked out at the hopeful faces of the candidates. I will always cherish his response:

'No they cannot. It'll be enough to have to look at the fuckers in the Dáil for the next four years. Drive on.'

Whether Charlie was in power or spitting venom from the opposition benches, entertainment was guaranteed. Even though the joke was at our expense, we laughed and laughed.

~

In a democratic republic people should not think in terms of having laws other than those that allow private citizens to make their own free choice in so far as these private matters are concerned . . . The politics of this would be very easy. The politics would be to be one of the lads, the safest way in Ireland. But I do not believe the interests of this State, or our Constitution and of this Republic, would be served by putting politics before conscience in regard to this. There is a choice of a kind that can only be answered by saying that I stand by the Republic and accordingly I will not oppose this Bill.

Desmond O'Malley, TD, speaking during the Dáil debate on legislation broadening the availability of contraceptives, 1985

With the advent of the 1980s, the country my grandparents had fought for still bore many of the outward trappings of a Catholic nationalist state. The Angelus bell still tolled on radio at noon and at six in the evening. The day closed on television with the playing of our national anthem, 'The Soldier's Song'. The cardinal and his bishops were still given a respectful hearing in the media, and their views were listened to carefully by the occupants of Government Buildings. But change was accelerating.

Ireland's entry into the EEC a decade previously had helped to transform the economy and the universities were turning out some of the most highly qualified graduates in Europe. In Limerick, where I'd learned my journalistic trade, the local Institute for Higher Education predicted the coming technological revolution and prepared its students to reap the benefits. Unemployment peaked at a staggering 17 percent in 1986, but after that it was a story of steady, sure improvement. The ground was being prepared for a boom that would see the country of emigration transformed into the fastest growing economy in Europe.

With our exposure to Europe, and the influence of radio and television, and a highly educated younger generation, the country's stern Catholic ethos was under threat. The issue was only how long it would take to remove the constraints on achieving a more pluralist society. The early battles were depressing. The Pro-Life campaign ended with victory for the Catholic right, who succeeded in having the Constitution changed to include a specific protection for the life of the unborn. The campaign was characterised by vicious displays of intolerance, crazed interventions by several parish priests who fell back on visions of hell and damnation to frighten their flocks, and a full-on charge by the Catholic bishops and the papal nuncio.

The hierarchy laid down the only course of action for good Catholics: 'We are convinced that a clear majority in favour of the amendment will greatly contribute to the continued protection of unborn human life in the laws of our country,' they announced. The country voted in the Pro-Life amendment by a majority of more than 60 percent.

A referendum on divorce in 1986 ended in victory for the anti-divorce lobby, much of it achieved through the incompetence of the government which sponsored the legislation and the cunning of the arguments proposed by the Catholic right.

Farmers were encouraged to believe that divorce would lead to the dismemberment of family farms up and down the country.

In a society where land tenure was regarded as a sacred right, it was a shrewd ploy. I remember travelling to a big farm in County Kilkenny and asking a farmer why he wouldn't accept the government's promise that land would not be sub-divided in cases of divorce. 'A politician's promise is like a hoor's kiss,' he replied, thus settling the argument. Much of the clergy, inspired by the hierarchy, correctly regarded the media, particularly RTE, as acolytes of liberalism. As I was leaving the area, a plump young priest pulled up at the door of a house where I'd stopped to ask directions. He saw my tape recorder and frowned. I noticed a large bunch of anti-divorce placards in the back of his car:

'Father, would you do an interview?' I asked.

'I wouldn't,' he replied. Then he said: 'And you know what? You can fuck off for yourself so you can.' He was *cute* enough to make sure I had the tape recorder switched off before he made his un-Christian suggestion. Then he turned his back and returned to the car.

On the streets of one large market town in County Tipperary, I vox-popped local shoppers. There was an evident confusion between divorce and sex. One would naturally lead to an explosion of the other:

'It's a dirty old thing. I've always kept myself clean and there's no way I'm for divorce,' said one woman. 'I have a son and there's no way I want him getting stuck with that old stuff.'

When I tried to follow up, she simply told me I knew what she was talking about. There was nothing else that needed to be said. *You know well what I'm talking about* is one of the great standbys of Irish argument, especially in relation to a matter as uncomfortable as sex. *That old stuff.*

Yet there were a few, even in this rural backwater, who

spoke strongly in favour. I particularly remember one old woman who was walking to the shops with her daughter and granddaughter. She looked haggard, poor, with a cigarette voice that wheezed up from her chest: 'I lived with a fella who beat me and the children. I had my share of it. I don't want her to have to put up with the same nonsense.'

As the child of a broken marriage, I found it hard to be detached on this issue. On the day of the referendum my mother called early in the morning to say she had voted. She was making sure I too went to the polls. 'Every vote is important,' she said. My father also supported divorce. He had no wish to re-marry himself, but he knew plenty of people trapped in the limbo between separation and divorce. He was a social liberal and the intervention of the bishops, and the bitterness of the rhetoric directed at the pro-divorce lobby, had re-ignited the anti-clericalism fostered in the classrooms of his boyhood.

He loathed the intolerance unleashed by the Catholic right and remembered the hypocrisy of a country which had made conditions so intolerable for unmarried mothers that they felt they had no option but to take the mail boat to England for an abortion. We could live with abortion as a nation so long as the deed was done in England. It was another example of an 'Irish solution to an Irish problem'. As for contraception and divorce, he believed they were not a liberal or conservative cause, but basic civil rights in any civilised society.

When the divorce referendum was defeated my mother was furious. 'The selfishness of them. The bloody selfishness,' she said. But within the decade there was a second referendum and the pro-divorce lobby won. By then the Catholic Church was beginning to come under siege over clerical sex abuse scandals and revelations about the affair between the country's best known bishop and his housekeeper. The once mighty pulpit squeaked but a majority of the people stuck fingers in their ears. I was far away when I heard the news but I cheered out loud.

~

Later that year there was an upheaval in my personal life. It happened in the middle of one of the biggest moments of my career. The annual interview with the Taoiseach normally took up the entire radio programme and ranged across domestic politics, Europe and the endless trauma of the Troubles. The editor had decided to give me a chance, testing me to see if I had the makings of a regular presenter.

The interview had been going for about half an hour when I noticed a flicker of disturbance outside the glass. But there was no message from the producer in my headphones to suggest anything might be wrong. I ploughed on, challenging Garret FitzGerald over public spending and getting an avalanche of figures for my trouble; a favourite tactic of his was to retreat into detail, sure that the audience would assume great wisdom on his part and complete ignorance on the part of any interviewer who was bold enough to interrupt. I performed reasonably well, succeeding in annoying Garret's press officer with my questioning on Northern Ireland.

When it was over the editor ushered me out of the studio, suspiciously quickly I thought, and into the corridor, away from FitzGerald and his team of handlers. I thought things had gone well. What was this stern look about?

'I have some very bad news,' he said. And then, very quickly, added: 'There was a call in the middle of the programme, your father is in hospital. St Vincent's. He's had a heart attack. Don't panic, he's going to be okay. Trust me. He will be okay.'

I didn't wait to say goodbye to Garret FitzGerald. I ran out of RTE and raced to the hospital.

I found my father, sleeping, with tubes in his nostrils and

mouth, a drip in his arm and wires leading from his chest to a heart monitor. He looked grey. Old and grey. I went and sat by the bed. A nurse came over.

'Are you his son?' she asked.

I said that I was.

'He's going to be fine. Don't worry. He had a bad turn but he'll make it.'

She turned to walk away then suddenly did an about turn.

'I knew you were his son. You're the living image of him. The colouring and . . .'

Here she paused.

'. . . and the nose. That fine nose. I hope you don't mind me saying that!'

~

Later my father woke up and we spoke very briefly.

He held my hand tight. He told me that he was afraid.

'I've been laid low, old boy. What are they saying about me?'

I told him the hospital staff were sure he'd make a good recovery. 'Try and get back to sleep.'

'Will you come back in tomorrow?' he asked.

I promised I would. Then he tried to lean forward towards me, grimacing from the physical effort. I told him to lie still. Then I leaned over and kissed my father goodnight.

I cannot remember how long he stayed in hospital. But when it came time for him to leave the doctor in charge said Éamonn would have to go into short-term residential care. He needed constant monitoring and the guarantee of regular meals and comfortable surroundings.

I had not expected him to like being institutionalised, but he seemed relieved to be going from one hospital to another. He looked smaller now and he walked more slowly. For the first time in my life I saw my father as an old man. When I dropped him off at his new hospital he turned to hug me. His body felt much slighter, the arms thin and struggling to embrace.

~

I had made plans to move north well before my father's heart attack. He was subdued when I told him. It was unusual for him to state an opinion on anything I did with my life. I think perhaps he felt that he did not have the right. He had been absent for so much of my childhood and was keenly aware of his own failings as a parent. But he emphatically did not want me to take the job in Belfast. 'It's a mad place up there,' he said. 'They're a different race of people to us, the Catholics and the Protestants.'

We were sitting over tea in the Pronto Grill when I told him about the job: radio and television reporter with RTE in Belfast. At last the chance to cover a war and hone the skills that might take me to Africa. I had been getting impatient in Dublin, watching the calendar as the months slid towards my twenty-seventh birthday. I would have to be out of RTE within the next few years if there was going to be any chance of becoming a foreign correspondent. I had some advantages. I had developed the 'plausible manner, a little literary ability and rat-like cunning', famously recommended as essential qualities by Nick Tomalin, the *Sunday Times* reporter killed on the Golan Heights. To his recipe I would add a prodigious stamina, insatiable curiosity about the world and deep insecurity. My father saw these traits in me. He knew that getting to Belfast could be my ticket to other, bigger stories.

But it didn't sway him. 'Aren't you doing well enough here? You've got a good job on the radio, you could buy a house here,' he said. His tone was gentle, not hectoring. Then I reminded him of something he'd told a friend of mine a few years before. The friend was trying to decide whether to give up broadcasting and go back to newspapers. 'You told him that a man must follow his star,' I said. 'That's what I'm doing now.'

Like many southerners, my father regarded Northern Ireland with a mixture of bewilderment and fear. He had been brought up to understand that the 'Six Counties' were part of the Irish Republic, the fourth green field with which the South would eventually be reunited. As a young man he'd been a romantic nationalist who was suffused, as I had been, with the poetry of blood sacrifice.

While researching for this book I came across a dog-eared copy of Seamus Heaney's second collection of poems, *Door into the Dark*, published in 1969, the same year the Troubles erupted. My father had borrowed the book from a local library and had forgotten to return it. It is one of the few mementoes I have of him. Leafing through the collection I saw where he had folded over the top of the page on the poem 'Requiem for the Croppies' about the failed rebellion of 1798.

> *Terraced thousands died, shaking scythes at cannon.*
> *The hillside blushed, soaked in our broken wave.*
> *They buried us without shroud or coffin*
> *And in August the barley grew up out of the grave.*

The onset of the Troubles changed my father. The sight of blackened body parts being shovelled up by firemen after the IRA attacks on Bloody Friday – 21 July 1972 – took the romance out of revolution. Watching it all from the South we were horrified, alienated by the violence. As the conflict in the North wore on, the South mentally disengaged. There were moments when atavistic passions ran high, like the Hunger Strike of 1981 when the hectoring voice of Margaret Thatcher awakened deep within us the folk memory of callous Britannia, and Bobby Sands ascended to Parliament and then to martyrdom on the rising tide of Irish anger.

But mostly we ignored the North. The stock response in

Irish homes when news of another atrocity came on television was to wish the place out of existence: *I wish they'd cut it off and let if float off into the Atlantic.* To many southerners the northern accent became synonymous with complaint – an angry, aggrieved tone that lectured us for being sell-outs to the cause, or, when the complaining voice was Unionist, warned us to keep our hands off precious Ulster. The impulse to shout 'You're fucking welcome to it' was barely restrained. To the average southerner, as to the average Englishman, the word Ulster meant incomprehensible hatreds and endless whining. Whatever was going wrong had nothing to do with us.

My father didn't fall into the category of 'average southerner' though. His understanding of the problem grew more complex with time. He read the newspapers and listened to the arguments; he had made the effort to examine the real history of his own past. Over the years he progressed from his idealised view of Robert Emmet and Patrick Pearse, towards a disappointed realism, seeing them as brave but flawed men.

When I look back now I think his worries about my moving north had more to do with us being separated than they did with politics or the violence. Unspoken, but I am convinced very much on his mind, was the thought of another heart attack. The doctors had told me he was vulnerable to another coronary but that with exercise, good food, no alcohol or cigarettes, he had a very good chance of surviving for a long time. He was not drinking at this time but I wondered how long that would last. *'That's the end of it now. No more. It takes too much out of me.'* He would say things like that often. But he was too intelligent a man, and he understood too well how alcoholism worked – the vicious, pernicious, unrelenting power – to believe his own promises with absolute certainty.

As I left for the North he asked: 'You'll stay in touch, won't you?'

I promised that I would. Of course I would.

CHAPTER THIRTEEN

North

> *As it comes back, brick by smoky brick,*
> *I say to myself – strange I lived there*
> *And walked those streets.*
> 'In the Lost Province', TOM PAULIN

The letter said we had actually started somewhere up north. The Keanes were landowners, the woman wrote. They were really *O'Cathain* or *O'Kane*. It is a name from the County Tyrone badlands. They were our ancestral lands. Her maiden name was Keane and she had sent the letter to another family member.

Her letter detailed various relatives who had done well for themselves. One had gone to America and got involved in local politics, another had become a governor of Assam. Then she told the story of going to visit County Tyrone, looking for the land where the Keanes had originated. She visited the home of a Protestant ex-army officer. During the evening she said the colonel had asked her name. After she told him it was Keane he said: 'These used to be your lands.'

This had infuriated the woman. She finished the letter by saying that when the recent Troubles first started the colonel's son had been put in a ditch with a hood over his head and shot dead. 'A long time coming,' she wrote.

By the time I read that letter I had long left the North of Ireland. I had lived through the killings and funerals. I did not write to her. *A long time coming.*

~

It was an earlier round of the northern conflict which inspired my parents to give me the name Fergal. The name is derived from the Irish words '*Fear Gheall*' or 'bright man'. I was not named out of passion for the Irish language but after a dead IRA man. 'Boy' is a better word. Fergal O'Hanlon was only seventeen years old when he was killed. He died during an attack on Brookeborough police station, County Fermanagh, in Christmas week, 1957. O'Hanlon died with another teenager, Sean South, from Limerick city. Both would later be eulogised in ballads, the guarantee of immortality for Republican gunmen. O'Hanlon was celebrated in the song 'The Patriot Game'. '*I was taught all my life, cruel England to blame/And so I'm part of the patriot game.*'

The border campaign in which O'Hanlon died was an incompetent mess. By the time the campaign sputtered out the IRA was finished as a military threat to Orange domination in Ulster. But the deaths of O'Hanlon and South inspired a revival of romantic nationalism in the South. I grew up with my head full of romantic notions of blood sacrifice. My father taught me Republican ballads. '*Whether on the battle field or the gallows high we die/Oh what matter when for Erin dear we fall . . .*' Éamonn performed in benefits for the fiftieth anniversary of the Easter Rebellion in 1966, and a year later took to the stage of the Gate Theatre in the role of Robert Emmet, hanged and beheaded after an abortive uprising in 1803. One of his most celebrated roles came in a drama about the United Irishmen's revolt of 1798: Éamonn won Ireland's main television acting prize for his role as the doomed hero in *When*

Do You Die Friend. The play is based on the diaries of the rebel Michael Farrell. Some years ago I was given a tape of the film. My father is magnificent in the role of Farrell.

The clear role of the idealistic hero was one he would aspire to all his life. Years later an academic would write of the performance: 'There was a haunting sincerity and a high moral tone to it that made the viewer want to hold his head high at having inherited such traditions.' Though he was a romantic, my father knew enough of what had happened in the War of Independence and the Civil War to grow up with an ambiguous view of revolutionary violence. He loathed the violence of the Provisional IRA. The stories he heard as a boy – murders, betrayals, torture – were part of the cause of his worry about my going to Belfast. What had happened around Listowel was as bad as anything now being experienced in the borderlands of Fermanagh and Tyrone.

The way my father told the story the dead man was a British soldier. That's why the ghost was green. It was khaki. The army colour. You had to stay awake all night to see him. And it didn't always happen. Sometimes he came and other times he didn't. Nothing happened when he appeared. He just floated in through the window and around the walls of the room. 'It's like he was searching for something, like he hid something in the room,' Éamonn explained. The ghost was killed by the IRA on the street outside my grandmother's house. He was a British officer and he was walking up the street. Then two IRA men ran out and shot him.

It was more than thirty years before I found out who the ghost really was. The IRA shot everyone who worked with the Crown: British soldiers, fighters with irregular units like the Black and Tans, policemen and ex-soldiers who formed the auxiliary police, neighbours who were informers, and a well-known local landlord. In those days Ireland was awash with killers in and out of uniform.

The story behind the ghost began in the village of Ballylongford, a few miles from Listowel. One night an Irish police inspector, Tobias O'Sullivan, arrived in Ballylongford with several lorry loads of Black and Tans. The troops proceeded to terrorise the local population and promised vicious retribution if they didn't give up supporting the IRA. The Black and Tans had already murdered several unarmed men in the nearby district of Knockanure.

O'Sullivan had nothing to do with the Knockanure episode, but he had distinguished himself by leading a bayonet charge when his men were outgunned during an IRA attack in neighbouring County Limerick. This action made him a marked man in the eyes of the IRA and a plan was laid to assassinate him. On the appointed day three gunmen arrived in Listowel. They'd been told by local spies that O'Sullivan walked from Mass in the Catholic Church to the police barracks at the same time every morning. Two men waited in a pub near the barracks, and close to my grandparents' home. Another stood on the street keeping watch.

O'Sullivan came walking up the street. But the watcher noticed something that must have made him stop and think. The policeman wasn't alone. He was holding his six-year-old son by the hand, the two of them walking slowly up Church Street. But if the watcher had second thoughts he quickly banished them. As O'Sullivan drew level he crossed the road to the pub and gave a signal to the trigger men sitting inside. They walked out and across the road, raised their guns and shot Tobias O'Sullivan at point blank range. His son started screaming. Screams that echoed up and down Church Street. They would have heard the shots and screams in the Keane family home a few doors down. The killers ran off down a lane and escaped across open fields.

Many years later the army of the new Irish state sent historians out into the countryside to compile an oral history of the

War of Independence. One of the men who'd killed Inspector O'Sullivan told his story. It is a faithful account of what happened that morning. But he left out one crucial detail. There is no mention of the little boy holding his father's hand. Every war I've ever covered has been vicious. And every war is maggoty with lies. The biggest lie of the lot is that you can fight a clean fight.

That was the huge lie in the country in which I grew up: the 1916 Rebellion and the War of Independence were 'clean' fights. Years later when the IRA was bombing civilians into little pieces, I frequently heard how they were bringing the old IRA into disrepute. The common refrain of official Ireland was that 'they'd never have done anything like that'. Granted they didn't stick car bombs in the middle of Irish cities without giving a warning. But they did most of the rest. We couldn't acknowledge that. The memories were too recent and painful; our culture too secretive. We made triumphs of our tragedies and ghost stories of our atrocities.

~

I first went to the North at the age of seven. It was 1968, the year before the Troubles exploded, and my mother was taking a class from her school to visit Belfast. Tension was starting to rise in working-class districts of Belfast and Derry. There had already been some civil rights demonstrations against the manifold injustices of Unionist rule. The demand for equal rights for Catholics had been met with a Protestant backlash, which gathered pace as the Stormont government of Sir Terence O'Neill made concessions. An extremist clergyman named Ian Paisley was busy fanning the flames, telling Protestants that the Civil Rights Movement was the vanguard of a papist, nationalist conspiracy.

To us Paisley was a frightening figure. I would meet his

like again and again in conflict zones around the world. He preached intolerance but surrounded himself with a patina of respectability; his words inflamed hatred but he kept a clear distance between himself and those who did the actual killing. When Ulster needed calm he created fury; when it needed words of peace he spat hatred; when those exhausted by conflict tried to make peace he stood outside the process, bellowing betrayal.

In the late spring of 1968, Paisley was hardly known outside Northern Ireland and we were only vaguely aware of the Civil Rights Movement demonstrations. Travelling north on the bus as a child I was more struck by the physical differences and the changes in the landscape than by any political tensions.

We passed the border outside Dundalk and headed along the fringes of a dark forest into the meagre lands of South Armagh – all scrub and stone here, ragged looking farmhouses, small fields that became drumlins that in turn became mountains – until we reached South Down and I saw bigger fields, well tilled and prosperous with herds of fat cattle and solid farmhouses, pebble-dashed and shining clean. I had passed from Catholic Ulster, the land of the defeated, the supplanted, into the country of unionism, the land of the conquerors.

We were travelling on a motorway now, the first I had ever seen. The lanes seemed extraordinarily wide, the cars looked shiny and new. I saw a cricket ground. A red post-office box. A Union flag. This last I remember registering as strange. My flag was the Irish tricolour. I could not understand how we could travel from one part of Ireland to another and see the flag of a different country. But I forgot my perplexity in the excitement of arriving in Belfast. My mother took me to a model-soldier shop. I was ecstatic. It was bigger, more various, than anything at home. The sweets were different too and we paid with English money.

The city itself was disappointingly small to a child from

Dublin: it was orderly and much quieter. Later, on the way back, we stopped at Newcastle, a small town overlooking the Irish Sea. The tide was out and I wandered down to the stones and rooted around, looking under them for shrimps and eels. Over the span of more than thirty years, one word describes how I remember the North: *sleepy*. It was neat and sleepy.

Within a few months the long sleep would be over. On New Year's Day, civil rights protesters attempted to march from Belfast to Derry. They were set upon by Loyalists at Burntollet Bridge, outside Derry, and the images of Protestant extremists beating students were flashed around the world, a fitting addition to the convulsions of Paris, Chicago and Prague. By August the old certainties which had defined life in Ulster for generations were about to be rent asunder. Rioting and sectarian warfare spread throughout the working-class areas, where Catholics and Protestants now faced each other in huge mobs.

The Irish government said it wouldn't stand idly by, and then did exactly that. The British army was deployed, initially to a Catholic welcome, to replace the Protestant B-Specials and an exhausted police force. The IRA split and emerged as a far more effective and ruthless organisation. Loyalist paramilitaries re-organised and set about killing as many innocent Catholics as they could. There were plenty of political initiatives, all of them doomed because the men of violence were left outside, or kept themselves outside, the process. It became a bloody stalemate. Which was pretty much the story when I arrived in Belfast to work as a journalist almost twenty years later.

~

My first home was in Carmel Street, in what is known as 'the Holy Land', a neighbourhood of classic Belfast red-bricked terraces with names like Jerusalem Street, Damascus Street and Palestine Street. My room was on the top floor, and on the warm evenings of late May I would open the skylight to allow air to circulate. From overhead came the sound of the army helicopters, a perpetual drone over the skies of Belfast. They looked like fat, lazy insects hovering above Divis Mountain, but they were always watchful, the 'eye in the sky' day and night. There was another sound that rolled up the Ormeau Road, and rattled all night along the avenues of the Holy Land, what Louis MacNeice called 'the voodoo of the Orange drum'.

I went to live there permanently in 1986. By then some 2,793 people had been killed in the modern wave of the Troubles. Nearly another thousand would die before the violence ended.

Numbers came to dominate my journalistic life. How many died in a particular attack; how many children did they have; how many pounds of explosive were used to make the bomb, or to prepare that booby trap; how many people attended the funeral; how many troops were being deployed for the marching season; how many guns did the Provos import from Libya? As if the mathematics might help us make sense of the madness. For the record, in the year 1987, 106 people were killed in Northern Ireland: 45 of them were civilians, 16 were policemen, 3 were soldiers from mainland regiments, 8 were members of the overwhelmingly Protestant Ulster Defence Regiment, 26 belonged to Republican groups and 6 were Loyalists.

I cannot remember how many killings I reported. Or the number of funerals. They were all the same. And all different. It usually began with a phone call, a tip-off from a local or a policeman, or the half-hourly broadcasts on Downtown Radio. And then we rushed to the car and headed towards the white tape. At nearly all the crimes scenes the police cordoned the area with tape, an endless binding rope of white that wound its way from Belfast through every small town and village where blood was spilled. Sometimes we got there before the police. We learned to stand well back from the body. Booby traps. Stick a bomb on a corpse and you can kill any policeman, soldier or medic who comes to investigate. In the more remote parts of the country we often arrived after the police had left and found the relatives, angry or somnambulant, sometimes seeming unaware of our presence as we moved around them filming, asking questions, and enquiring whether they had a photograph of the deceased.

~

Years after I left Belfast, a group of Northern Irish journalists produced a book detailing all of the murders of the Troubles – names, places, dates, explanations. I immediately bought a copy. The book, *Lost Lives*, begins with the first killings in 1966 and ends more than three decades later in July 1999.

One Saturday evening I sat down at home with the book and leafed through the section dealing with the 1980s when I had been based in Belfast. Reading the lists of names, I remembered events that had been buried for over a decade. Each death listed – and they are too numerous to describe here – evoked a particular memory for me:

Joe McIlwaine, a twenty-year-old part-time soldier with the UDR, was shot by the IRA at the municipal golf course where he worked as a green-keeper. I remember the words of my colleague Gary Honeyford, an experienced 'Ulster hand', as I was leaving to cover the funeral: 'Remember he is an individual. Find out something about him, something personal to show that he is not another statistic.'

Nathaniel Cush, a married father of two and a former soldier who worked in the Tomb Street post office. I heard the bomb which killed him. It rumbled up the city to the RTE offices on Great Victoria Street. At his funeral I caught the eye of a child walking behind the cortege. I had never seen an expression so distant, so hurt.

Brendan Burns and Brendan Moley, two IRA bomb-makers, were killed when the device they were preparing exploded near Crossmaglen. I walked around the area a day later. Tiny pieces of human remains were scattered in the grass near the barn where the bomb detonated. 'Don't step on that,' said Johnny Coghlan, the camera-man, pointing to a little shard of bone and flesh.

Gillian Johnstone, a twenty-one-year-old Protestant civilian, was shot by the IRA as she sat in a car with her fiancé outside her home in the lake lands of County Fermanagh. At her funeral in a remote country church-yard I saw an elderly man with white hair stand amid the headstones, away from the main group of mourners, shaking his head from side to side, over and over. The IRA later apologised for the murder, but not before making the entirely untrue claim that her boyfriend was a member of the security forces.

Sometimes the atmosphere at funerals could be intimidating. If a Loyalist paramilitary was getting buried the television crews usually stationed themselves at a distance: the hoodlums who made up the ranks of the UDA and UVF enjoyed nothing better than beating up cameramen, always the most exposed figures by simple dint of the equipment they needed to carry.

Once or twice at funerals of UDR personnel a family friend or a serviceman would enquire which television station we represented. When the name 'RTE' was mentioned they might politely ask us to keep a distance. We came from the South and in the minds of these people we were, if not quite the enemy ourselves, at least the kith and kin of those who were attacking them. Having one's ethnic identity count in this way was alien to me. The first time I was angry. I wanted to say 'Why are you blaming me? I hate this as much as you do.' But I was silent. You cannot harangue heartbroken people, and besides, I reminded myself continually, I was there to witness, not to become embroiled.

By then murder – the daily, unspectacular, tit-for-tat killing – had a script of its own. A man shot in bed in front of his wife and children. A man shot on his way to or from work or abducted on his way from the pub. It was murder choreographed according to daily routines. There were some 'spectaculars' as well. Big bombings aimed at the military, as well as atrocities against civilians, such as the Enniskillen Remembrance Day bomb. Such attacks increased the volume of condemnation but within a day or two the old rhythm had returned and we listened to Downtown Radio and waited to hear the accompanying lyric. '*A part-time member of the Ulster Defence Regiment has been shot dead in County Down*' or '*Gunmen have shot dead a man in West Belfast. Police say the killing was sectarian.*'

At every graveside there were sobbing family members. Some mourned for the victims of killers, others for killers who had themselves been killed. Some found consolation in faith, others were inconsolable.

~

Some of my early assignments involved an unexpected level of adventure and, in retrospect, a surprising degree of hilarity. Shortly after arriving I was sent to cover the build up to the twelfth of July parades in the notoriously tough Tigers Bay area of north Belfast. This Protestant ghetto looked exactly like the Catholic ghettos of north Belfast, the only difference being the Union flags and red, white and blue kerbstones which declared the Britishness of the inhabitants. It was not a wise place for a southern Irish Catholic to start asking questions of *any* kind. But innocent of the local temper I blundered in.

While the camera crew were setting up their equipment I noticed a petite old lady standing on her doorstep. She smiled. I smiled back. Encouraged by her initial display of sociability I wandered across the road, vaguely aware that the cameraman, a veteran of these streets, was calling my name. Whatever it was I would deal with it once I'd spoken to the old woman.

She smiled again as I approached. 'Are you lot from UTV [the local television company]?' she asked.

I towered over her. She reminded me of my grandmother back in Cork. I caught the smell of baking drifting from her kitchen.

'Actually, no,' I said. 'We're from RTE.'

The effect was instantaneous.

'*RTE!*' she screamed, in a voice that was ten times her size. 'You're from *RTE!* Well, let me tell you something . . .'

At this I stepped backwards off the footpath and onto the road.

'I've only one thing to say to you. Get away to fuck, ye Fenian bastard! Go on. Off with ye.'

So I did what any sensible man would do confronted by an irate Loyalist granny. I ran. She continued screaming; expletives flew past my ear like stones. '*Fuck off back to Dublin. Go on with ye's.*'

Passing my colleagues at a sprint, I shouted: 'Run for it, lads. She's bound to draw attention.' Leaving our dignity behind we jumped into the car and sped away. Crossing out of Tigers

Bay and onto the ring road the cameraman looked in the mirror and, catching my eye, warned me to keep my mouth shut from then on.

There was a similar encounter, though not provoked by me, a few years later when a southern priest arrived in the Loyalist heartland of the Shankill Road on a self-declared mission of peace. The Shankill was the most anti-Catholic street in the world, a stronghold of the main Loyalist paramilitary groups and the place which spawned Lenny Murphy and his Shankill Butchers, a sectarian murder gang which specialised in cutting the throats of, and then mutilating, Catholics whom it abducted at random. So strong was the enclosed mentality of the place that Protestant journalists I knew would shudder at being sent there on assignment, let alone a chap with a Gaelic name like Fergal and a fine, broad southern brogue. A Catholic priest preaching on the Shankill Road would have been similar to Malcolm X giving a lecture to the Ku Klux Klan.

But the priest was one of those eccentrics who believed absolutely in his own powers of persuasion, a religious absolutist of the kind who regularly decorated bonfires in past centuries. I arrived just as he was getting out of a car at the top of the Shankill. It was the middle of the morning, a blessing because it meant the more vicious of the paramilitary types might still be sleeping off their hangovers, or crawling to one of the Loyalist pubs for a cure.

The priest was dressed in an orange kilt and knee-length socks, of the kind favoured by participants in Irish dancing competitions. His knees were knobbly and pale. The upper half of his body was clothed conventionally, but potentially fatally for the Shankill Road, with the collar of a Roman Catholic priest. He had with him a tape recorder and a bundle of leaflets. The leaflets explained that he was a priest from the South who was dancing his way around Ireland for peace.

A colleague whispered in my ear. 'This eejit will get killed.

We'd better stand back and be ready to make a run for it.' Already a small crowd was beginning to gather, at this stage more perplexed than anything else. That was about to change. The smiling priest pressed the play button on his tape recorder and a blast of Irish ceilidh music uttered forth. He then started to dance, knees flying in the air as he did a poor version of a reel. The assembly grew larger.

At first the crowd, mainly made up of women, laughed. There were a few cat calls and jeers. Then somebody read the leaflet.

'A *Fenian fucking priest*,' screamed a harridan standing behind me. As the realisation dawned that the dancer was a cleric from the hated Roman Church and not some advance promotion from a circus, the crowd became menacing. They did not see a good-natured, if wildly eccentric, man doing his own misguided bit for peace, rather a demon made flesh who had come to make fools of them. 'Ye think you're funny. We'll give ye funny,' a man called out.

By now the priest's smile had disappeared. He was dancing much faster. The crowd pressed in. 'I think you should stop,' one of the reporters called out to him. He nodded, reached for his tape recorder and switched off the music.

The leaflets were abandoned as he set off at a trot down the Shankill Road, followed by journalists who in turn were pursued by the shouting crowd. We escaped unharmed. But only just.

The priest would later achieve infamy by running onto the track in front of Formula One cars during the British Grand Prix of 2003, and the following year, during the Athens Olympics, when he leapt in front of the lead runner of the marathon four miles from the finish, and destroyed his hopes of winning.

∼

I started out seeing the North as a place in which to advance my career. It was a province at war in which an aspiring war correspondent was duty bound to serve his time. Most of the big names in Irish and British journalism had done their stint in Belfast. But it ended up being something quite different. The North got into me. I travelled through my own ignorance and pre-conceptions and I was changed, in some fundamental ways. The North was where I sorted out a lot of what I believed in and what I was willing to take a stand for.

I would leave with a visceral loathing of tribalism in any shape or form – the sly sectarianism of men in suits and clerical collars, the slick justifications of the politicians who spoke for the murder gangs, all the weasel words of justification masquerading as expressions of concern. I could not alter the fact that I was an Irishman reporting a war on the island of Ireland. I might declare myself 'journalist'. Not a Catholic journalist. Not an Irish journalist. Just a journalist. But I was living out part of my own history. Every Irish journalist covering the Troubles who was born on the island came to the story freighted with the weight of the Irish past.

In the wake of IRA atrocities there were some in the South who publicly agonised over their own Irishness. After Bloody Friday, La Mon Hotel, Enniskillen, they would cry: *It makes me ashamed to be Irish!* To hell with that, I thought. I could not accept that green or orange fascists with guns would dictate the terms of my identity. I would not, I promised myself, be corralled by their idea of what it meant to be Irish. Republicans would argue that my own state had been born of bloody revolution. After all, my own family were part of that struggle. But I did not see the violence of those years as a justification for the Provo campaign. Rather that the killing, and especially the Civil War, should have acted as a warning.

Some of what I experienced was disarmingly familiar: in church there were the same Catholic rites of my youth, but practised with a conviction unknown to my generation in the South. There was the music of fiddles and tin whistles in the pubs near the docks, the same leaden skies in winter.

But in other places I felt inexpressibly alien. On the Falls Road I shared the same religion but none of the 'passionate intensity' of the marchers who protested each August on the anniversary of internment. How could I, who had grown up without army searches, the threat of Loyalist murder gangs, the struggle to assert an identity, how could I call myself one and the same with them? I was called 'Free Stater' and 'Sell Out' by young men and women who judged me by my accent. To them I was a citizen of the southern 'statelet' and a representative of a broadcasting organisation that had banned their leaders – Gerry Adams, Martin McGuinness and others – from the airwaves.

I felt an alien too when I visited the small Protestant churches of the borderland. They were little structures of timber and tin that rang with the sound of the accordion and tambourine and where the faithful spoke in tongues – the hinterland of fierce believers, the biblical farmers evoked by Derek Mahon:

> *Yes, you could*
> *wear black, drink water, nourish a fierce zeal*
>   *with locusts and wild honey, and not*
> *feel called upon to understand and forgive*
>   *but only to speak with a bleak*
> *afflatus, and love the January rains when they*
>   *darken the doors and sink hard*
> *into the Antrim hills, the bog meadows, the heaped*
>   *graves of your fathers . . .*

It was the quieter people I met who defined the country. A man like brave John O'Neill hemmed in by hatred up in

Ligoniel, whose son was murdered and who sat down every day to paint his landscapes. They became my landscapes too: the winter snow high on the glens of Antrim, the haunting northern sun on autumn drives to Ardglass and Coney Island, and summer afternoons on the beach at Cushendun.

My North was a place of bombs, assassinations, funerals, voices of hatred, loss, stalemate, frustration, bewilderment. But it was also a place of gifts. The friends I made there did not define themselves as Catholic, Protestant or Non-Believer. We were close because we could see each other as purely human, our tribal baggage cast aside. They took me into another Ulster: Ken Kelly, the taxi driver negotiating the barricades with me in Loyalist areas, showing me a Protestant face that was generous and hopeful; Alan and Jeanette Murray in whose home overlooking Belfast Lough I was fed and entertained with stories of growing up in east Belfast, in the shadow of the shipyards. And there were other southern exiles like myself: Paddy and Patricia McEntee with whom I played guitar and dreamed of home, exiles in a place we sensed was not really ours. And when I eventually left Belfast it would be a bitter wrench in a way I could never have foreseen.

CHAPTER FOURTEEN

Marching Seasons

Time and place – our bridgehead into reality
But also its concealment!
'Carrick Revisited', LOUIS MACNEICE

For any journalist with hopes of becoming a war correspondent the marching seasons of the mid-1980s were the best of training grounds. The annual exercise in triumphalism, dressed up as an important cultural tradition, had been a rallying point for troublemakers for generations. There were several flashpoint areas where the routes of the Orange parades passed through, or close by, Catholic areas. Even the most ardent advocate of pluralism and tolerance would have struggled to see the cultural value in armies of Orangemen, followed by beer-swilling bandsmen, marching through the Catholic areas reminding the 'Papes' of old defeats.

The eve of the twelfth, the so-called eleventh-night celebration, was dreaded by Catholics living in areas close to march routes. One of these was a small nationalist estate near Ballynahinch in County Down, an area of prosperous farm holdings and a Protestant majority. The estate was essentially a one street cul-de-sac where the minority had learned to keep their heads down and mouths shut during the marching season.

Those who could escaped across the border for the two tense weeks in the middle of July, part of a great annual migration to County Donegal prompted solely by fear of their neighbours.

On the eleventh night I decided to position myself in one of the Catholic houses near the end of the cul-de-sac. I seem to remember a family of five: a husband and wife with two children and a grandmother. Through the early part of the evening we sat drinking tea, listening to the rattle of the drums from the Loyalist estates, waiting for the moment when the bandsmen would move out to assert their dominance. There were RUC officers on duty at the entrance to the estate, among them a young community policeman who told me he thought the whole business was insane and the marchers should be kept out. The Catholic residents spent the evening walking to the end of the street, checking on the proximity of the march.

By nightfall, around 10 p.m., we could hear the bandsmen approaching, drums hammering and the fifes blasting: '*Oh give me a home where there's no Pope in Rome and every day is the 12th of July . . .*' The last Catholics cleared off the streets and locked their doors. Had it been a bigger estate there might have been a protest, but this little cul-de-sac was too exposed and its residents too few. The mother in the house took the children into the kitchen. The father and grandmother stayed in the front room with the lights out, listening to the sound of the march growing louder. By now you could hear the voices of Loyalists shouting above the drums. I stood directly inside the window, trying to observe the scene outside through a small gap in the curtains. The sound of drums, fifes and shouts echoed around the cul-de-sac. I felt the windows rattle.

Then there was screaming. I pulled the curtains back and saw that across the road a man had emerged from one of the houses. He was shouting at the marchers. His voice was drowned out in the din. The man was gesturing furiously with his finger, pointing towards the exit from the estate. A ring of

222

policemen stood at the gate to the house. One of them was shouting at the man to get inside. As he did some of the Loyalists broke away from the procession and converged on the police line, screaming abuse. A woman came out, followed by several younger men. For a second it was hard to tell if they were going to join the man or try to persuade him to come inside. The policeman in charge was agitated. I could see him waving his hands in the air. By now everybody was screaming: Catholics, Loyalists, police. But the bands were so loud they were all reduced to lip-reading. The woman and the younger men pulled, pushed the man inside. He was red-faced with tears streaming down his face.

I was so busy concentrating on the action across the road that I'd failed to notice a breakaway group at the tail end of the march. There were now so many marchers milling around in the middle of the road that some were able to slip behind the thin police line. The marchers had seen me looking out of the window and were now running towards the house. I noticed them at the last moment and pulled back. A brick shattered the window. Glass flew across the room. The noise suddenly became much louder, blasting through the broken window. Inside the house people were shouting and crying. I remember children's voices screaming and the mother trying to comfort. Then the grandmother rushed towards the door. Before anybody could stop her she was walking out into the middle of the marchers, an elderly woman who had lived through decades of such provocations. I raced after her with my tape recorder running.

The Loyalists seemed utterly perplexed by her appearance in their midst.

She stormed straight up to a tall man near the head of the march.

'Who are you?' she shouted.

'My name is Jim Wells,' he answered.

'And what are ye but?' she asked – *What do you do for a job?*

He answered that he was a councillor from Ian Paisley's Democratic Unionist Party.

The old woman gave him the full force of her anger. Nothing could deter her. Not the fact that she was so massively out-numbered or any of the angry shouts from his companions. She had seen the children in her house terrified and the older people humiliated and Jim Wells was going to know how she felt. He tried to make the usual claims about the right to march. But Wells was reduced by this old woman and he knew it. When she had finished, still shaking with anger, the old woman went back to the house and made tea for the family.

By 1984 the marching issue was dominating the political agenda between the British and Irish governments. Dublin was demanding that police prevent Orangemen from parading through flashpoint areas around Portadown in County Armagh. But the merest whiff of Dublin's involvement in the re-routing of parades drove Orangemen to apoplexy with the ever-helpful figure of Ian Paisley on hand to fan the flames and remind the Loyalists of their sacred right to rub Catholic noses in the mud.

Ironically it was Margaret Thatcher, ostensibly the most Unionist of Prime Ministers, who showed courage in facing down the bully boys in the Orange Order. With the same unbending attitude she displayed towards the Republican hunger strikers, Thatcher ordered the police and army to pre-vent Orange marchers entering the Catholic 'Tunnel' area at Obin Street in Portadown. There were two principal Catholic districts in Portadown and the Tunnel was the most exposed. It essentially consisted of one street clinging to the edge of the town centre and surrounded by Loyalist territory.

To the Orangemen the sight of the RUC lined up in full riot gear to defend a Catholic area was an unparalleled affront. I stood behind the security cordon at Obin Street and watched the Orange marchers hurl themselves repeatedly against the police lines. The impression was of an army of spoiled children too long used to having their own way at last being confronted, and erupting into a gigantic tantrum. At first they jostled and punched.

'Incongruous' hardly described the scene as men in immaculate suits and bowler hats wrestled with the RUC officers at the front of the line. All the while the bands played, the sentimental wheezing of the accordions providing a homely accompaniment to the day's savagery.

Then the hard men in their ranks started throwing bricks and lumps of metal, steel railings were ripped up to become javelins soaring through the air. After two days of rioting I found myself ducking when birds swooped over, only realising at the last minute that they weren't missiles aimed at the police. It was nerve-racking but extraordinarily exhilarating. I felt completely in my element, just as I had during the small riot in Dublin. Surrounded by violence and chaos I was focused and calm, observing and recording the battle, pushing as far forward as I could until the police would allow me to go no further.

I was absorbed by the extremes of human emotion on display. I knew that these riots were not the 'mindless violence' described by many British and southern politicians and echoed by an ignorant media. There is no such thing as mindless violence, especially not in Ulster. The killing was firmly rooted in the processes of the mind. Fear and anger created the hatred and if hatred wasn't a psychological condition what was? The Loyalists feared that my people, the southerners, wanted to dominate and rule over them. Being prevented from marching down Obin Street was the harbinger of rule from Dublin and Rome. The northern Catholics were regarded as the fifth column, whose agitation for civil rights was no more than a ploy to undermine the Union.

The IRA campaign, with its targeting of Protestant police-man and soldiers who had Protestant wives and children, brothers and sisters, mothers and fathers, reinforced the sense of siege. When the IRA killed a young Protestant man on a border farm, offering as their justification his association with the UDR, they were acting according to careful psychological calculations. Ratchet up the pressure. Keep them afraid. Fear was the most powerful weapon in the hands of ideologues on both sides. With fear you could terrify those on your own side who might be less than enthusiastic about killing; fear of the other side's killers also enabled you to pose as a defender of the community.

Fear made it a win-win equation for the preachers of intoler-ance, and for all the killers and their apologists.

~

John O'Neill Jnr, the son of the landscape painter, would travel home from work along the Crumlin Road. The Crumlin ran between the Loyalist Shankill on one side and the mixed Antrim Road on the other. Here Loyalist murals were embla-zoned on gable walls, swearing fidelity to an Ulster of the imagination – the country of Protestant dominance which had vanished with the first chants of the civil rights marchers nearly thirty years before. Peace walls divided Catholic and Prot-estant, the red brickwork designed to blend in with the newly built council houses. There were fifteen of these walls in north and west Belfast. This architecture of division enhancing the sense of murderous claustrophobia which pervaded the poorer districts of the city, as Yeats put it of the island as a whole: '*Great hatred, little room.*'

In my memory, this part of Belfast is always dark and slicked with rain, a place I am always glad to leave. I would never walk here. Not out of choice and never, ever, at night. This was the Shankill Butchers' territory and the memory of their campaign strikes a primal fear into the hearts of Catholics. They rode in black taxis and were flagged down by unsuspecting Catholics on their way home from the pub or social club. The journey always ended in mutilation – a body dumped on waste ground or in an alleyway, throat slit from ear to ear. Abducted by them or their ilk, it wouldn't matter that I was a journalist. Religious identity would be enough to qualify for an appalling death.

John O'Neill died because he was a Catholic. He was twenty-five years old, a house painter who lived with his father and mother and three siblings in Ligoniel, the tiny Catholic enclave at the top of the Crumlin Road, and about half a mile from Ardoyne. From the hills around Ligoniel you looked directly down at the city with the Lough and the gantries of Harland and Wolff to the left and straight ahead, across the valley, the Cregagh Hills of the Protestant east. The Catholics of Ligoniel were the most beleaguered in the North. To get in and out of their area they needed to pass through Loyalist territory. They knew that if their Protestant neighbours wanted to rampage through Ligoniel it would happen long before the police were able to do anything about it.

So the people on John O'Neill's street kept quiet. They didn't assert their Irishness by painting their streets with the green, white and gold of the Irish tricolour. They did not decorate their gable ends with the names of dead IRA men. They lived in fear.

On the evening of 15 March 1986, John O'Neill went for a drink with some friends in the city centre after finishing work. The following morning his body was found lying in a stream in a Protestant estate near to his home. John was so badly beaten that his brother was only able to identify the body because of the distinctive red hair. The same hair as his mother and father and brothers and sisters, the only part of his physical identity which the killers were not able to obliterate. In court it came out that John had gone to a Protestant social club to meet some friends from work. His father, John Snr, said it would have been typical of him. Young John didn't differentiate. He worked with Protestants, why wouldn't he socialise with them? Given the sectarian history of the area where he lived that might have been a naive attitude.

But look at the history of the Troubles and you'll find plenty of examples of people who believed they would be safe; maybe it was because of a particular personal relationship, or the simple belief that because they meant nobody harm there could be nobody who would harm them. John O'Neill's killers had it in their minds to do him terrible harm.

At the social club John was attacked and beaten, then dragged outside and beaten again. At the time people spoke of a large stone and knives – police said a 'blunt instrument' – being used. It was frenzied killing. Nothing else could explain the relentlessness of the marks and cuts.

On the night after the body was found John O'Neill Snr went to the scene. His son's corpse was in a local mortuary now waiting for burial. John Snr walked right into the middle of Loyalist Ballysillan. He is a small figure and he has a bad limp, but in his anger and grief he feared no man. In the falling rain he crossed the open ground to the stream and when he found the place where John was mutilated he stood still and imagined his son begging for mercy, calling out for his family and then dying knowing that his family could not hear him. He came close, he believed, to hearing his son's voice; something of that lost energy lingered on the hillside.

The murder brought an unaccustomed silence to the O'Neill house. People moved quietly from room to room as if stealth would help them avoid brushing up against the one giant truth which dominated their existence. A son, a brother, was gone forever. The murder was the first sectarian assassination I reported.

~

After three years I felt the country closing in me; it was too small, too bitter, too lost, I told myself. And I was bored. My career was in the doldrums. The little chart I'd written all those years before in Limerick, detailing my plans, was looking more and more like a foolish indulgence. At the rate things were going I would be forty years old and still racing off to cover a bomb on the Falls Road. The alternative was going back to Dublin and a job in the RTE newsroom. But I felt alienated from the South.

The people down there were bored with their fellow islanders north of the border. Bored. I cannot think of another word that better describes how people expressed themselves. Many condescended to the barbarous provincials of Ulster. In four words they had decided what they thought. *To hell with them.* All of that violence. The invocation of martyrs. The tricolour fluttering above the housing estates. The tributes delivered in Irish. The endless accusing finger pointed south. The culture of complaint. *To hell with them.*

The IRA's war for national reunification had done more to antagonise southerners than anything the Unionists could have devised. Thirty years of violence in the North had made the shibboleths we grew up with embarrassing. The old rebellions were no longer commemorated as great national events. Like devout Catholicism they were becoming a fringe interest.

The South to which I returned for weekends and holidays was feeling the first spasms of economic growth. Emigrants were returning. Unemployment was declining. New factories were opening.

At dinner parties in Dublin I learned to say nothing about

the North. I was quiet when someone who had never been north of the border launched into a tirade. Sure there was nothing to be done with the place, they said. How could you help people who wouldn't help themselves? It was a sick society. They were all bigots. All they did was complain. At the opposite end of the spectrum there were the closet IRA supporters – the well-named 'sneaking regarders' – who naturally deplored all acts of violence but said I had to understand the context in which bombs were being stuck under people's cars, and why the sons of Protestant farmers were being shot on border farms.

Mostly the Dublin conversations were about normal life. I had been too long up north by then to appreciate the southern idea of 'normal'. People spoke of their new houses, renovations, foreign holidays – *Barbados or Provence this year?* – or the second home in the countryside. Rural Ireland had become fashionable now. A politician from the Labour Party said that we were now a post-nationalist and post-Catholic state. That wasn't quite the truth. If pushed to make a choice, most people would still have counted themselves as nationalist and Catholic, but they were no longer sure what these things meant. Most embraced the pleasures of new money and left it to the academics and the opinion page writers on the *Irish Times* to worry away about what it meant to be Irish.

After a while I stopped going to Dublin every weekend. Although it was a convivial place, and I always felt a surge of relief when crossing the border into the South, I was alienated by what I saw as southern complacency. I could no longer join in with the jokes and condescensions about northerners without feeling I was betraying those whose funerals I reported every week.

Stuck in my northern fastness, with only my feelings of superiority to keep me warm, I was starting to have troubling visions of becoming the defeated retiree I'd met in the *Irish*

Press on my first day. 'Don't let the bastards grind you down,' he'd said. I didn't need *their* help. I was doing a good enough job on my own. I was full of the old insecurity. Dublin was out as an option. If Africa was going to happen it would have to happen soon. Anne told me to wise up. 'If you want it, stop whining and get out there and start looking.'

Every Monday, like young journalists across Britain, I went to the newsagent's and bought a copy of the *Guardian*. Monday was the day for media jobs. This particular Monday I saw an ad for the BBC. There were two jobs: Ireland correspondent, based in Belfast, and Dublin correspondent, based down south. I applied, hoping for an interview. If nothing else it would be good experience. A week later a letter came calling me to interview and asking me to send on a tape of any script I wanted. I wrote a personal account of some of the violent incidents I'd reported on in the previous year, in a style emulating the despatches I had heard on my favourite programme, *From Our Own Correspondent*, on Radio 4.

The interview took place at Broadcasting House in London. A phalanx of managers interrogated me about the BBC's recent coverage of a story in Ireland. I was critical. Not for the first time my big mouth ran away with itself. I flew back to Belfast convinced I'd blown my chance of ever becoming a foreign correspondent. Then a man called Bob Eggington, the home news editor, called from London to offer me a job.

'I thought I blew the interview,' I said.

'They liked the tape,' he replied.

Bob Eggington said the BBC wanted me to be Ireland correspondent based in Belfast. First I would have to come to London for a training course.

After putting the phone down I jumped up and down. 'I've done it. I've done it,' I shouted.

A cameraman friend came rushing in from their room next door. 'What have you done, Bunter? [a nickname I'd picked up as a result of enjoying good lunches at a next-door café run by an Italian of dubious background].'

'I'm out of RTE,' I said.

'But are you out of Belfast?' he said.

'Eh. No. But it's a start.'

'Call me when you're at Aldergrove with a one-way ticket out,' he said.

I didn't mind the teasing. My confidence was back and given time, I was sure, I would be clearing the dust of Belfast off my heels.

~

The atmosphere at Broadcasting House was very different to RTE. There was little of the easygoing banter. Mistakes were noted. Every morning at 9 a.m. the editors would troop into the office of Jenny Abramsky, a daunting figure, diminutive in size, but with a laser stare and terrifying powers of recall.

In those days the BBC was more than usually addicted to acronyms. Jenny's was ENCAR (Editor of News and Current Affairs Radio). Abramsky didn't miss a single news broadcast. She was a pure journalist, and not one of the tedious brigade of office politicians and minor advantage seekers who proliferate in large corporations. Senior editors sat in a circle around her, nervously waiting to be interrogated about stories missed, lead-ins that were badly written, or interviews that went on too long or were too short. One of them carried a small rubber squash ball which he massaged relentlessly, waiting for his turn to be harangued or praised. I was intimidated and impressed. She was as quick to give credit as criticism. I had the sense that every word I wrote would be studied carefully for grammatical precision and factual accuracy. In that respect it was a step back to the days of the *Limerick Leader* and Brendan Halligan with his slashing red biro.

My first encounter with Ms Abramsky would not have convinced her that I was a sound prospect for the future. On my first day a secretary was instructed to teach me how to use the BBC's internal computer system. The system allowed you to access the international wires and to file scripts for programmes and news bulletins. Unbeknown to me the first line of every story typed in the reporter's script appeared at the top of computers all over the building. So for example if a reporter wrote: *Israeli troops today attacked a Hezbollah base in Lebanon and killed a large number of militants,* the news editors across the building would be immediately alerted. One of these editors had the responsibility of reading out the top line of any dramatic breaking story on the internal tannoy system and sending a news flash via computer to the BBC's regional offices.

In complete ignorance of this system I sat down for my computer lesson.

'Type in a made-up story,' she said.

Without thinking twice I wrote the following: *The Reverend Ian Paisley has resigned from politics. He made his announcement in a statement issued just minutes ago in Belfast.* Pleased with my handiwork I sat back from the computer. Then a voice boomed from the tannoy:

'Services here. Breaking news story: Fergal Keane says the Reverend Ian Paisley has resigned from politics. Repeat. The Reverend Ian Paisley has resigned from politics.'

I literally slid out of my chair onto the ground. The secretary dropped the phone on which she had been pursuing a long conversation with a friend.

'Oh no, it's only a made-up story,' I shouted.

'Ring them now. Now before it goes on TV and radio,' the secretary cried.

I picked up the phone and rang the desk. There was a horrified response.

'Oh dear Christ. Are you sure?'

'Yes, I'm positive. I'm sorry.'

There was a strangulated yelp from the other end of the line. He hung up.

A millisecond later the tannoy burst into life once more. The voice was a pale shade of the confident announcer of a few minutes before:

'Eh, Fergal Keane says that was a computer error. The Reverend Ian Paisley has not resigned from politics. Repeat: the Reverend Ian Paisley has not resigned from politics.'

I looked to my left and saw the secretary with her head in her hands, slumped over the desk. I became aware of several figures approaching from the management end of the room. It was the foreign editor, the man in whom my hopes of becoming a foreign correspondent were vested, who reached me first, followed in short order by the home editor and the managing editor of radio news.

'What the fuck was that about?' said the foreign editor.

Christoph Wyld was an old Harrovian and not usually given to outbursts of bad language. 'I mean really. It's not on. Do you know what would have happened if that had gone on air?'

At this point the managing editor chipped in. 'You, my friend, would have been out of here on your arse and we would have been humiliated. Paisley would love to prove that there is a conspiracy against him by the BBC and you very nearly obliged him.'

The secretary, to her eternal credit, spoke up:

'It's my fault,' she wailed. 'I told him to write a practice story. He didn't know it was the wrong file and the story might get picked up.' This generous admission helped to mollify the managers. By now phones were exploding all around.

One was a call from Belfast demanding to know what had happened. The story had been seconds away from going to air on the main afternoon news bulletins in Northern Ireland.

Then a phone rang with the distinctive steely voice of Jenny Abramsky on the other end.

I sat down and mentally prepared myself for the sack. If the boss herself had heard it I was surely finished. I listened to the managing editor explain the drama and make as convincing an argument as he could for mercy. They spoke for several minutes. At the end I saw him smiling.

'What did she say?' I asked.

'She said that you're not to be such a bloody fool ever again.' For several weeks I worried that Paisley would hear about it and create a rumpus that would force the BBC into sacking me. But it would appear the old firebrand had more to worry him. (At the time of writing – nearly fifteen years after the offence – there is no sign of the Reverend Paisley resigning from politics.)

Nobody held it against me, and the other reporters in the Broadcasting House 'pool' were a genial bunch. I had been warned of terrible backstabbing but compared to the highly political atmosphere of RTE, let alone the *Irish Press* beforehand, the BBC was more reminiscent of a gentleman's club. I never saw a punch thrown.

There were other new recruits besides me. I met one of my future closest friends while doing an overnight shift on the *Today* programme. Alan Little had just come in from recording a feature on a Salvation Army night shelter; he had the look of a lugubrious Celt about him, and before he opened his mouth I had divined that he was either Welsh, Irish or Scottish. It turned out to be the latter but he had a talent for self-mockery that confounded all the melancholy stereotypes. Little would go on to become one of the best reporters in the BBC's history; a man of rock solid integrity and a wise ear on the other end of the telephone in times of crisis. In an age of broadcasting clones without a fresh idea in their heads, he remains a beacon for me.

I loved the new job. I was reporting for programmes like *Today* and *The World at One*, the cream of radio broadcasting, and I was effectively my own boss, reporting to London but with the freedom to pick my own stories and work my own hours. I worked frenetically. My compulsive nature was a definite asset in journalism. I pushed myself harder. I came to the office earlier and left later than anybody else. The hero-grams – brief epistles of praise – started to arrive from London.

Soon there were positive noises from the foreign editor. When I joined I'd told the BBC I wanted to get to Africa eventually. The existing Southern Africa correspondent still had a few years left to run but I was told that if I kept producing good work in Belfast I would be a strong contender for a move to Johannesburg. A new white president, F. W. de Klerk, had been elected. There was talk about the un-banning of the ANC. Negotiations were under way for the release of senior leaders. Nelson Mandela was said to be preparing for the moment when he would emerge from prison after nearly twenty-seven years inside.

For the first time since I'd climbed the stairs to the editorial room at the *Limerick Leader* my dreams of Africa and of becoming a foreign correspondent began to look like realistic goals.

I was 'a high flier', the sort of energetic, do-everything-he's-asked, annoyingly enthusiastic chap the newsroom executives love. As for drinking, I had managed either to stay off it, or at least drink very little, for several years. I didn't find it a battle then. Not in the way it would become later. When I drank I worked hard to control drink. But I always drained the single glass of wine or beer with the sensation that I had been cheated, that something vital to me was being denied, and I was always conscious of the rueful shadow of my father at my shoulder.

During this time, work helped me trample alcohol underfoot. It also took me further away from my father. I had begun to put distance between us after I left Dublin. Now that I'd joined the BBC and worked every hour of the day and night I no longer saw him regularly. Weeks could pass without any communication. I was an inconsistent son. I made promises I did not keep. I would promise to call him and not call. I would tell him that I would visit and not visit.

Inconstant is one word for the way I behaved. But it is only part of the story. It doesn't explain what was going on underneath. I could not make my father fit into the picture I wanted. I wanted guarantees. No more drinking ever; a maturing into kindly old age; wisdom and dependability; a man who would be a grandfather to my future children. I decided that I could not live on the rollercoaster any longer, wondering if he would stay sober or fall once more. I did not want the late night phone calls promising love, or the others that came in the morning saying sorry or, when he was deep into drink, the calls that never came at all.

But who was I then? That depends on who is answering the questions. Those who knew me only as a journalist saw a young, ambitious man who was destined for the top – quick with banter in the office, popular. But in personal relationships I was a taker. I was dependent, needy, manipulative, and quick to use the pain of my past as an alibi for selfishness. *Poor me. If you had the childhood I did you would be the same.* The same sad, imploring eyes with which I had scavenged affection as a child now looked into other eyes and dared them not to feel sorry for me, refused them the right to be angry when I took and took and then vanished into myself. Those who were closest to me saw a man who retreated into silence when he was challenged, who could not communicate feelings, a man with the self-obsession and compulsiveness of the truly driven; a man running.

CHAPTER FIFTEEN

Visitor

> *. . . This, you implied, is how we ought to live –*
> *The ironical, loving crush of roses against snow,*
> *Each fragile, solving ambiguity.*
> 'In Carrowdore Churchyard', DEREK MAHON

One of my last meetings with my father was in Belfast. I asked him to come up for a few days and stay in the house at Carmel Street. I collected him in Dublin and we drove up the east coast. Perhaps because they are some of the last memories I have of him, they are the most vivid. My father hummed away to himself as we drove north. As far as I knew he had not been there in many years. Not since the theatrical tour on which I was conceived.

'Is Belfast changed much?' he asked.

'An awful lot,' I said.

'Is it dangerous?'

'No. You're fine with me. I'm living in a grand safe place.'

Outside Dublin we pulled off the road onto the strand near Skerries and got out of the car. He could only walk slowly now and was out of breath after a short distance. It was sunny but the wind whipped sand into our faces. We sat down on the beach, looking out towards the Irish Sea. Out of the blue,

I asked him why he had never learned to swim. As a child I had asked him often to come to the seaside and swim with us but he always demurred.

'I was always afraid of drowning,' he said. And then he burst out laughing. Understanding the joke immediately, I laughed too and put my arm around him.

In Belfast I drove him around the city's trouble spots. I showed him the peace lines and the army barracks. He saw the military and police on patrol and the IRA slogans all over West Belfast. My father was genuinely appalled. To a man born in the bitter aftermath of the Civil War, Belfast evoked many feelings, not least a sense of the futility and waste of such conflict. We drove up the Falls and across Lanark Way to the Shankill and down to the motorway and across to the east and the gantries of Harland and Wolff, with my father reminiscing about Louis MacNeice with whom he'd worked in London in the 1950s. He said they had drunk together in the George pub near Broadcasting House. 'A gentleman,' he said, 'but awfully hard to get to know.'

The following day we drove up to the Glens of Antrim and visited the grave of MacNeice at Carrowdore churchyard in County Down. The Glens are beautiful at any time of year but my father had come to see me in the spring. Life was starting again across the folding mountains; the brutalities of the city were so distant that you might have thought we had entered another country.

At Cushendun we got out and walked and my father reminded me of the time when a cousin of mine had slapped a horse I was riding, on the beach at Ballybunnion, near Listowel. The horse had bolted and carried me across the beach. I cried but managed to hold on to the animal's mane until it eventually stopped a few yards from the water's edge.

'But you weren't there that day,' I said.

Thinking that I was reproving him, my father became quiet. Before I could speak, he looked at me.

'I meant to be,' he said.

We drove back to Belfast along the coast road, skirting the Paisleyite towns of Larne and Antrim, coming back into the city around the big outcrop on Cave Hill they call 'Napoleon's Nose'. As we came into the city my father asked if we could drive up to Duncairn Gardens, a Loyalist area close to one of the north Belfast peace lines. There was a guesthouse there, he explained, which he remembered from his time as a young actor playing at the Belfast Opera House. The boarding house was run by a Protestant lady called Mrs Burns, who played host to theatre companies from all over the British Isles. Éamonn had stayed there with my mother in 1960, not long after they married.

Mrs Burns was a good host, he said. She would wait up for the actors and have supper ready for them when they came back from the evening's performance. My father remembered her Ulster fries, the vast plates of rashers, sausages, black puddings, eggs and soda farls, and the friendly atmosphere of her kitchen.

Back then it would have been hard to see any public evidence of sectarian division on Duncairn Gardens. The tension was bubbling away but visitors from the South would have struggled to detect the signs. Paisley hadn't yet exploded onto the scene in a major way, the first Loyalist killings of Catholics were six years away and a travelling theatre company from the deepest South was still welcome. In my father's memory, Duncairn Gardens was still a prosperous street of large red-brick houses, whose owners took the most intense pride in the appearance of their homes. It was a place of conspicuous respectability, revelling in order. But the sectarian geography of north Belfast invited disaster for Duncairn Gardens. One half of the long street was largely Protestant, abutting Tigers Bay, while the other led onto the Catholic New Lodge.

When the Troubles erupted this proximity turned Duncairn

Gardens into one of the worst flashpoints of the conflict. Thirty years of war had wrought appalling change. Where houses had not been bulldozed they were boarded up. There was broken glass on the footpaths, rubbish, weeds, small pieces of masonry, slogans of paramilitaries and swear words scrawled by bored teenagers. Mrs Burns and her house were gone. The place was hollowed out. We drove up and down the road several times, my father shaking his head at the strangeness of it all.

Living in the South people saw the devastation in short segments on the television news. It was remote, not something they were encouraged to connect to their own history, a self-contained mess that had arisen out of purely local perversions. But after the raw experience of the Belfast peace lines my father made the connections. As we drove back towards the city centre he spoke about the Civil War and the atrocities that had taken place near his home.

'Look how long it's taken us to get over that,' he said. 'This will take longer. How will people ever get on again after what's happened?' In Duncairn Gardens, amid the ruins, my father saw the land where history had carried us, and I think he was shaken.

~

The trip to Duncairn Gardens had confirmed what my father had suspected for a long time. He would not live to see the United Ireland for which his mother and uncles had been will-ing to sacrifice their lives. It depressed him. It wasn't so much the fading hope of unification that made him sad but the vicious stalemate he found in Belfast. The violence repelled him.

But I knew his melancholy was only partly to do with poli-tics. His health was poor. The heart troubles of the previous few years left him increasingly short of breath, struggling to keep up when we went for walks. He apologised for holding me up. My father was aware of the shadow of death, unable to ignore what followed him, the draining away of the life force which had seen him through so many tribulations. In Belfast he had been reminded of the young man who, three decades earlier, had played at the Royal Opera House to rousing applause and great reviews; at Duncairn Gardens he went in searching for a glimpse of that person and the young woman he'd loved, my mother. What he had found was rubble and broken glass.

On the last day of his visit we were driving along the Ormeau Road when I pulled up at traffic lights. It was a frosty morning and Éamonn had wrapped up well. Still he found it cold. My father said it reminded him of the time he worked for the Hudson Bay Trading Company. The cold would skin your hands, he said. And the smell of the beaver skins was the worst thing imaginable. He made a sucking noise of disgust through his teeth.

To my certain knowledge my father had never travelled further than France. Now he was talking about his days on the frozen wastes of the Canadian Arctic. I did what I always did when he fantasised. I nodded. I laughed to myself. But later I worried that his mind was slipping badly. *The Hudson Bay Trading Company? Beaver skins!* I wondered if it was the onset of senility or whether the booze had wreaked such havoc on his brain that he truly believed his own stories.

'Desperate it was,' he said, 'the coldest place I was ever in.'

Years later, after the death of my father, a man wrote to me from an address in Bristol. His name was Paul Piercey and he'd been a friend of my father in London during the late 1950s. They were both aspiring actors, although Paul said he quickly understood that my father was the real talent. My father had taught him all the skills he knew. He was patient and loyal. On the occasion of Paul's twenty-first birthday my father had given him a copy of the *Collected Works of William*

Shakespeare and wrote on the flyleaf a dedication urging his friend to have a happy life. Acting work was in short supply so they took any other work they could find. The strangest job of all, he explained, was working for the Hudson Bay Trading Company in Covent Garden market. The rooms were freezing cold and the animal skins stank to high heaven.

'Are you sure about that?' I asked, as if somehow my father and Paul had concocted the story between them. But Paul was sure.

He remembered the mornings when they headed from their flat in Chelsea to the fur warehouse, cursing their luck but desperately needing the money. Afterwards, if they went into a bar for a drink, the other customers would edge away from them, the reek of furs still clinging to their clothes. My father had been telling me the truth after all. I had followed the instinct honed by years of listening to exaggerations and excuses and chosen not to believe him. I cannot say how grateful I felt to Paul Piercey. He had given me a small but extraordinary gift, a picture of my father to contrast with all that was negative and choked in my heart.

My father continued to write. One letter came from a hospital run by nuns in the Irish countryside, where he had gone to recover from the effects of drinking. Even in this bleak predicament he kept a sense of humour, though he continued to do battle with authority:

Denis Murphy's sister, Betty, has made an arrangement on my behalf that I will enter what was formerly known as 'Moran's Hotel' in Church Street, Listowel, as a guest with a comfortable room and three meals a day from the 1st of October next. I will give it a go for a year or two. My heart rejoices. Like Dante released from the Inferno . . .

Then, referring to the head nurse at the hospital, he wrote:

She told me this morning that I could stay on here for the rest of my life and 'Die a happy death with us all round you'! Jesus laughed!

~

PEADAR: *Is there no hope for him?*
TRASSIE: *He is too old to fight now!*
Sharon's Grave, JOHN B. KEANE

My cousin's call came late on a Sunday night, the first Sunday of January and the day before my twenty-ninth birthday. I'd gone to bed early and was woken by Anne:

'Conor is on the phone from Listowel. Something is up.'

Conor Keane was John B's second eldest son and my best friend in the family. We were close in age and had once shared a flat together.

I sat at the end of the stairs and picked up the phone. I remember every detail of that conversation.

'How are you going?' asked Conor.

'I'm okay. What's up?'

'He's gone,' he said.

For a few seconds I didn't understand what he meant. 'Gone?' I knew he meant my father but 'gone' where?

'He passed away a short while ago. It was very quick,' said Conor.

My father had suffered another heart attack. I had prepared myself for this moment for so long but now that it had happened I did not know how to react. I did not feel shock. Nor was I overwhelmed by grief. I felt numb, as if I were observing the scene and the person on the phone receiving news of his father's death was somebody else.

~

My father had gone home to live in Listowel not long after he came to visit me in Belfast. With his RTE pension he was financially secure. My father was well loved in Listowel. There were friends and family all around him. The locals still called him 'The Joker' and he filled his days with reading, writing and walking and the morning and afternoon visits to the bookie's. He visited John B's regularly and was offered a room in his house. But Éamonn preferred to keep his independence; he'd lived on his own for nearly two decades and liked to come and go as he pleased. Instead my father took the room he was offered in a guesthouse opposite the police barracks and just a few doors up from 15, Church Street, where he had been born and reared. Not long after settling in Listowel he was granted one of the wishes of his life: Hollywood called.

After long negotiations my Uncle John B's play *The Field* was about to be made into a major film, with Richard Harris and the American actor Tom Berenger in leading roles. Other parts were to be taken by Brenda Fricker and John Hurt – the latter would play a local rascal and intriguer, the 'Bird' O'Donnell. The play was based on a real-life murder case not far from Listowel in which a man had killed his neighbour over the ownership of a patch of land.

The Field is set in Ireland towards the end of de Valera's period as leader, that period in the late fifties when all the dreams of self-sufficiency, of a happy Gaelic nation for a Gaelic people, had foundered. The play reflects a very different idea of rural life to the pastoral idyll espoused by 'the Chief'. It is about land hunger, but there is much else in it besides. Denial of unpleasant truth is a central theme. My uncle understood well that Ireland's sense of itself in the late de Valera era depended on suppressing truth, and this play about a single murder can be seen as an evocation of a much larger crisis. The culprit is never brought to justice. Nobody in the local community is willing to give evidence to the police. To do so would be regarded not only as a betrayal, but would force them to acknowledge publicly the awful wrong that had been committed. As the local bishop says in a sermon to parishioners in Act II of the play:

> Five weeks ago in this parish, a man was murdered – he was brutally beaten to death. For five weeks the police have investigated and not one single person has come forward to assist them. Everywhere they turned, they were met by silence, a silence of the most frightful and diabolical kind – the silence of the lie.

My father loved the play. He felt my uncle had come closer than any living Irish playwright to capturing the hard truths that underpinned rural existence, and in the voices of the characters he heard the wit and toughness of the cattle jobbers on fair days in his youth. In the acclaimed stage and television productions my father had played the part of 'Bird' O'Donnell with Ray McNally as the murderer 'Bull' McCabe. McNally had been due to play the part of the 'Bull' in the film but had died of a heart attack before filming began.

For my father there might have been some upset at playing a relatively minor role – as a village matchmaker – but if there was he showed none of this on set. John Hurt remarked on how helpful he had been. 'If you have played a part and somebody comes from abroad to play it, it is very easy to be difficult. But Éamonn was never that.'

On set Richard Harris befriended my father and even insisted that the producers keep him on after his scenes had been finished. 'Harris loved his company. He was kind to him and your father would keep him going for ages with stories and jokes,' a relative told me later. I know that Éamonn would have been flattered with the attention and with his incurable optimism would have looked at his small part as a foretaste of much greater things to come.

After the film he came back to Listowel and resumed his routine. When Christmas 1989 came around he sent me a copy of the *Collected Stories of Raymond Carver*. Carver's stories and poems were filled with the kind of characters my father would have known from his own life. They were men and women who lived on the last chance. Among them were a high proportion of alcoholics, like Carver himself, who was now sober, and who wrote movingly and more beautifully than any writer I know of the desperation of each drinking day. I believe now my father was sending me a message about his own drinking and mine. He had been sober for a long period when he picked up a drink on that last Christmas. His heart could take no more.

~

We drove south in the early morning of 8 January 1990. It was twenty-nine years and two days since my father had arrived at the hospital in London to celebrate my birth. There were very few cars on the roads. Ireland was still on holiday. The country was grey and freezing, all the colour leached out of the fields and hedgerows. I remember crossing the Cork border into Kerry and passing down narrow roads, seeing mountain streams in flood, rushing with dark water.

This would be a very public funeral and I was nervous – conscious of the fact that for the next twenty-four hours the family would be watched and commented on; there would be newspaper and television people, and a film crew who were making a documentary on the life of John B.

The town of Listowel looked empty when we arrived. At John B's pub they were getting ready for an influx of mourners. My uncle put his arms around me. 'He went peacefully in the end,' he said.

The funeral home was situated near the bend on the road leading to Ballybunnion and the farm at Lisselton where I'd gone with my father as a boy. A few memories flickered, momentarily knocking my detachment. I saw him on a summer's evening in 1968 rollicking with laughter at the story told by some old relative, and later that same week buying a bag of chips to share in a café above the beach at Ballybunnion; and that evening when he caught the small brown trout on the banks of the Feale.

Then the undertaker came and ushered me back to the present. He had the pious expression of the professionally lugubrious, but I was glad of his skill, the ease with which he helped me navigate the journey of my father's death and burial.

My father looked peaceful in death. At last the long sleep from which there would be no waking with remorse. I stood looking at him and then leaned forward and kissed his forehead. It was cold, like a windowpane in deep winter.

Then I sat with my relatives, facing the door through which people were already coming to pay their respects. The mourners came in large numbers, slowly shuffling past, praying over the coffin and then shaking our hands. 'Sorry for your troubles,' they said, again and again. I shook hands firmly. I made eye contact with everybody and thanked them all for coming. There were cousins from far out in the country, people I hadn't seen since I was a boy, and there were actors, poets, politicians, some of whom I recognised and others I knew only by name. For several hours they passed, and then we rose and went out into the dark and followed the coffin through the streets and down to the church in the main square. I walked alongside my mother, a quiet, dignified woman remembering the past with every step.

There were more prayers. Afterwards we went to John B's pub and I spoke to a man from a newspaper and to another on the phone. I listened to many stories about my father that night. *Sure he was a lovely man . . . He'd always stop and give you the time of day . . . He was the gentlest soul you could meet . . . We used to have great times together, your father and myself . . . Do you know there was no badness in him at all . . .* I had the feeling I have heard so often described by others caught in moments of trauma, that of floating far above the scene, observing the comings and goings, hearing the words as a benign noise, grateful but in the end hardly hearing them.

We buried him the following morning. At the funeral mass I read prayers of the faithful along with my siblings. The cortege wound slowly up Church Street, past the house where my father was born, and then the guesthouse where he had suffered his last heart attack. We carried him the last yards to his grave in the cemetery by Gurtenard Wood. There were more prayers and an actress read a poem. I cannot remember what it was. A camera crew circled around us. Then I spoke. I quoted from F. Scott Fitzgerald's *The Great Gatsby*. Éamonn loved that book. He identified with Gatsby's extravagant romanticism, and like Fitzgerald's hero, he had gone on believing in his own dream, all of his dreams of love and artistic perfection, until the end:

He had come a long way to this blue lawn, and his dream must have seemed so close that he could hardly fail to grasp it. He did not know that it was already behind him, somewhere back in that vast obscurity beyond the city, where the dark fields of the Republic rolled on under the night. Gatsby believed in the green light, the orgastic future that year by year recedes before us. It eluded us then, but that's no matter – tomorrow we will run faster, stretch our arms further. . . And one fine morning –

So we beat on, boats against the current, borne back ceaselessly into the past.

Later that year *The Field* appeared in Irish cinemas. There was a glittering premiere in Dublin. Richard Harris was widely praised for his portrayal of the Bull McCabe and won an Oscar nomination for Best Actor. The documentary on John B's life appeared and contained a scene where Richard Harris is shown enthusiastically welcoming my father. 'Éamonn, Éamonn, my friend,' he said. My father would have loved that; he would have seen it as an affirmation of his place among the front rank of Irish actors. Richard Harris had fought with alcoholism himself and I am sure he understood my father's struggle and what this film role meant to him.

I saw the film in a rural cinema. When my father appeared on screen, looking old and tired, I felt a surge of pride, proud for myself and for him. I wanted to shout to the other people in the cinema: *Look, there's my father up there with Richard Harris*. And then my father spoke his lines. That shocked me. Because the voice wasn't his. It was nothing like his rich, true timbre.

I heard later that my father had been so physically weak on set that the microphones struggled to pick up his lines. In one scene my father was required to climb a hill to the Bull McCabe's cottage. As always with film there were several re-takes. 'Every time Éamonn came up the hill, his breath had gone completely. I felt we should have carried him,' one of the film's producers said. Normally my father would have been called to come into the studio and re-dub the voice himself, this time without the exertions of climbing the hill. But he was dead before they could ask him.

CHAPTER SIXTEEN

A Journey Back

A father's no shield
For his child
We are like a lot of wild
Spiders crying together
But without tears.

'Fall 1961',
ROBERT LOWELL

I went back to Belfast after my father died. There was little to be tidied up in the way of his personal affairs. Éamonn owned almost nothing when he died. That would not have struck him as in any way pathetic or sad. He was never greedy for material possessions. What little he had he would have given away to the first poor person he met. If this could be frustrating for a family member to witness, it was also a tribute to his genuine capacity for kindness.

Back in Belfast I worked more frantically than before. I shut my father out. I did not want to think or feel about him. Perhaps it's truer to say that I did not know what to feel. Feeling should be instinctual, shouldn't it? But there was only a numbness in me, and I could not cry for him. I felt taken over by a deadness. I could only sleep when thoroughly exhausted. That sleep was always fitful. There were so many nights I woke in a cold sweat and lay there, feeling lost but unable to say why. To speak his mind and feelings a person needs to know them. The reckoning would come later.

~

Throughout this time I did not drink. The temptation did exist. And I could easily have constructed justifications: *Sure you deserve one after what's happened. A few pints to steady the nerves. Nobody will blame you if you do. Just because your father was one doesn't mean you are too . . .*

What stopped me then? I believe it was nothing more complex than my will. It was still strong enough in those days. And as before, working hard was a perfect substitute. It brought me praise and that praise was my drug. It also brought me to the attention of the foreign desk of the BBC. It was said that I was promising material. Hints were passed from London that I might think about applying for a foreign post in another year or two.

A month after my father died I watched Nelson Mandela walk free from prison. It was a Sunday evening and I was sitting in the Belfast newsroom of the BBC. I was thrilled by the images, carried along on the extraordinary emotion of the moment. People were beaming and cheering in the newsroom. But later that evening I succumbed to an ignoble thought. If Mandela was out of prison, surely liberation was close at hand, and where would I be then? In bloody Belfast following coffins and listening to ranting and weasel words.

The ANC and the South African Communist Party had been un-banned; exiles were returning to South Africa, and already there were talks about the political future and elections. Then luck intervened. The resident BBC correspondent decided he wanted to come back to take up a new post. His job was

swiftly advertised and I was called for interview. I had prepared well. The years of reading and immersion in African
affairs paid off.

I had just come through the front door of my home in Belfast
when the phone rang. 'Welcome to foreign,' the voice said.
'You are the new Southern Africa correspondent.' Chris Wyld
was an avuncular fellow who was affectionately referred to by
his underlings as the 'Young Master', but whose gentlemanly
demeanour did not entirely conceal a steely core. 'Bloody good
interview,' he said. 'Even the boffins from Bush House were
impressed and you know how hard they are to please.'

I knew I stood a good chance but I still felt awed. Southern
Africa correspondent! There was still much of the naive provincial about me and when I let out a loud cheer down the
phone line I think the foreign editor was taken aback. I imagined people at parties asking what I did for a living and my
answering nonchalantly: 'Oh, I'm a foreign correspondent
with the BBC.' What magical words. I called everybody I
knew. In Listowel John B let out a loud cheer. 'Your father
would be dancing in the street. I'm sure he's at it in heaven.'
The *Limerick Leader* carried a short story and photograph:
'*Leader* man off to Africa for BBC.'

A few days later I flew to London to have lunch with the
press secretary at the South African embassy. Before we went
in Chris Wyld gave me a mild warning, delivered in the most
genteel manner. 'I know you're probably very anti-apartheid,
old fruit, but just oblige me with this Johnny and avoid any
rows. He's a monstrous bore but remember you need him to
stamp the visa.'

The press secretary was a former newsreader with South
African television, sleek and jowled, as big a bore as Wyld had
promised, and still whining about Michael Buerk's coverage
of the State of Emergency. 'I hope we won't have any such
bias from you, Mr Keane,' he said.

Then he asked me where I came from.

'Ireland?' he exclaimed. We had hit a potential snag. 'The Irish aren't very good friends to South Africa, are they?'

I knew what he was referring to. A few years before a young woman shop worker had refused to sell South African fruit in a Dublin supermarket. She was suspended. Her colleagues joined her on strike. The affair quickly became a cause célèbre in Ireland. When the shop worker and some trade union allies tried to visit South Africa they were arrested at Johannesburg airport and deported. Though a minor drama in the great story of apartheid, this display of courage by one worker had rankled with the South Africans, worried maybe that it would add to the pressure on big companies to disinvest from the country.

Wyld kicked me under the table, as if to say: *Don't start now.* But instead of attacking I went into Celtic blather mode. 'Ah, sure, not at all. We love everybody.' I bordered on the unctuous. At this point my boss erupted into a booming laugh, as notable for its insincerity as its volume. The dreadful South African seemed satisfied.

I half feared that the embassy would look up their files and find my old rejected applications or some reference to my clandestine visits in the 1980s. I flattered myself. By then the white spooks had more to worry about than the record of a BBC correspondent. Mandela was out of jail. The ANC was organising across the country. The black majority was on the march. And the white state was caught between reform and repression.

My only communication from South Africa House was an instruction to go to the Chelsea and Westminster Hospital for a tuberculosis x-ray. South Africa was suffering a massive increase in TB cases. I didn't know it then, and the white government wasn't too concerned to find out the cause, but the upsurge was linked to a deadly new phenomenon: HIV.

The embassy approved my work permit and told me I was free to go anytime I wanted. So, in early October, as the southern summer was beginning, I left Belfast and flew to South Africa. The idea was that I would travel alone at first, find a place to live, get into the swing of the job. But I was not happy. I was still running. I had been for years.

~

On board I am seated towards the back of the plane in the middle of a group of disabled athletes returning to South Africa from a competition in Britain. They are excited and happy to be going home. I am travelling to South Africa because I want to escape. So I head for the country of dreams. In South Africa the light will banish the slow ache that has been fastening around my heart for months. But as the engines start up and we taxi out to the runway I feel my hands starting to shake. I have flown a thousand times so it cannot be panic about the journey.

The plane lifts clear of London and points towards the Bay of Biscay and south to Africa. By the time we reach our cruising altitude the young South African on my right has noticed my shaking hands. He has some communication disability and speaks with difficulty, but I know that he is asking what is wrong with me. I cannot reply. I am not only shaking now but crying too. I stand up and climb across the people sitting to my left, and a teardrop falls on the bare knee of a girl. She looks up into my face and she is afraid. I make it to the toilet and lock the door and I cannot stop shaking and crying. I want to get off this plane. I want to run home. But I am being catapulted through the night. I clasp my arms around myself and sit there. Waves of fear rise and subside. I throw up until there is nothing left. But the violent action of vomiting stops the shaking for a few seconds. Then it comes back, worse than before. There is a knock on the door. A South African accent. 'Is everything okay in there?'

I cannot form words. I make a sound. It is not a word exactly but enough to convince the stewardess that I am okay.

I repeat my mantra. Everything will be all right. I go back to my seat. I am lucky because the flight is not full. There is a row of empty seats at the back and I lie down. But sleep will not come. I shake still and cry. Dawn is a red streak across the horizon. We are crossing from Central to Southern Africa. Then the plane shakes. Not a violent movement but different from the usual bump and drop of turbulence, a shaking that is accompanied by a grinding noise. Lights come on. The captain's voice tells us there is nothing to worry about. Just a technical problem. Holy Jesus. I am in the middle of what feels like a mental breakdown and the plane has decided it might crash. We are diverting to Windhoek in Namibia. We land safely.

At Windhoek the desert heat blasts into my tired, red eyes. The other passengers are in a hurry to get off the plane. But I can only shuffle. It feels as if switches have been turned and the power run down, throughout my body. We are herded into a departure lounge to wait for another plane.

The panic subsides. I don't know why this should be so, but for the next few hours I am quiet. A new plane comes. I fall asleep on the short journey up to Johannesburg. I get a taxi from the airport to my hotel in the white suburb of Rosebank. This is a neighbourhood of beautiful mansions, long tree-lined avenues where the October jacarandas spill purple flowers on the streets. It is also the beginning of the storm season; great banks of cloud are forming behind the communications tower in Hillbrow, a mile or so downtown.

In my room the panic returns. This time it will not go away. There are no moments of reprieve. I phone everybody I can think of: family, friends. At first I do not say that I think I am going mad. I talk about South Africa. The weather. I say there is a storm going on outside my window. There are flashes of lightning like nobody in Ireland could imagine. One second the city is grey and rainswept, the next it is bright silver. But I cannot keep up this façade for long. My voice cracks. I choke on words.

I hear worry in the voices at the other end of the line. Get a doctor, one says. But I resist this idea at first. I can make it through this. Just a panic attack. I've had them before. It will go away. I stand up and start walking around the room. Back and forth. I sit down again. I stand up. Up and down. Then I walk to the window. I am walking from the window to the door. Maybe twenty times, thirty times. And so on. Then I pick up the phone again. I dial my grandmother's number in Cork. Before she can answer I hang up. I realise that if I speak I will frighten her, because my voice gives it away, the sheer terror of not knowing what is happening to me.

The room is too small. I go out. One of the black porters calls after me. 'You okay, sir?' But I keep going. The rain has stopped but the streets are still glistening. I walk quickly through a shopping area and on towards a main road. There are cars racing along here. Most of them seem to be coming out of town because it is late afternoon. I stop and lean against a bus stop. There are mainly black people here and they are looking at me: a young white man panting for breath and with tears flowing down his face. 'Get a doctor.' The words of my loved ones come back.

'Is there a doctor near here?' I ask a young black woman. She says she doesn't live here.

I go into a bakery and ask the white owner. He says I should walk along the road towards town. He thinks there is a doctor's surgery about half a mile away, on the other side of the road.

It starts to rain again. Not heavy but before long I am wet

through. I start to walk along the road towards town. I try to cross to the far side. Suddenly there are car horns blaring at me. I am like a drunk weaving through the traffic. It is too thick, too fast and I retreat. I slump down and sit on the ground beside a block of flats. An elderly white woman comes up to me.

'Are you in trouble?'

I manage to say that I am a visitor and that I feel ill.

'Why don't you ask your hotel to call a doctor?'

She offers to walk with me back to the hotel. It is an extraordinary gesture of trust but I am incapable of forming words to thank her properly. The old woman is not frightened by this. She puts a hand on top of mine and steers me towards reception and asks the lady to find me a doctor.

The doctor comes within half an hour. He is in his fifties, slight of build but with a strong handshake and a smile. He talks softly to me. His voice is deep, rich, reassuring. He tells me I need to sleep. He gives me a strong sedative. When it does not work and I am calling him in panic several hours later he returns and is again calm and tells me that he would like to put me into hospital for a short while. I agree. I want to be safe, watched over, asleep.

I don't remember much else, except that the hospital is a private clinic on the outskirts of the city. In the hospital I am given more tranquillisers and put on a drip. I fall into a deep, drugged sleep. Early in the morning I feel a hand tugging at my sleeve, pulling me out of the deep fug of tranquillised slumber. A nurse is standing over me. She takes my temperature and gives me a tablet.

Then I hear voices. There are African workmen on scaffolding outside the window. I cannot understand the language. It is Zulu, I think. They talk through the morning, an easy murmuring conversation, occasionally broken by laughter. The nurse comes back and tells me about her own son. She is a 'coloured' – a South African of mixed race who in that time, just after the release of Mandela from prison, was still denied democratic rights. She tells me that her son wanted to go to university but never had the chance. Apartheid kept him out. 'That's how it is in this country still,' she adds.

I nod but cannot think of anything to say. I sense that the ward sister disapproves of me. Or it may be she is simply perplexed. How must I appear to her? This is a hospital more used to dealing with physical traumas. I have no sign of any injury. To this nurse I am probably no more than another spoiled white.

'Do you mind if I ask something?' she says.

Before waiting for me to nod or speak, she continues.

'Look at you. You are a healthy and successful young man. Yet you are here in hospital. What happened to you?' she asks.

But I cannot answer her. I do not know where to begin or end. Only years later do I begin to understand.

~

Nearly a year after my father's death I went back to Listowel. I'd returned to Ireland after the collapse in South Africa, wintering in old places, half haunted by them, half desperate for the familiar. I had written to John B a few weeks after getting back. I told him in brief outline what had happened. He wrote back immediately. My uncle told me not to give a damn what anybody thought of me. 'Come down and see us,' he said.

I took the train to Tralee from Cork. The fields along the Bandon River were flooded and the hedgerows and woodlands stripped of their colour, everything spent and shrivelled. I was spending my days chain-smoking, writing bad poems, listening to music, afraid. I moved from one day to the next as if from room to room, the same rooms always with the same grey light falling through the windows and nowhere reached at the end of walking. I heard the voices of those who loved me, but I could not talk to them or face them or explain to them.

What are you thinking?

Oh, nothing.

What's wrong with you?

Nothing. Honestly. I'm fine. Just thinking, that's all.

Christ, you just sit there, saying nothing. You act like you are the only person in the world.

And this last is true. There is no place more self-obsessed than in the grey rooms of depression. I'd become a conversation with myself. To all others I was silent. So silent I would have driven Mother Teresa to anger. I was still seized by night panics and so I would sit up late, smoking cigarette after cigarette, a light always burning somewhere nearby, scribbling furiously and watching for the dawn coming up over the steeples of Cork.

Back in the city of my boyhood I walked the streets and hills by night, out along the Mardyke and up the Western Road, and across by the university to the Glasheen Road, passing the places where I had walked years before with my first girl, feeling comfort in movement. I went to the places where I had once been so happy, as if it were possible to step from one time into another. There is a line of F. Scott Fitzgerald's which talks about 'the real dark night of the soul being at three o'clock in the morning every morning'. So it was with me as I made my nightly rounds.

Messages came from the BBC. They were kind and reassured me that my job was secure. But I had grave doubts by now that I would ever get back to South Africa. The way I was stumbling around I'd be lucky to do the courts for the *Cork Examiner*. I feared that I would never return to work, or that if I did somehow the word would leak out among my colleagues: *he had a mental breakdown . . . a flaky character*

... not to be depended on. Depression is the obliterator of confidence.

~

John B was waiting for me at Tralee station. He hugged me tightly. 'Come on away. Mary has the dinner ready for you in Listowel.' I travelled back with him to my father's town. He talked most of the way, about what was happening with various plays of his, what the Abbey planned with one play or the Olympia with another, and about his books which were selling in phenomenal numbers. In Listowel Mary welcomed me with dinner and a few sympathetic words. After dinner John B suggested going for a walk. We went to Dirha bog where we'd gone the day eleven years before when I needed his help to get a job in journalism. He wore his peaked countryman's cap and an anorak buttoned up to the neck against the cold.

'You look strained,' he said, 'but you'll be all right. The Keanes are hard men to put down.'

He reminded me not to worry about what anybody thought. I have no memory of my own side of the conversation.

'Whatever is up we'll always love you,' he said. Which at the time was the most precious thing he could have said. My uncle, my hero. John B talked about his own life and how years before when he was a young writer and the Abbey rejected his plays he'd wondered if the struggle was worthwhile, but that the hunger to put words on paper had kept him going. Like he'd said in this same place years before: *'If I couldn't write I'd go stone fucking mad.'*

Then he talked about my father. He was the cleverest man he knew, John B said, and the most impractical. 'Christ knows, he wasn't an easy man. And I know ye had it hard. But he was very proud of you. He was always talking about what you were doing, right up to the end. I know he'd want you to get better and go back to work. You can do so much. It's all there if you want it.'

The following day he dropped me back to the train. As I got out of the car, he gave me a hug.

'We're always here if you need us.'

The fact that I came back from mental breakdown is less a tribute to my own powers of recovery than it is to those who endured the long alienating silences, the self-absorption, the evasions, and still found it in their hearts to give love. I was also helped by a wise doctor at his cottage in the County Cork countryside. Tony Humphreys listened to me, asked some probing questions, told me that I should not feel shame because of what had happened. Then he gave me the most enduring insight of my life: my happiness was my responsibility alone. No person, alive or dead, could change that. Nobody else was responsible if I was unhappy. It would take me many years, and no end of pain for myself and others, to find a way of fully accepting that truth.

~

By the summer, 1991, I was ready to go to South Africa. This time I travelled with Anne at my side. She was excited by the prospect of going there; it was a country we had got to know and love together, and she knew she would find work as a freelance reporter. Yet after the last year she was naturally more wary of me, wondering if the man she had married would fall again. But Anne had a fidelity to those she loved that I could hardly have guessed at.

In writing about someone with whom you are still in love, it is difficult to have perspective; the best writing of all seems to be about the love affairs that have ended. Because ours is a continuing narrative I must be wary of the danger of idealising, or looking back and writing fine words out of guilt as some consolation for the price our relationship has paid for my career and the crises of my adult life. I can only assert what is to me so clear: our meeting each other was the best thing that ever happened to me.

As people we could not have been more different. Where I was impulsive she was cautious; where I talked a great deal, she was a listener; where I was inconsistent in friendships, she was relentlessly loyal; where I veered from high to low, she maintained a steady rhythm. Her assurance then, and so many times later, was that everything would be all right.

~

On the way out to South Africa we stopped off in London. My grandmother, May Hassett, was being treated for cancer at the Royal Marsden Hospital. May looked smaller, reduced by old age and the disease that was attacking her body. She described the shrinking of her life back in Ireland. Everything was circumscribed by pain and effort. She could no longer take the bus from her home into town to shop, and so she no longer had stories of the people she met; she was frightened of being burgled – a conman had got into the house some time before and robbed some of her savings; the laughter was gone from her voice. My grandmother upon whom I had depended so much as a child was preparing herself for death. My final memory of her is of a little old lady standing at the top of the stairs in the hospital, still calm and smiling as the life of the hospital buzzed around her. She knew for certain then what I only suspected, that this would be the last time we would see each other. May went home to Cork and was hospitalised again.

Just before she went into hospital in Cork I had reason to call her. It occurred not long after I went to Africa. I'd been despatched to Zaire to cover a coup attempt by mutinous troops. They were attempting to rid themselves of the dictator, Joseph Mobutu. It was a terrifying journey full of drunken soldiery, extortion, and intense physical discomfort. After a hair-raising trip from Njili airport to a hotel in the capital, Kinshasa, I finally managed to get an international telephone line, no easy thing in the Congo of the Mobutu era. Knowing that my mother was at school teaching, I telephoned May Hassett, assuming that she and the rest of the family would be hanging on desperately for news of the Congo crisis and my role in it. The phone was answered with the usual warmth:

'Hello, love!'

I started to explain where I was, but was cut short.

'I'm sorry now, love, you'll have to call back later. *Coronation Street* is on.'

Click. The conversation ended, my precious international line vanished. I laughed at that for hours afterwards.

I got the news of her death over another long distance phone line. I was in Johannesburg on a crisp winter's morning. May had passed away in her sleep at the Bon Secours Hospital in Cork. I grieved for her but it was not the distracted, confused grief I had felt for my father. My grandmother had lived a hard life but she died in happiness, telling people that she was leaving to join the ones she had loved and lost – her dead children, her dead husband – and that nobody should feel sorry for her.

CHAPTER SEVENTEEN

Beloved Country

... And the earth that has been crying out for rain has been given blood.

Rumours of Rain, ANDRÉ BRINK

At the Chicken Farm squatter camp in Soweto I see a mother standing over her son's body. The ground around him is black with the blood. It looks like oil has been spilled. She has placed a newspaper over him. It is winter on the high veld and there has been a sharp wind blowing down from the Drakensberg for days. The wind keeps whipping the paper away and the mother struggles to hold it down, trying to offer her dead child some dignity. It is an unfair contest. The wind is too strong. It eventually blows the paper away. All the time she keeps up a constant wailing. It is much worse than anything I can see or smell. It fills the air.

I see so many strange things these days. In Tokoza I see a little girl hand a basin of warm water and a baby's bib to her mother, who then proceeds to clean up the blood that is leaking from a corpse at the end of their garden. In the same township I am on patrol with the army, stuffed into the back of a large armoured car, when I hear the soldiers shouting. One of the voices says: 'Oh, Jesus Christ ... oh, Jesus' and I look out the small slit window and see a pack of dogs coming towards us. In the middle is a small dog carrying an object in its mouth, like a dog carrying a newspaper, except when it comes closer I can see that it is a human arm. It belongs, or belonged, to a skeleton with the chewed remnants of a head attached that lies further up the road.

The skeleton is that of what police call 'an unknown male', a victim of township violence during the night. Nobody knows who he is or whether he supported the ANC or Inkatha.

Milton is waiting to meet me in another part of the township. When I tell him what I've seen he says he hopes the man took a round in the head before the mob got him. A man who took a direct hit to the brain was, relatively speaking, lucky. That way he had no idea what the mob would do to his corpse; he wouldn't be alive when the petrol was poured on and the flames exploded and they hacked and beat him.

Then Milton says that we shouldn't hang around: 'Let's go baba before the shit starts up again.

All kinds of bad things come to pass. Our friend Joe Mogotsi tells a story about going into one of the Zulu hostels where they are making weapons. The Zulus here support Chief Buthelezi and they hate the ANC. Joe films in a room where they are making spears and axes. Then as they are getting ready to leave he slips away from the group to try and get some GVs – general vision shots – which would help to expand the piece. He goes into a room where a group of men are sitting and talking. The smell in here is terrible. As Joe is explaining to the Zulus who he is and where he is from, he feels drops of liquid on his shoulder. Then he looks up and sees, hanging on string like clothes on a washing line, the severed private parts of a number of men. The liquid is dripping from these. The Zulus see that he has seen this and they become angry. Fear is what stops him from retching there and then. But his clothes stink so much afterwards he throws them away.

Milton teaches me that you don't wear a seatbelt in the townships. It means too much time spent fiddling around if the car is hit and you need to make a run for it. He says that when you stop at a roadblock in a township you should always reach for the hand of one of the kids and hold it while you explain who you are and what you are doing. Someone who feels your pulse, the warmth of another human hand in his, may think twice about killing you instantly. It buys you time, he says.

And you always call them 'comrade' – 'com' for short – and talk softly, talk them down from their high plateau of craziness and rage, because if you try to act the hard man the fourteen-year-old with the gun will know that he has all the aces, and if he kills you it won't matter to him because he has been killing for a long time.

We have hundreds of these roadblock conversations. They go something like this:

'Hey, Com'owzit?'

'Okay. How are you?'

'Okay too. We're from radio. From overseas. The BBC. You heard of BBC?'

Most of them have no idea what the BBC is – in those days World Service radio is largely listened to by white expatriates, and the more liberal English speakers.

'Radio, eh? So what you want here? You sure you're not cops?'

Hearing this a few of his friends sidle over.

'Cops. Are they cops?'

I feel my heart starting to accelerate. Boom, boom, boom. I am convinced they can see it pounding against the wall of my chest, like a demented animal trying to escape from my body. A boy with a Bob Marley T-shirt and a large stone in his hand has started asking questions.

Then I produce the ANC press pass.

There are smiles. African handshakes all round.

'Go ahead, my brother. No problem. You are okay. Okay.'

And on we go. Every day. Roadblock after roadblock.

Milton has become an expert on ballistics. He says that a round from an AK-47 will blow you off your feet and then tumble and dance inside your body before blasting its way out, the exit wound as big as a fist. The BBC flak jacket can stop an AK-47 round, but white neo-Nazis have titanium-tipped sniper rounds that will go straight through it and blow you to eternity, pushing the Kevlar fibre from the flak jacket into your body to speed the journey. And if they manage to get a head shot . . . well, imagine a ripe melon being smashed with an axe and you have the picture.

Even with Milton, who knows everything you could know about the townships and their narrow margins, I feel afraid so much of the time. And yet I feel at home in this craziness. I am more alive than at any time in my life. After the collapse the first time out, the slow journey back to health, the fear of never getting here, of never being a foreign correspondent, I am back doing what I know I do best. I am on the front line, risking it all, our own correspondent calling out his news down a crackly line from Boipatong, Kathelohong, Soweto, with the sound of shooting or chanting rising in the background.

They can hear it in London and in every place around the world where there is a short-wave radio: 'Over now to our Southern Africa correspondent, Fergal Keane.'

When my first dispatch is broadcast my mother calls and says the neighbours have been on the phone to say I was on the radio. She is excited and, I know, relieved. This is South Africa in the last years of apartheid. In a single week I have had breakfast with Mandela, sat in the homes of impoverished shack dwellers, and listened to white right-wingers tell me of their plans for revolution. Before all of this ends we will count the bodies of friends and we will thank God that we survived. And I will learn that for everything terrible that happens, the Africa of my childhood dreams – my 'beloved country' – exists, and is every bit as beautiful as I had hoped.

~

Our first morning was cold and bright. I was nervous as we stepped onto South African soil. Not because of the war I knew was raging in the townships, but because the last time I came here I failed. There was much to prove now. I knew that for all their kindness my BBC bosses would be watching carefully. The first few months of existence as a foreign correspondent are invariably difficult. You want to make a big impression. You desperately need to avoid making mistakes. After what had passed in the last year I felt the pressure more than most.

We arrived in the middle of the township wars. People were dying in their hundreds in the townships around Johannesburg. On the radio as we drove in from Johannesburg airport the news was reporting battles between Zulu hostel dwellers and township residents. It was the start of the short southern winter and the grass was burned brown already. There would be no rain for months. I would become used to bitterly cold mornings in the townships, waiting for the sun to warm us up as we trawled for evidence of the previous night's killings. The wind kicked dust into our faces when it blew in from the plains of the Free State or down from the Drakensberg mountains, and on killing days we covered our mouths with scarves, fearful of what the wind might lift and carry.

The war was a day job. I left in the morning carrying a flak jacket instead of a briefcase. By the evening we were back in the office drinking cold beer. We flitted out of the black world and back into the white. One of the most troubled townships,

Alexandra, was less than a mile from my home. At night we could hear the fighting around the hostel. But we were protected from Alexandra and its troubles. There was a huge motorway and several concentric rings of housing where Indians lived, a buffer between black Africa and the white suburbs.

I came back to alcohol in South Africa. It wasn't a dramatic return. A few glasses of wine or beer with the other reporters. You would come back from townships and drop the flak jacket on the floor before heading straight to the fridge to feel the sweet iciness of a can of Castle Lager. And when that first draught of beer hit home it was like somebody had pulled a cord and all the tension came rushing out of you like air.

I rationalised picking up again by saying that my life was under control. The traumas were behind me, and, given what we were seeing in the townships every day, a man needed a calming beer in the evenings. Besides, drinking didn't affect my work; I had never been more productive and I had strict rules about only drinking when the story was filed. I had it under control. But I knew that every time I finished my beer and said 'enough', a longing persisted, the old sense that somehow I was being cheated. On the few occasions when I did drink too much I always sank into a black gloom. And it would linger on through days when I didn't drink at all. My father only ever came to me in dreams back then. He had been dead more than a year and with work I could push him out of my conscious mind. But he turned up in sleep. I cannot remember the exact pictures, only that I always woke feeling hollowed out and afraid.

Many drank a lot more than me. A few drank less. I only knew one reporter who didn't drink at all. Like most wars, the township conflict created the perfect conditions for drinking. War made the domestic world seem trivial. The conditions of normal life were suspended. We lived as though the war was all that really mattered. The conflict had created an informal group of correspondents, producers, cameramen and photographers who became known as the 'Bang Bang Club'. I didn't see myself as part of any club, but I ran around the same streets, dodged the same bullets and I drank and swapped war stories with them.

I was fond of those 'Bang Bang' boys. They were brave, sometimes stupidly so, but you knew that if a bullet took you down on a township street they would stop to drag you out of the line of fire. Most of them were South African whites who'd been forced to serve as conscripts in the apartheid army. I think they wreaked their revenge by going into the townships to expose the brutality of the police.

Anne says now: 'It was a crazy bloody time.' Objectively speaking I can agree. But I know that part of me will always long for those days. We all felt the adrenalin rush of the fighting moment, the excited camaraderie of young men together in danger, living the dream of being war reporters. Every one of us had read Michael Herr's book *Despatches* and wished we'd been around at the time of Vietnam; we hated the violence because of what it did to ordinary people, but we couldn't deny what it did for us: the sense of moral purpose it gave us, the sense of being totally alive in a way none of us had ever experienced before, the sheer insane excitement of it.

~

We lived at the end of an avenue of trees and shadows, behind steel security gates, in a rambling house that had been bequeathed to us by the previous correspondent. It was built in the 1970s hacienda style and rented to the BBC by a grizzled old landlord who'd come down from Rhodesia after independence, and who rarely lost a chance to moan about the blacks.

There was a huge garden, invisible from the road because

of the profusion of trees. Jacaranda. Flame Tree. Pine. Outside
the front door there was a large flower bush which seemed to
be in blossom for most of the year. It sent a cloying perfume
wafting into the face of anybody arriving and leaving the
house. It was called Yesterday-Today-and-Tomorrow. That
scent of flowers stayed with us through countless departures
and arrivals, often going to and from places which stank of
tear gas and death.

Whenever I smell it now I remember the house on Wood-
burn Lane in the manicured dullness of Morningside, in the
northern suburbs of Johannesburg. Only the black people
walked anywhere. They were domestic servants and migrants
from the countryside looking for work. White South Africans
drove everywhere, and *everywhere* meant the shopping malls
or the houses of friends and occasionally a trip out into the
bush to escape the tension of the city.

In the mornings we woke with the first light and the sound
of birds, more numerous and strange than anything I'd ever
heard, like the hadidas, the sacred ibis, screeching as they lifted
into flight, their pterodactyl shapes silhouetted in pairs against
the morning sun.

We lived in a world of conspicuous luxury. There was a
swimming pool and a huge patio area for parties, and a sitting
room into which you could have fitted several families. The
two of us rattled around in the house of many rooms. We had
come from living in a small terraced house in Belfast. For all
the tension of Belfast life, we had still been able to walk to
work and to the shops, we knew our neighbours and we had
made friends across the sectarian boundaries. In Johannesburg
we entered a world as divided as it had been nearly a decade
before when we first visited South Africa. Not only racially
divided, but where the concept of neighbourliness hardly
seemed to exist in our wealthy white community. In four years
of living in South Africa we met our neighbours once – at the

With Anne in Crossroads township near Cape Town
in the year of liberation, 1994.

ABOVE: Sylvestre Gacumbitsi when we tracked him down in 1994. I would face him in an international court ten years later.

BELOW: At Nyarubuye church where Hutu extremists murdered thousands of Tutsi civilians. The stench of corpses was overpowering.

LEFT: The Benaco camp in Tanzania in the early summer of 1994. Hundreds of thousands of Rwandan refugees fled here after the collapse of the genocidal regime in the country.

ABOVE: With the *Panorama* team at Benaco camp in 1994. Setting up: Hamilton Wende, Glenn Middleton and me.

LEFT: Valentina photographed two years after the genocide in which her parents and brothers were murdered. She survived for six weeks hiding among their corpses.

ABOVE: With Valentina in Rwanda. This was taken at the turn of the new century. The change in Valentina is remarkable.

BELOW: Valentina on her visit to London. She came to testify at a public commemoration for the victims of the Rwandan genocide.

ABOVE: With my best friend, Milton Nkosi, son of Soweto.

BELOW: With Daniel in Dublin shortly after we returned from Hong Kong in 1997.

With Glenn Middleton, putting together a piece for the Ten O'Clock News in Tikrit in the shadow of the recently fallen Saddam.

Doing a piece to camera on a Baghdad street just after the fall. In those days it was still possible for a reporter to stand and talk to camera in most parts of the city.

At the Iraqi border on the morning we set out for Baghdad. It was a terrifying journey.

On the Shat el Arab with the Royal Marines. After Iraq I realised I could no longer do 'hot' wars.

Me back in Ardmore. 'Alive, sober, loving and being loved',
as Ray Carver so wonderfully puts it.

local police station where we had all converged at three in the morning to complain about loud music coming from the house of another neighbour.

Anne wanted a home. Instead she got a fortress. We had alarms and electronic gates and panic buttons, lights that flashed on if intruders came into the garden; there were bars on the bedroom windows and a 'rape gate' so that if the burglars did get through the first line of defence the bedroom was at least protected. At night, when all the doors were locked and the alarm panel set, we retreated behind the rape gate and listened to the sounds of a fearful city: sporadic gunshots as some nervous or drunk neighbour fired at the shadows, and once a deafening hail of automatic fire when the police tracked a big-time gangster to a house a few streets away. His body and that of his girlfriend lay on the pavement the following morning. There were so many mornings when we woke exhausted after nights of tossing and turning, imagining we could hear intruders in the garden.

Sometimes we hit the panic button and the gunmen from the Armed Response Team – often working-class Afrikaners who didn't make it into the police – would come jumping over the wall, torch beams crisscrossing the garden until they were sure nobody was hiding in the bushes. Once the garden lights flashed on and we heard voices, right outside our window. Anne hit the panic button. We locked ourselves into the bathroom. Then we heard a loud commotion outside. The Armed Response had arrived and collared a suspect. There was shouting. Rough voices were threatening somebody in Afrikaans. A torch light shone through the window.

'Sir, this one says he works for you.' The voice was young, barely an adult. I looked out and saw a young Afrikaner with a shotgun in one hand and Peter the gardener held in a head-lock with the other.

Peter worked for the landlord and lived at the back of the

house. He had a weakness for drink and would occasionally disappear for weeks. This time he had been out late with his friends and was so drunk he'd got lost in the garden. The poor man had come within seconds of being shot dead by the Armed Response Team.

Crime and the fear of crime dominated every social gathering. At dinner parties with white South Africans we heard one horror story after another. An atmosphere of barely restrained paranoia prevailed. When I told whites that I spent nearly every day in the townships, they were aghast. Most had never been near a black area in their lives. Fear kept them out and apartheid legislation made double sure.

We never heard what black South Africans felt. They weren't usually invited to those dinner parties. I once asked a hostess why. 'How would they get home to the townships?' she replied. You would get to meet black people at the *braais* organised by other foreign correspondents, but these were usually big affairs, not a place for serious conversation or developing friendships.

Yet the story of my time in South Africa would become defined by an extraordinary friendship. When I arrived at the BBC in Johannesburg early in 1991 there wasn't a single black employee. All of the cameramen, producers, fixers were white. Mostly they were English-speaking university graduates who had drifted into media work when the riots started back in the 1980s. They were almost universally nice people and some of them are good friends of mine today. But given that the politics of the future was being shaped in the townships the absence of black staff was a poor state of affairs. They might be hired on an ad-hoc basis but that couldn't substitute for the benefits of bringing someone with township knowledge and contacts onto the regular staff.

It wasn't a deliberate policy of racist exclusion. I believe it was simply thoughtlessness. The white correspondents from

Europe and America came to a country where blacks had long been regarded as fodder for menial labour, and in which well-educated young white boys would always have the advantage when it came to being hired. When I brought up the issue I was told that there was a shortage of suitable black journalists. But to be frank the BBC and the other networks weren't actively looking for them. The problem extended to the way foreign networks covered South Africa. Far too much attention was paid to the actions of white parliamentarians, far too little to the emerging political groups in the townships. Just as we did in our hiring policy, we paid undue attention to the white community because we identified with them, both consciously and sub-consciously. Because the leaders of the black community were either locked up or in exile we tended to think that blacks had nobody to speak for them, as if the everyday voices of the townships could not mediate the truth of their lives, and would have to remain dependent on the campaigning of white liberals.

This changed with the rise of charismatic anti-apartheid figures such as the Reverend Frank Chikane and, above all, Archbishop Desmond Tutu, and the emergence of militant activists in the townships. As it became clear from the late 1980s onwards that change was coming, we woke up to the real power dynamic of South Africa. It came from the factory floor and from the streets of squatter camps and townships all over the country.

~

I would have learned very little of the black reality in South Africa, and I would have missed so much of the country's intimate beauty, the love of life and optimism at the heart of the place, had I not had Milton Nkosi for my guide and friend. We experienced death and tragedy together and I was there when he claimed his birthright as a free human being in the elections of 1994; he has remained my best friend because I believe he knows me best.

In the townships he watched my driven moods, my determination to succeed and be the best, and he called me back to sanity when my determination to get close to the action brought me into mortal danger. I could pick out so many fine qualities, but it was his humanity, the willingness to see the possible good in all South Africa's people, that drew me close to him from the start.

The relationship of correspondent and producer in news is delicate. At its best they work together to get the best story. But ego gets in the way. Most often the correspondent's ego. Stick a man or woman in front of a camera and microphone and they become altered beings. When there is a triumph the correspondent takes the praise. When it's a disaster blame is sprayed everywhere, and frequently at the producer. It has been this way since broadcast news was invented. The average news producer also knows that the reporter usually carries more clout with the bosses. This is particularly true for producers hired locally. To whom do they complain if the reporter walks all over them?

This was complicated in Milton's case by the racial dynamics of South Africa. The white man – even a journalist with liberal credentials – was treated with habitual deference in most of his encounters with black South Africa. So when we hired Milton I was wary that he might be in awe of me. I was wrong. My new producer was self-confident and bright. He was also very funny. When I met him first Milton was working as a 'runner'. He ferried tapes in and out of the townships for Visnews – the international news agency which shared an office with the BBC.

I'd just come back from a press conference at ANC headquarters when he appeared in the doorway. He was eating a hamburger at the time. Fast food of many kinds – from burgers to biltong, the dried meat beloved of Afrikaners, to scraps of goat meat plucked from the braziers of township hawkers – would be a constant theme in our lives. We ate on the run.

I was struck by the fact that he waited until he'd finished the food before speaking. It suggested self-assurance. The man would talk when he was ready. 'I heard you might be looking for someone to work with you?' he said. Not: 'Please, Mr Keane, can you give me a job.'

Then Milton Nkosi smiled. It was the kind of smile that is already halfway to being a laugh. It also sparkled with mischief. I was disarmed by him. So instead of saying what I would have said to any prospective job applicant: 'Can you write me a letter and drop it off along with a CV?' I invited him to sit down while I made some coffee. Then I asked him to describe what experience he had.

'Where do I begin?' he asked.

'Wherever you want. Whatever you think is relevant to the job.'

'Suppose it's all relevant?'

'Then tell it all.'

So he did.

Milton was a child of the age of rebellion. He'd been born in 1966, six years after the Sharpeville massacre when scores of unarmed demonstrators were shot down for protesting against a law which required them to carry passbooks in order to enter white areas. Milton's father Henry had been active in the ANC Youth League and secretly worked for the organisation after it was banned. His mother Bridgette worked in Johannesburg in a white-owned factory that made outfits for domestic servants. Henry's tribe of origin was Swazi and his wife was a Tswana. Under the grand apartheid of Prime Minister Hendrik Verwoerd they both technically belonged in separate black homelands. But tribes were never part of the political discussion in Soweto, Milton explained. 'My folks were South African. I was South African. That was how we all saw ourselves.'

One of Milton's earliest memories was listening to Henry's most prized album, a recording of Miriam Makeba and Harry Belafonte singing songs of the struggle. 'What I remember was that me and my brother Twoboy were sitting with my dad. He put this record on and said we should listen to it, but he had the volume turned down to level one so you had to really strain your ears to hear it.

'Now in the townships if you have a record you play it at top volume, we're not big on noise control. When I asked him why it was so low he said: "Boy, don't you understand if someone hears this and reports us to the police I can be arrested!" That was the first time really I understood something was seriously wrong with this country. They can stick you in jail for listening to a song!'

Milton's father had been forcibly removed from the township of Sophiatown in the 1940s. As well as being the home of township jazz, Sophiatown was the parish of the great anti-apartheid campaigner Father Trevor Huddleston, and it was much too close to the white city to be allowed to remain in black hands. The black homes were levelled and a new white suburb built called Triomf or 'Triump' – with the blunt stupidity and spectacular insensitivity for which apartheid would become infamous. Henry Nkosi was sent to live in Orlando West in the south-western townships or, as they were becoming known, 'Soweto', a constellation of what were then called 'native locations' like Meadowlands, Dube, Orlando and Zola.

Growing up in Orlando West, Milton was hardly aware of the white world outside.

'The only whites I encountered were very hostile people. They were cops or people who worked for the Bantu Administration Board. They were whites who ruled the lives of blacks. Later when we were a bit older and went into the city you got to know whites as people who would make you get off the sidewalk if they were passing. The only nice whites I knew were the priests in the township. There was an archbishop who confirmed me into the Anglican Church and I remember that even though he was important, a big white man, he talked to me like I was a human being the same as him.'

In the southern winter of 1976, Milton was a pupil at Belle Higher Primary School. On the morning of 16 June, the school sang and prayed as usual at assembly and then filed into class. Halfway through the morning Milton heard singing coming from the road outside. The whole class jumped up and looked out the window:

'There were loads of school kids outside singing and chanting. They were shouting "Away with Bantu Education" and waving signs. The police were there too and shouting at them to disperse. So we stand there watching and notice that the crowd is getting bigger and more and more police are coming too.'

The teacher told Milton and his classmates to hide under the desks. Soon after that the shooting began. Tear gas filled the air. There was a lull and it sounded as if the demonstration had moved on. Milton ran outside.

'There was blood everywhere. It was on the road, on the windows of cars. Some of the kids started to pick up stones and went to where the police were and started fighting with them. I ran home 'cos I was worried where my kid brother was. The lady who was minding us while my parents were at work said he hadn't arrived. I ran out looking for him. Man, it was the longest ten minutes of my life. As I am looking for him this kid I know called Mayibuso comes down the street with a small boy in his arms and I can see in the distance that the kid is bleeding. He was wearing a uniform just like my brother, and for a moment I thought it was him. Then he got close and I saw it wasn't and Mayibuso just said: Go home, go home.'

Milton found Twoboy. Later he found out that the child being carried was eleven-year-old Hector Petersen, the first victim of the Soweto riots. A photographer came on the scene and caught the image of the dying boy being carried away from the rioting. It became one of the iconic photographs of the struggle and would devastate the lives of all connected with it. (Mayibuso would die in exile in Nigeria.)

The Nkosi boys were not township radicals. Henry and Bridgette were solid ANC supporters but they wanted their sons to be educated, and they urged them to stay off the streets as violence erupted again in the early 1980s. But both boys were caught up in the escalating crisis that would lead to the State of Emergency in 1986. Twoboy was on his way home from school when he was caught up in a riot and shot with a rubber bullet, and Milton was taking part in a demonstration against the army when he was arrested on the eve of the Emergency.

'They stuck these army patrols outside the school. It was like having to go through a checkpoint every time you went into school. So we got mad and were shouting at them. Then it all kicked off. They were beating us and we were running in all directions. I ended up hiding in a toilet with another guy when the door bursts open and these two blond, blue eyed Afrikaners with guns are screaming at us.' Milton was taken to a police station and there experienced one of those small epiphanies that shape a consciousness.

He was sitting in a back office with the other detainees. The police had placed a vicious dog in front of them. Every time they spoke or moved the animal growled. What worried them most was that their names hadn't been taken or their finger-prints recorded. This was at a time when the police were 'disappearing' activists. It occurred to Milton that he could be tortured and killed without anyone being the wiser. The police would simply deny he'd ever been arrested.

The same thought had occurred to a young policeman arriving on duty.

'This white guy comes in and sees us. Then he shakes his head and starts saying he is sorry.

'He said he had been conscripted and didn't want to be in the townships at all and that what was happening was wrong, and that he was a pharmacy student at the University of Cape Town and just wanted to go back and finish his work. Well, this young cop got rid of the dog and made sure we had our names put in the station log book and our prints taken so they couldn't just kill us and dump our bodies. I won't forget that ever. It was the first time I'd seen a white in a uniform behave decently. It showed me they weren't all evil.'

~

Had Milton Nkosi not walked into my office and asked for a job I know I might now be dead.

The notion of the faithful guide who saves the Bwana is such a wretched colonial cliché that I half draw back from describing how Milton kept me safe. But I do so because we never saw each other as anything but equals, and when he intervened to help me in dangerous times, he did so as my friend.

His ease with people is a legend in South African journalism. Once when we were surrounded by a group of hyped-up Zulus, waving their axes close to my face, Milton reminded them that he was a Swazi, a tribe that is regarded as an offshoot of the Zulus, and spoke in the patois of the rural areas from which they came. After a few minutes of this we were being welcomed like best friends.

On another day, a day of madness in Kathlehong, we were following some ANC leaders on a tour of burned-out houses when a sniper opened fire from a nearby hostel. The bullets chipped the concrete of walls where were hiding, and sent little spouts of dust flying in the air. As we ran around frantically, I saw a photographer colleague, Abdul Shariff, running in the direction of the sniper. Then a few minutes later he was running back along with a team from Sky News. More shots rang out and Abdul screamed and toppled over. I saw his body being pulled past us and shoved into a car. There was more gunfire. I felt a strong hand pulling me down. It was Milton. We rolled on our stomachs towards the roadway and then inched along to where he had parked the car. As we reached it Milton jumped in first, started the engine and screamed, 'Get the fuck in now.'

Then he spotted something to our left, behind the cluster of houses near to where Abdul had been shot. 'There's someone wounded,' he said.

A reporter we knew waved at us. A few seconds later we were helping a young journalist from the South African Broadcasting Corporation into the car. A bullet had whipped past, grazing her side, just missing her stomach. As we sped down the road to get to hospital and away from the shooting the car hit some gravel and went into a spin.

Milton stayed cool. He took his hands off the wheel and allowed the spin to finish. The SABC woman got to hospital. We got out alive.

When my BBC colleague John Harrison was killed covering the violence before the elections, it was Milton who drove with me through the night to recover his body, through an area where neo-Nazi gunmen and ANC radicals were setting up roadblocks and shooting at will. In the anguished aftermath of that death Milton was the strong, confident one, and I leaned on him and listened to his counsel. Before I met Milton

I was ignorant of black lives. I had a learned understanding of apartheid, but with Milton I began to hear the voices that would have been hidden from me without this sensitive interlocutor.

CHAPTER EIGHTEEN

People Are People

People are people because of other people.
South African proverb

Milton used to call me 'Irish'. Or 'Paddy'.

'Hey, Paddy, get your ass into gear. It's all happening.'

Had it been an English voice I might have bristled, the old atavistic impulse ready to jump at the perception of a slight. But Milton and I had gone beyond all that. We teased each other continually.

'So, Paddy, when are you going to invite the squatters to come and share your house? We're going to take it anyway when the revolution comes.'

Or:

'So, Paddy, when are you Irish going to come and help us drive the Boers into the sea?'

I would remind Milton that in colonial times Irishmen had helped both the British and the Boers to keep the blacks in their place.

'Ah, I knew it,' he would reply. 'You are just imperialists like the rest of them.'

'Not so, comrade. Don't talk to me about oppression. You lot are just youngsters. Three hundred and fifty years is nothing. Try seven hundred years of the Saxon boot on your neck.'

'Don't give me shit, Patrick – I'll tell those hillbilly Zulus you're an ANC communist and they'll kick your ass.'

And so we went on bantering through the countless waiting hours and long journeys.

By the time South Africa's first multi-racial elections approached in the southern autumn of 1994, Milton and I had travelled to every corner of the country. Much of our reporting was based on the violence that threatened to derail the transition. But my friend taught me that war was only part of a complicated equation. He continually pushed me to see how black people lived, to listen and try and negotiate a way past the ritual response of 'we are suffering' which greeted every microphone and camera in the townships. People most definitely *were* suffering. But black lives were also joyous and creative; an amazing dignity and generosity were preserved in places where one would have expected meanness and anger. Like Swanieville.

~

Swanieville was where I reported my first African massacre. It happened the day after I'd arrived from Belfast, and several weeks before I met Milton for the first time. I was woken by my bleeper. At least ten dead, it said, maybe more. Swanieville was what apartheid planners called 'an informal settlement'. These were the squatter camps to which the rural poor flocked in the 1980s and '90s, destroying the dream of grand apartheid with its plan for blacks to be contained in 'independent' states in the remotest, most impoverished parts of the country.

The settlement at Swanieville took its name from the local Afrikaner farmer who had rented some of his land to poor people from the ANC heartland of the eastern Cape. On the other side of the highway, close to the white town of Krugersdorp, was a hostel stronghold of the Inkatha Freedom Party.

Just a few hours before my bleeper went off, a party of hostel dwellers had attacked Swanieville. Anne came with me and we sped out along the highway to the west, keeping an ear to the local radio bulletins. *702 Eyewitness News coming to you from the heart of Johannesburg . . .* The death toll was rising. More than twenty, the radio now said.

I saw the smoke from the side of the road, thin trails of grey floating up over the settlement. We turned off the main road and crossed a sandy track. Closer in we swerved to avoid a police armoured-personnel carrier coming the other way. After that we saw a line of refugees. They walked past us, some sticking their hands out for a lift, others looking as if they were in a trance, trudging forward with the few possessions they'd managed to salvage. Closer in I saw that the smoke came from smouldering shacks. People picked at the wreckage of their homes. *Homes.* I hadn't thought of these corrugated shacks as homes until Anne used the word.

'My God, look, they've lost everything. All their homes must have gone up in the fire,' she said.

Then I saw women and children, sitting around in small groups, wrapped in blankets, not saying anything and watching us with wary expressions.

We got out of the car and started to walk along the line of shacks. I saw patches of blood where bodies had been lying. Then I saw a body. It was a man lying face down, with his head on his arms, as if he was sleeping. He looked like a drunk, someone who had fallen here during the night. At any moment he might wake, look around him and stand up shakily before weaving his way home. But there was blood coagulating around his head and neck and on the ground where he lay. Somebody had struck him with a machete or an axe. The cuts were open and flies were already pestering the wounds.

The camp was located on the open veld. There was no protection from the winter wind. The smoke from the smouldering shacks was now joined by swirls of dust. It floated across the dead man and blew into our faces. We recorded some interviews. The people told a story that would become familiar to me in the years ahead. The Zulu war party descending after dark. The screams and shouts. The burning. Shots and small explosions as braziers were knocked over and paraffin lamps thrown to the ground. Some of the squatter camp residents described how they had seen white men accompanying the attackers.

It would later be established that the police had helped the hostel dwellers. Throughout this period the President, F. W. De Klerk, denied that there was official collusion in the slaughter. De Klerk did not himself order or organise the killings, but like any other South African he could see what his security forces were up to, and he was bitterly castigated by Mandela for doing little while the townships burned. De Klerk's assertion was that the violence was caused by fighting between blacks, a matter of regret but not the responsibility of the white state. Now we know that elements within the police and military intelligence worked to foment the violence and took part in attacks. It suited his purpose to have black South Africa divided, to allow Buthelezi's supporters to weaken the ANC ahead of the electoral battle he recognised as inevitable. Not for the first time in my life I realised that a man could be capable of acting for the good – in De Klerk's case by ordering the release of Mandela – and yet also be guilty of cynical disregard for human rights.

I believe De Klerk ordered Mandela's release because he recognised that to keep him in jail would ultimately lead to an unstoppable black revolution. But in releasing him De Klerk thought he would be able to control the process; after all, blacks had been controlled in every sphere of their lives up to that point. Just as Gorbachev learned in the Soviet Union, De Klerk would find that long-restrained forces would sweep away his plans. The truth which Anthony Trollope recognised in the nineteenth century – that South Africa was a country of black men and always would be – could no longer be avoided. The time was coming when whites would have to accept the share of power that their minority status had ordained for them.

That time would come too late for the dead of Swanieville. But before the elections I went back there with Milton. At his urging – 'Paddy, you've got to really see how these people live' – we arranged to spend the night at the camp, sleeping in one of the shacks. The plan was that we would talk to residents and make a feature for the *Today* programme. Most of the people we spoke with beforehand said we were mad.

'You'll be robbed or killed or both.'

Anne was more sanguine: 'It can't be any more dangerous than what you are doing every day.'

Which was true. Since the massacre Swanieville had been quiet. The worst violence was taking place on the East Rand.

The most concerned were Milton's black colleagues. Most were regular township residents who regarded squatter camps as sinkholes of violent crime, and many of their residents as unreliable hillbillies. But Milton said he'd spoken with the local ANC. As long as the hostel dwellers didn't attack again we would be fine.

On the appointed night we drove out to Swanieville. At first things didn't go well. I heard a youth on the corner shout: 'Get that white fucker out of here.' It was understandable given the role of the white state in the violence that had nearly destroyed the camp. Milton was as ever an emollient figure, walking from shack to shack explaining our presence, deliberately spending longer with the younger elements, and playing up his own 'struggle' credentials.

'I told them about my background. A prince of the struggle,' he joked.

'Did you tell them you spent a week in jail and not twenty-seven years?' I chided.

He laughed. 'Don't be a wise guy. I am saving your white ass.'

That night was bitterly cold. A woman named Maria had invited us to be guests in her home. She had created two 'rooms' by draping a curtain across the middle of her shack. The shack itself was constructed of pieces of corrugated iron, plastered with old magazine pages for decoration and hammered together into a rough box shape. It smelt of paraffin. Some ten million black South Africans lived in similar conditions. In summer they were roasted by the sun and drenched by the afternoon rains; in winter the cold whipped through the many gaps in the iron and drove out any heat. Sometimes a child or an animal would knock over a stove and a shack would be set on fire, and because the shacks were all so densely packed together, the flames would spread. Every year, thousands were made homeless in this way. Yet still people flocked to these locations. In the city there was the chance of work. Back in the over-grazed, soil-eroded and corrupt homelands there was nothing.

It was one of the most physically uncomfortable nights I can remember. Milton and I lay on a double bed with wind slicing across us. Even though we were fully dressed and had a blanket it was impossible to sleep. There was the cold, the barking of the dogs, the noise of reggae blasting from another shack, a couple arguing, a baby crying. Noise travelled through these shacks like the wind. We talked about the chances of another attack by hostel dwellers.

'Nah. They've made their point. Anyway, the publicity would be too bad for the cops,' I said.

'You think those fuckers care about bad publicity. Come

on, will you! Look at everything that's happened,' Milton replied.

'But this place has been taught its lesson. The ANC is quiet out here. There are other places they want to harm more.'

It was one of those eternal 'calculate the odds' discussions beloved of journalists in conflict zones.

Milton nudged me. 'Look, man, if we keep talking like this we are going to frighten the shit out of ourselves.'

So he started talking about his love life. He was between girlfriends and bored.

'Hey, man, I don't know what my heart is telling me these days.'

'I don't care,' I said. 'I want to go to sleep.'

Just as the sun was coming up I heard a noise. Milton was wide awake too. It was a scratching sound, like somebody trying to pick a lock. I immediately thought of our car.

'What's that?' I whispered.

'Fucking *Tsotsis* – gangsters,' Milton replied. Then we did what any sane person would not do – we both jumped off the bed and ran to the door. We both hit it with such force that the shack trembled.

I genuinely feared it would collapse. Milton eventually got the door open and we lunged out. The thief stood directly in front of us, unconcerned, almost arrogant. It was a chicken, a scrawny beast that had been picking away at some seeds lodged in the hubcap. Milton aimed a kick and the chicken took off squawking into the veld. Then we heard laughter. Across the road a man was washing himself, and laughing uproariously at us. It wasn't every day that a white boy came galloping out of a shack after being terrorised by a chicken.

People Are People

Vat is verby verby
what is past is past.

Nelson Mandela, at his inauguration as President of South
Africa, May 1994

If I ask myself why South Africa mattered so much to me, why
it still does, I come up with a variety of reasons. The things
that attracted me as a lonely, dreaming child – the sunlight,
the landscape, the mystery of a 'wild' continent, the promise
of escape – are all still part of the attraction. But over time
something much deeper emerged. It had to do with hope. And
also with how we face the past.

In my work I told the stories of people who were bereft.
They had lost loved ones, seen their homes destroyed. They
had been shoved from one part of the country to another; they
had been classed as less than human under the law, they were
despised and humiliated.

But there was dignity in these camps. I saw it in the way
people like Maria had plastered their walls with the brightest
pages from magazines. Paltry decorations, I know, but a little
statement: *We know that we are cast down but we are not
defeated.* And I saw it too on numerous mornings driving into
the townships in the direction of the war, passing the lines of
schoolchildren in their uniforms going the other way. They
were children whose parents had risen early to wash and give
them breakfast, who had scrabbled to find the money to buy
them books and clothes, and who believed that in the next
generation all of this suffering might stop.

I saw it in Mandela's eyes one morning in a private breakfast
room at the Carlton Hotel in the middle of Johannesburg. Here
he was sitting with just three of us around a small table, gently
advising the waiter to bring him only very cool porridge because
the years in jail eating cold food had made him unable to bear

291

anything too hot. I cannot remember too many of the words he said at that table. I know he spoke of his determination to make sure that elections happened soon, and of how betrayed he felt by De Klerk, who had failed to act to stop the violence. But the words don't matter as much as the quiet strength he exuded.

On another day in a different place, I sat with him while he talked about the collapse of his marriage to Winnie Mandela. By then she had become a notorious figure, convicted in court of kidnapping a fourteen-year-old boy who was later found murdered. The old man was sad. He was vulnerable in a way that I had never seen before. The icon of millions, the confident figure I had watched addressing rallies in the townships and leading the ANC into negotiations, had been replaced by someone frail and heartbroken, a man counting the cost to his family of his own determination to lead. Yet Mandela knew that a nation watched every expression on his face and hung on his every utterance. So he came back.

Mandela was no secular saint. I believe that was his great strength. Watching him over the years taught me that a man is not great because he is different from other men. It is because he is like them, vulnerable to all of the same temptations, stupidities, vanities, but able to come through these, humbled but still hopeful.

~

On the day Milton was due to vote he collected me from home after dawn. We drank coffee in the kitchen. 'Can you believe it, eh?' It was Milton talking.

'No. After all that's happened.'

It was chilly and parts of Soweto were blanketed with mist. The April sun was slowly burning through. I thought of all the mornings we'd come here to count the dead. Now we counted queues.

They were everywhere. Outside schools and churches and civil offices. They were the longest lines I'd ever seen. Everybody we met was happy. I stopped to speak with an elderly woman and asked how long she'd been waiting.

'Since last night,' she replied.

'Weren't you uncomfortable waiting that long?' I asked.

'Young man, when you have waited all your life to vote a few hours in the cold is nothing,' she said. Then she laughed. Everybody was laughing.

All that year I had a line of script I'd been waiting to use. The line that would say to me and the listening world that apartheid was over. And so when I filed my despatch for the morning news it began as follows: *White rule on the continent of Africa came to an end at 7 o'clock this morning.*

This wasn't only about South Africa. In that Soweto churchyard Milton and I were watching the end of a terrible proposition: the idea that men could rule over other men because their skin was a different colour. From the Cape to Cairo white men had ruled this continent for over three centuries. They had taken its wealth, sold its people as slaves and then abandoned them to civil war and despotic leaders. If this last white government in Africa could end and be replaced with a real democracy then it might act as a rallying cry for the rest of the continent, an example of the possible.

I waited in the car as Milton went to vote. When he came out he was beaming. Years later he told me what he'd felt:

'You know, I went in and put this x on the ballot paper and I said to myself: "Is that it? Is that all we've been fighting for, sticking an x in a box?" Then as I walked out of the place and I saw all those people who were still coming in, my people, the people of the townships, and I saw the looks on their faces, that look of hope, that concentration! Yeah, then it hit me what it meant, and I could feel the tears in my eyes.'

Milton and I set up our mobile recording studio outside the

polling booth. Later that afternoon his mother, Bridgette, came to vote. On her way out she was accompanied by an elderly man, a neighbour of the Nkosi family called Simon Kaptein. We were reporting live to London at the time and I asked Bridgette and Simon to join the discussion.

Bridgette spoke of the beauty of the moment of voting. This Soweto woman who had spent her life making uniforms for the servants of white South Africa had been given an extraordinary choice that day. 'I never expected to live to see this,' she told me.

Then I turned to Simon Kaptein. He told how he had been 'banned' by the state for five years and how his sons had been tortured and harassed by the security police. He himself limped because of a beating he received from the police. I asked what this moment meant to him. He paused very briefly and then said: 'Today I became a human being once more.'

～

Milton Nkosi followed Mandela's example. My friend was not free from anger over the past. But he did not allow it to degenerate into bitterness or what the Holocaust survivor Primo Levi called 'the bestial vice of hatred'. In the years after liberation there was a Truth and Reconciliation Commission to investigate the crimes of the apartheid era. It achieved some success but was criticised by many for allowing the perpetrators and benefactors of apartheid – particularly the white leadership – to escape any form of justice.

A commission can go some way towards establishing the truth. The writing of a 'real' history can create a climate of openness in which reconciliation becomes possible. But true reconciliation is a journey that happens between individuals. It cannot be ordered by the state. Along with millions of South Africans, Milton is still making his journey. It may not end for generations but the point is not the destination. It is in the willingness to keep moving. There is a South African proverb. It says: *People are people because of other people.* Milton explained it like this:

'It's like John Donne and "No Man Is an Island". The same idea. We get our humanity from how we treat others.'

CHAPTER NINETEEN

Limits

We were overwhelmed, you see. We were overwhelmed by this great evil, by these acts of wickedness.

BROTHER OTTO, German clergyman, speaking to author in Kigali, Rwanda, June 1994

No two events could have been more different or could have told me such contradictory things about human nature. If one rejuvenated my capacity for hope, the other took me directly into the presence of evil. As the South African elections approached and I busied myself with preparations for coverage, an event occurred in a tiny African country far to the north which would change the lives of millions. The plane carrying the President of Rwanda, Juvenal Habyarimana, was shot out of the sky as it came in to land in the capital, Kigali. Soon after his death the killings started. Within three months up to a million people would be dead.

Though far closer physically than South Africa was to the terrain traversed by David Livingstone, Rwanda was not the Africa I had imagined as a boy. It was a land of absences. Nobody in their right mind, no matter how desperate their childhood circumstances, would ever have dreamed of escaping to Rwanda.

Rwanda was a civil war which was turned into genocide. It happened because educated men took the decision that it should happen. I had seen civil war in the South African townships and in Angola; in Northern Ireland I had seen people murdered for no other reason than that they were Catholic or Protestant; I had grown up listening to my father's stories of the communal atrocities which occurred in the Irish Civil War.

But my father, and his forefathers who fought in that terrible war, would have been driven to appalled silence by Rwanda. In the hills of Kerry there were limits. The war was fought among combatants. The idea of exterminating communities would have been unimaginable. Though there had been massacres in South Africa, they were not directed at the wholesale destruction of one tribe. That is not to say that in Ireland or South Africa or anywhere else, people were unaware of the idea of genocide. All of us who were children of the latter half of the twentieth century knew about the Holocaust; we had read about the Hitlerite injunction to murder justified with the phrase that men were merely 'biological Plasticine'. Some more of us may have been aware of the genocide of the Armenians at the hands of the Turks at the beginning of our century.

But these horrors existed as historical abstracts. When my mother pressed *The Diary of Anne Frank* into my hands as a child neither of us could imagine that I would one day find myself watching a genocide unfold in Africa.

I was not a victim of what happened in Rwanda. I was simply a witness. Yet bearing witness has its price. I am not talking about the nightmares so many of us suffered in the immediate aftermath of the genocide. Rather, the challenge which Rwanda represented to the way I wanted to see – and still try to see – the world, the knowledge it gave me about humanity.

What made Rwanda terrible had nothing at all to do with Africa. There was nothing uniquely African or Rwandan about the horror. I was and remain haunted by the universality of the lessons I learned, not only about mankind in general, but also about myself and the limits of my courage.

~

A few experts believed Rwanda or Burundi would be the next big drama. There had been massacres in Burundi a few months previously. Some estimates put the death toll at more than 100,000. In Rwanda there was fighting between the government and rebel forces. The rebels had been attacking since 1990 and had twice come close to capturing the capital.

Both states were caught in the same ethnic trap, and both had experienced periodic bouts of slaughter in the forty years since independence. In Burundi and Rwanda the ethnic balance was about the same. Hutus were 85 percent of the population, Tutsis around 14; an indigenous pygmy group called the Twa made up the remaining 1 percent. The big difference between the two states was who ruled who. In Burundi the Tutsis lorded it over the Hutus. In Rwanda the situation was reversed.

Both states had the misfortune of having Belgium as the colonial power. When you think Belgium in this context think of King Leopold. Irish people know about Leopold because our adopted son, our patriot hero, Sir Roger Casement, who died for Ireland on an English gallows, made his name exposing the human rights abuses under the Belgian king's rule. That was over one hundred years ago. Leopold set a benchmark for plunder and cruelty in Africa that local leaders, despite their best efforts, have never been able to match. By the time independence came around, Leopold was long gone. But the cynical and manipulative hand of Brussels was still at work. Under colonial rule the Belgians used Tutsis as the proxy rulers. But when Hutus began to organise politically, the Belgians switched sides. Then came the revolution and round one of the bloodletting.

Thousands of Tutsis were massacred and driven out of the country. In the intervening thirty years Hutus jailed, tortured and killed Tutsis. These were the basic facts as known to a handful of Western correspondents.

There was another 'fact' (later we would discover it was a big generalisation): all Tutsis were tall and thin and all Hutus were small and squat. There were several other 'facts' floating around. The Tutsis had come down from the north, possibly Ethiopia, centuries before. They were aristocratic. They were natural rulers. A German colonial officer (Germans had ruled the two states before Belgium) allegedly remarked: '*Ze tall ones are all arrogant, ze short ones are all stupid.*'

By the time the slaughter in Rwanda was under way these myths dominated international perceptions. None of us then understood that Rwanda was a country in the grip of an extremist elite, who believed that their own survival depended on the extermination of the minority population.

At one dinner party there was talk about the chances of a conflagration in Rwanda or Burundi. A correspondent from one of the big American papers spoke up:

'I've got a solution to this,' he said.

This man had a reputation for wisecracks. Everybody stopped. There was some expectant laughter.

'I know what you do with these guys. You issue an order: "Please, all of you Hutus and Tutsis line up together on the border. Now first all you short ones step to this side of the border." Then you wait until they've crossed. Then you turn to the Tutsis. "Okay, all you tall guys join the other tall people on the other side." Then it's sorted. The Tutsis in one country. The Hutus in the other.'

There was laughter around the dinner table. Why not?

Laughter was the only defence. If you started crying for all that was happening at the other end of those UN aid flights into Africa, you'd be at it until the end of time.

~

I was at home when the call came. An old friend of mine was on the line. David Harrison was a *Panorama* producer, now in his sixties and one of the most respected film-makers in Britain. He'd produced the landmark series *The White Tribe of Africa*, on the Afrikaners, and another epic, *The Africans*, on the history and future of the continent. I'd helped him out with a few stories over the previous year. Now he was returning the favour. I was flattered.

Up to that point I'd been a radio correspondent who did occasional bits and pieces for television news. A television editor in London had remarked to a colleague: 'I'm not sure Fergal is really one of us. He's a radio man really.' In the goldfish bowl of the BBC such comments travel fast. I was determined to prove him wrong.

Harrison told me that *Panorama* wanted me to go with him to Rwanda: 'You know where Rwanda is?' he asked. I did. Vaguely. One of our producers had gone there the previous year to make a short film about the gorillas that lived on the slopes of the Ruwenzori Mountains. 'Lovely looking place, but creepy as hell,' she'd said.

~

The news footage that was coming into our bureau during April and early May 1994 showed corpses bobbing up and down in rivers. There was talk of a death toll that reached into hundreds of thousands. But at that time I was preoccupied by the momentous events in South Africa. I had just finished covering the inauguration of Nelson Mandela as President of South Africa and I was feeling exhausted.

Besides, the Rwanda story was on somebody else's patch. The East Africa correspondent had been sent there for news when the violence started the previous month. Another BBC correspondent, Lindsey Hilsum, had been on secondment with UNICEF in Rwanda when the catastrophe erupted, and had filed the first vital reports on what was happening.

I asked Anne what she thought, should I go? She wasn't sure. What little she knew of Rwanda suggested that it was a country out of control. But I was impatient to prove myself on television. And if the human rights abuses were anything as big as the reports claimed, then, I felt, I had a moral duty to go. But Anne had heard my 'moral duty' spiel before. It always ended with her left at home, worrying and waiting for a call on a satellite phone from some village with an unpronounceable name where people were inflicting unspeakable cruelties on each other. She listened, unconvinced. I said yes to Harrison. I heard later that I was only picked after somebody else dropped out.

~

As the MSF convoy approached the border [post at Akan-yaru], Zacharia saw a group of ten militia armed with machetes chasing sixty to eighty people who were running on the road 'like cattle in a stampede'. Zacharia recalled: 'In front of us there was a man who looked very elderly to me because he had white hair. He could not run so fast and he stumbled. The militia [member] took his machete and he hit him with the machete on the side of the neck, right there before our eyes, directly in front of our car. We could see the blood that was gushing out . . . it was done in such a professional manner that he was

301

cut . . . they were crying for help, "Take us in!" But we had raised the window glass and the doors were locked. We could not take anybody in . . . All these civilians, sixty to eighty of them were pursued and hacked to death.'

. . . When the awaited convoy arrived, the aid worker went to get in his own car to lead them across the border. As he did so, two women with babies on their backs, ignored by the crowd, murmured a plea to be taken in one of the cars. The aid worker feared that doing so would attract the attention of the crowd to the cars and the Tutsi inside whom they were hoping to get across the border. He recalled that 'I would have preferred dying on the spot to saying no to these women and condemning them to death, but that is what I had to do.'

From 'Leave None to Tell The Story',
Human Rights Watch Report, 1999

The border post at the Akanyaru River must be one of the most pleasantly situated in the world. As you come over from Burundi the river rushes along to your left. Rising from the banks are steep slopes covered in pine. It looks like Switzerland, hardly a hint of Africa. Further up the road – about half an hour's drive in normal circumstances – is Butare, Rwanda's second city. Butare was the academic and theological capital of Rwanda, site of the main seminary for the Roman Catholic Church and, in the old days, the home of the Tutsi monarchy.

When we turned up around the first week of June, the attempt to exterminate the local Tutsi was almost complete. There were pockets still hiding out, stuffed into attics or starving in swamps, but the Interahamwe militia would soon track down and kill most of the stragglers. The killing had started late there, thanks to the peacemaking efforts of the local mayor. But after a visit by the prime minister of the new interim government, he was arrested and killed by the extremists. What followed was a frenzy of murder. As in the rest of Rwanda, Tutsis were killed regardless of age or gender. By the time it ended in the middle of July more than a quarter of a million Tutsis had perished in and around Butare.

Throughout, the radio station Radio Milles Collines – Radio of the Thousand Hills – had been urging the Hutus to fill the graves, and around Butare they were already stuffed with rotting corpses. Financed by businessmen close to the government, the station had been pumping out virulent anti-Tutsi propaganda for several years. It combined this with the best musical play-list in the region and presenters who weaved jokes into their racist tirades. As the slaughter got under way at least one of the presenters read out the names of prominent Tutsis over the airwaves. They were killed soon afterwards. We heard the voice of Radio Milles Collines at many roadblocks.

~

At the border the soldiers were sleepy. There were beer bottles lying around from the previous night. A transistor radio played Zairean pop in the background, all jangly guitars and high, trebly notes. A few of the soldiers had already begun a new day's drinking. The men who were supposed to stamp our passports were playing draughts with bottle tops. I expected them to give us a hard time. After everything that had happened here, was still happening, they should have regarded a television camera with horror. Besides, they were losing the war. The Tutsi guerrillas were closing in on their remaining strongholds.

But there was an atmosphere of ennui. The soldiers seemed tired. *Glutted from killing*, I thought. They examined our visas – some of the last issued by the regime from its Burundi embassy – and waved us through.

It wouldn't have been so easy without the advance work

Rizu had done. Rizu Hamid was a BBC producer who'd grown up in East Africa, who spoke fluent Swahili, and whose blend of persistence and calm would help to keep us all alive. With astonishing bravery Rizu had negotiated her way through the border alone the previous week, travelling all the way up to Butare and making contact with the officials responsible for the slaughter. She had managed to secure the help of an army sergeant who would come with us through the checkpoints.

The sergeant's name was Patrice and he was different to the men on border duty. He was softly spoken and had a gentle manner. He said he believed that we wanted to get the Hutus' side of the story. Which was part of the truth. Naturally we assured him this was our sole aim. When it comes to staying alive I will stretch any truth. I wondered what part Patrice had played in the killing, but it was a question I could never ask. We needed him too much. 'Trust me, when you see what's ahead of us you'll be glad he's with us,' Rizu said.

I have forgotten now how many roadblocks we negotiated – twenty, thirty, more? But what will stay with me until the day I die is the terror. Had I been a well-equipped Western soldier I would have regarded these men with contempt. A single airstrike aimed at one roadblock would have cleared the road all the way to Butare. A battalion of paratroopers would have swept the killers into the Akanyaru River.

But the world had decided not to act and so this rabble was free to murder at will. We were journalists, without weapons, and any one of these men could have killed us without fear of retribution. Every white man and woman on this road was suspected of being in league with the Rwandese Patriotic Front – the RPF – or of being a Belgian spy. The Belgians who had sent troops to take part in the UN mission were hated: *'Belgique?'* they would scream at us. *'Belgique?'*

Each time we shook our heads determinedly and shoved our passports through the window:

'*Non, non Belgique! Je suis citoyen de Grande Bretagne. Je suis citoyen Irlandais.*'

What did they look like? Like nothing really. They were peasants. Men of no property. It was the time and place, our knowledge of what they had done, which gave them the power of terror over us. They swung their machetes and clubs, and dangled their hand grenades in front of us. Most of the ones on the way up to Butare wore ragged clothes and had bare feet and came from the villages lining the road. Their houses were all packed tightly together. The Hutus and Tutsis had lived cheek by jowl. As I saw the physical structure of rural Rwanda unfold, all my questions about why Tutsis didn't escape down to Burundi were answered. How far would you get when your neighbours were that close and were watching every move you made? It brought to mind the great line from Heaney's poem 'Funeral Rights', about the killings in Ulster: '*. . . each neighbourly murder*'.

At a few of the roadblocks the Interahamwe were intrigued by our presence. As well as surrounding the car and looking at the passports they wanted to know what was happening elsewhere. How was the war going in the rest of the country? I wasn't too honest about that one. The peasants were being fed a daily bulletin of lies by Radio Milles Collines. Victory was assured. The 'cockroaches' – the name they gave the Tutsis – were on the run. Given the circumstances I wasn't about to disabuse them.

The truth was that Butare would probably fall to the hated Tutsis within a few weeks. Once they even came close to the city the Hutu population would flee to neighbouring Zaire. Mostly the Interahamwe wanted to justify themselves. We were told repeatedly about how the Tutsis wanted to make them slaves again, as they had been in the colonial days, a theme relentlessly driven home by the radio station. There was a massive inferiority complex at work here, fostered over centuries, of Tutsi and colonial domination and which four decades of Hutu rule had done nothing to change. Quite the opposite. Rwanda's Hutu leaders had constantly reminded the peasants of the bad old days. It was an alibi for clinging to power themselves. *If you get rid of us, if you weaken the Hutu cause, then the feudal days will return . . .*

We made it safely to Butare. The town was an armed camp. Fearful and suspicious, a town of bad secrets. The army and the Interahamwe had set up roadblocks on every street. Ten years after the events I still cannot convey properly the sick fear I felt in that place. It contaminated every encounter. With so many hundreds of thousands dead you knew that it had taken a great many hands to do the killing. So the hands you shook every day – the soldier at the roadblock, the militia- man checking your passport, that man who welcomed you at the hotel . . . what had they done? Or the wife of the rector of the university who sold you beer in her hotel? What was her role? Did she kill; did she pass on information, denounce her neighbours? Or was she one of the brave few who hid a Tutsi or tried to smuggle them across the border? Later I found out she was one of the worst of the killers – a woman I had sat and joked with, and thanked for keeping our drinks cold.

Primo Levi talked about Auschwitz being a place where the atmosphere was 'impregnated with evil'. That was Butare in the time of genocide. I met a university professor, a sophisti- cated man – articulate, with a taste for a good glass of whisky – who told me over a drink one night: 'Killing is a terrible thing, but in war people are killed. That is how it happens.' He claimed to have seen no massacres. The local Tutsis had all fled, he said. That was his explanation for their disappearance.

Only later did I learn that Dr J. Birchmans Nshimyumure- myi, vice rector of the University of Butare, educated in Canada, had been an ardent supporter of the genocidal regime, a Tutsi-baiter on campus, and heavily involved in the work of the local security committee.

~

At night it was always quiet. Nothing moved on the streets. On the road outside our hotel there was a checkpoint. The Interahamwe had lit a bonfire. When it was burning well the shadow of the flames played against the windows. Once or twice I heard them laughing at night. I suppose they could have killed us at any time. We knew that but didn't talk about it. What would have been the point? We were there. We had risked the checkpoints on the way up, and would have to face them again whenever we decided to leave. Might as well get on with the job of recording what had happened here, what was still happening.

My colleagues, besides David Harrison and Rizu Hamid, were also close friends. It helped greatly in the fraught atmosphere of Butare. Glenn Middleton, the cameraman, and Tony Wende who did the sound and doubled as a producer, were both veterans of the BBC Africa Bureau. We'd come through the test of the township wars together, and we could share our fear and talk about our families back home. I had wanted Milton to come with me but he was exhausted and needed for other things back in South Africa. Now I am profoundly relieved he didn't come. With his sallow skin and thin, straight nose he would have struggled to convince the racial purists of the Interahamwe that he was not a Tutsi.

~

I would never have slept in Rwanda without beer and whisky to take me down at night. I saved my ration for the end of the day. I was controlling my drinking. But my mind was becoming a jumble of images. Everything I had seen and heard during these weeks flashed back and forth. Massacre sites. Individual corpses. The shells falling on Kigali. A five-year-old boy with his leg torn off at the knee. The woman on the ground at the Red Cross hospital, half mad with fear, screaming '*My God, my God!*' ...

Once I dreamed I could hear the sound of the dead breathing. It was a husky sound, like asthma, only it came from thousands of voices. It blew over me, louder and louder until I woke up, my heart pounding.

One morning we went to the mayor's office. The atmosphere at the roadblocks was getting worse. We needed a pass to move around town. Outside the municipal buildings was a large group of refugees. They were some of the last Tutsis of Butare. I had never seen a group of people so wretched. Their clothes were in rags. They stank of sweat and wood smoke. They were clearly terrified.

They had gathered there after being assured of the mayor's protection. Sylvain Nsabimana was a small, fat man who wore a floral shirt and came from one of Rwanda's smaller political parties. He was Hutu and had replaced the murdered Tutsi mayor. At the time we knew nothing of his predecessor's ousting and murder. Nsabimana seemed pleasant enough. He was the first cooperative Hutu official we'd encountered. He signed a laissez-passer and assigned one of his assistants to travel with us. I asked him about the Tutsis who were camped outside. I said I had a bad feeling they would be killed. 'No, I do not think they will be killed. They have no guarantees. But they will not be killed,' he replied.

I was too distracted to ask the obvious follow-up. What did that mean?: *no guarantees*.

I should have asked him but we were too busy trying to film what we could of the Interahamwe in action, without provoking them to draw their guns and knives in our direction.

Besides, the mayor had organised an evacuation of Tutsis to take place in the next few days. He seemed at that time to be a moderate character.

The evacuees were Tutsi orphans, children who had seen their parents butchered. Some of them were wounded. I saw tiny kids with bandages on their heads where someone had hit them with a machete and, through the half-closed doors of the trucks, wide frightened eyes staring out at me. It was getting hot by the time we departed. The Swiss aid workers who were evacuating the children left the doors of the trucks partially open so that some air would filter through. I can still hear their voices chattering like so many little birds, until they headed in the direction of the border, and then they went quiet.

We followed the convoy through a series of roadblocks. We'd been told that on the last evacuation the Interahamwe had tried to pull children off the trucks to be slaughtered. This time Nsabimana accompanied the convoy along with several soldiers. I thought of his words: *no guarantees*. He was right about that. On this road where so many had been murdered in the past few weeks nobody had a guarantee, least of all a Tutsi child.

The journey took about half an hour. I sat beside Rizu. She was calm. My hands were shaking. Militia would wander out and wave us down. We were directly behind one of the trucks. I saw a militiaman with a machete lean in and look across the faces of the children. It felt as if everybody in the convoy was holding their breath. Then he waved us through. We reached the border unmolested. I watched the orphans being escorted into Burundi, past the soldiers and the last of the militia. I don't remember seeing any of them turn to look back.

That evening we tried to go back to film the Tutsis who were encamped by the mayor's office but we were turned away by the army. The soldiers were hostile and we were frightened. Already I felt we'd pushed our luck far enough. The RPF was getting closer and the atmosphere inside Butare was becoming increasingly fervid. My aim in getting to Butare had been to try and understand the hatred behind the slaughter. I feared now that it might consume us. So we turned away. We walked back to the car, got in and drove back to the hotel.

Early the following morning, Rizu set out with Glenn Middleton on a last mission. 'Only two of us should go. Any more and the militia will get suspicious,' she said. Rizu had tracked down a priest who'd hidden Tutsis and had witnessed some of the local massacres. He was living in the countryside outside the town. The journey, by their account, was fraught. The roadblocks were uniformly hostile and the priest, when they found him, was too scared to talk.

We brewed a last cup of coffee and then headed for the roadblocks and the border, out of Rwanda.

~

Several years later Sylvain Nsabimana was arrested by the International Criminal Tribunal for Rwanda and charged with genocide. The indictment asserted that there was far more to him than being a protector of Tutsi orphans. We could only report what we saw him doing. In that time of fanatics he seemed one of the calmer voices. His lawyer emailed me and asked if I would testify as a witness at his forthcoming trial. He was one of several Butare defendants.

I had seen Nsabimana do something that was ostensibly good. But I now knew about the circumstances in which he had taken power and I had read human rights reports which alleged he was an active participant in the slaughter of local Tutsis. Because I believe in the principles of international justice, and because the right to a fair defence should be an integral part of that system, I said I was willing to appear. The case dragged on. There were occasional emails. Then literally as this book was going to the printers I heard from the lawyers that the defence would soon call its witnesses.

Let me set the specific case of Nsabimana aside and ask a more general question. In a place consumed by genocide is it possible to be a good man and a bad man at the same time? If human nature is complex in ordinary times, then multiply the complexity a million-fold in time of war. In Nazi Germany there were SS officers who spared individual Jews. And in Rwanda there were Hutu extremists who protected some Tutsis while sending others to their deaths. Men claim often in war crimes trials that they did their best to save the minority. They point to individuals whom they spirited across the border or hid in the roof of their home. Very often they are telling the truth. Or they will insist that they only killed or participated in the structure of the genocide because they had no choice, or because they hoped to mitigate the excesses of their colleagues.

Deconstructing the evidence and denials is the work of international jurists. But for the rest of us there remains the agonizing question: if I found myself in such a place and time how would I behave? Would I resist the clarion call of evil?

~

Years later I went back to Rwanda to make a film for the charity Comic Relief. Thousands of Tutsi women who had been raped during the genocide were now dying of AIDS. The British charity was raising money to buy them anti-retroviral drugs and to help them establish communities where they could feel safe and supported. Towards the end of the trip I met a woman who was already in the advanced stages of AIDS. She had just come from having some tests in hospital when we met. I asked her where she had been living when the genocide started.

The woman explained that she had been living in Butare. I

told her that I'd been there too, in early June 1994. I said we had filmed the Tutsi refugees outside the mayor's office.

'I was there,' she said. Then she told of how the Intera-hamwe would come at night and drag people away. Men and young boys were taken to be killed. Women were raped. When the RPF got close to the town they were all shoved onto buses by the militia and taken out into the countryside. Some were killed; others escaped. I asked if she could remember some white men coming with a camera. Yes, she remembered that, she remembered white men coming. And she wondered why we had not saved them. There were two other people with me, listening to the conversation, Kate Broome, a BBC producer, and Esther Mujawayo, a genocide survivor whose husband was killed by the militia in Kigali. I said to Esther to please explain that I was sorry. We had been turned back by the army. We were very afraid. The woman said she understood. I should not worry.

Later I ran through all of the scenarios. Would we have been allowed to stay with the refugees? Probably not. What would have happened when the panic of retreat began, and the Tutsis were shoved onto the buses? Would the militia have tolerated our presence? Again, almost certainly not.

But after listening to the woman in Kigali I was forced to recognise the limits of my own courage. If you have never confronted evil in the form we witnessed in Rwanda, it may be hard to understand how we, and other journalists in other parts of the country, were able to leave threatened people behind. But I would ask that you try to understand this: we were confronted by something far greater than our own capacity for bravery.

I remember something a French clergyman, Father Henri Blanchard, said to me in Kigali after he and a German colleague had been evacuated, leaving behind a group of Tutsi boys in a building surrounded by the militia. He said: 'Somebody said to me that when they got out of Rwanda they would be insane. As for me . . . I am left with lifelong questions. What did I do that I should not have done? What did I not do that I should have done?'

As a child I had yearned to be heroic. I imagined all kinds of scenarios in which I would be brave, laying down my life for some glorious cause. But in Butare that notion had not occurred to me. All I knew was that I wanted to escape from that terrible place. I wanted to live. I discovered that I was no hero.

CHAPTER TWENTY

Valentina

I thought everybody in the whole world was dead.
VALENTINA IZIRIBAGWAYA

The first time I saw her she was lying on a mattress. It was a makeshift clinic in Rusomo, not far from the Tanzanian border. There were about five patients, four of them children. The room stank of disinfectant and septic wounds. There were two nurses struggling to take care of the wounded. They had some dressings and a few surgical implements. But there was no medicine. The little girl was about twelve years old but looked two or three years younger. She was thin like a famine victim, with huge eyes and teeth that seemed improbably large in her emaciated mouth. We were told her name was Valentina.

One of the nurses knelt down and started to clean her wounds. Valentina had a dressing on her head, and another on her right hand. When the dressing on her hand came off I could see that there were only stumps of fingers left. The entire hand was rotting and had turned black. The nurse daubed some antiseptic liquid on the stubs. Valentina winced and then whimpered.

The nurse then stood up and began to peel the dressing away from her skull. It stuck to the wound. Valentina grimaced

314

and gave a low cry. The nurse paused and then, very gently, resumed her work. When the dressing came away I saw a large gash at the back of the child's head. Like the hand, it was starting to turn black.

The child ground her teeth together as the nurse swabbed at the cut. There were no painkillers. All we had were some Panadol tablets which we gave to the nurses, along with some sweets. With her rotting wounds and severe malnourishment it seemed to me that Valentina would die. Rwanda was a country full of the dead and dying.

~

Valentina Iziribagwaya came from Nyarubuye, a nearby village. To reach it you take a left turn from the main road to Tanzania and onto a narrow track. At places on this track your vehicle descends into thick bush. The light is obliterated and the leaves of banana plantations brush against the window of the car. In the rainy season it is hard to navigate this track. Cars can become trapped, wheels spinning impotently in the mud while local children peer from behind the bushes. But they don't shout as other African children would. This is a country of silences and reserve. If you cross the bridge over the small stream without your car sliding off, the road gradually rises, becoming ever steeper until you gain the high plateau and see, far off to the right, the plains of Tanzania.

The name Nyarubuye means the place of stones, and it sits on a hill overlooking the Rwandan border with Tanzania. If you stand on the hill close to the great red church at Nyarubuye you can see the silver line of the Akagera River separating the two countries. There are rocky outcrops all the way between Nyarubuye and the border. It does not look anything like the rest of Rwanda. There are banana plantations, as there are everywhere else, but the landscape is more like the savannah of the east than the lush forests of central Africa.

Everything in this community happened around the church. The Hutus and Tutsis of Nyarubuye share the Roman Catholic faith and every Sunday, and on feast days and holy days of obligation, they would pray and sing together. Like Ireland it is an overwhelmingly Catholic country. But in Nyatubuye the faith was imported in the last century by Belgian missionaries – stern-faced fathers with pointed beards, who came from Flanders and the small towns and villages along the Dutch border. They saw Rwanda as a host of savage souls to be claimed in the name of Christ. They designed the church at Nyarubuye in the 1930s and it was built with local labour, most probably Hutu. By the time of the genocide there were no white priests left in Nyarubuye. They had died and been buried with their predecessors in Kigali or had gone home, pale and malarial, to finish their days in Antwerp or Bruges.

Valentina lived about a mile from the church. To reach the site of her home you pass the church on your left and continue along the track, past the school buildings and a row of mud houses, turning left into the bush just before you get to the village dispensary. There are only some stones left now from the foundations of the house. They are blackened from fire. In the years since the massacre, the area has become overgrown.

Valentina lived here with her mother and father and two brothers. Their lives followed the pattern of all rural lives in Rwanda. Awake before dawn, Valentina would go down to the family's plantation and work, or help to prepare the breakfast or lead the cattle to pasture, and after a breakfast of maize or bananas she would walk the ten minutes down the track to school.

The school was old and dilapidated. There were no windows and pupils sat crowded together on long wooden benches. Another girl told me how the teachers would ask the Tutsis in the class to stand up. In this way she became aware of how few there were compared to the Hutus. It was in school that Valentina became conscious of her *Tutsiness*. Valentina played games at break-time and sometimes the children would ask to see the palms of her hand: 'They said they could tell if you were Hutu or Tutsi by looking at the palm of your hand. But it was just a game, nothing serious.'

The history taught in the schools emphasised ethnic differences. It was Hutu history: stories of the downtrodden, enslaved masses and the glorious revolution which had destroyed Tutsi feudalism. In 1990, when Valentina was eight years old, the rebels of the RPF invaded from neighbouring Uganda. The exiles had lived in refugee camps since the Hutu revolution of 1959; many joined the Ugandan rebel movement that ousted Idi Amin in 1979. With military training they planned for a return to Rwanda. For years the Hutu state ignored the refugee problem and refused to countenance their return home. The RPF invasion shocked the Hutu state. The rebel advance was swift. They were only repelled with the intervention of French forces. But the invasion had triggered a merciless crackdown on the Tutsis living inside Rwanda. Valentina recalls that 'at that time people began to change. Even if you were playing with other children, they would pick a stone and tell you that they can kill you and nothing will happen to them.'

In the years that followed, as the civil war continued, the state began to demonise the local Tutsis. Thousands were killed. Many more were arrested and jailed. The radio propagandised against them. In the words of one writer, Gerard Prunier, Rwanda became 'a claustrophobic, airless hell'. Valentina, a child of a rural village, could sense things were wrong, but neither she nor her parents had any inkling of the disaster that was about to befall them.

When news broke on 6 April 1994 that the Hutu President Habyarimana had been assassinated, Radio Milles Collines immediately blamed the Tutsis. Many of the Hutu men of the

Nyarubuye district had joined Interahamwe groups and they now roamed across the hills attacking and setting fire to Tutsi homes. At night they hid out in the banana plantation and watched the flames rising from homes across the valley.

Mayor Sylvestre Gacumbitsi was the most powerful man in the district. He would become a key figure in my Rwandan story, someone who would follow me past the borders of place and time, a sinister presence which frightened and angered me, and which I would one day have to return and confront.

Soon after the President's plane was shot down Mayor Gacumbitsi visited the Nyarubuye area and said the Tutsis would be safe. Gacumbitsi was an archetypal Big Man of rural Africa. He had been hand-picked by President Habyarimana and was faultlessly loyal to the ruling party. His local influence extended into every area of life: he controlled the municipal land – a key power in an overcrowded country – and anybody who wanted a state job had first to go through the office of the mayor.

Gacumbitsi also controlled the municipal police force. When he came to Nyarubuye, Valentina was playing with some friends and saw the convoy arrive; the tall and well-built mayor with tribal scars on his face spoke loudly and gathered the local population around him:

'We were told not to leave our homes. To stay where we were and we would be safe . . . I don't know how it is in your country, but here when you lead people you are respected,' Valentina remembers. A few days later word came that the mayor had instructed the Tutsi population to gather at the church.

Thousands grabbed whatever possessions they could find and headed for the compound. At Nyarubuye church there were numerous outbuildings. Some of these housed diocesan offices, others were part of a Catholic school. As they arrived, the men, women, children, including many babies and elderly people, set up camp in the buildings. Many more were forced to sit out in the open. Soon the place was filled with the crying of children, and the thick, acrid smoke of hundreds of wood fires.

The local priests who lived there decided to flee to Tanzania. For the refugees this was a bad sign. From time to time Hutu men would approach the church and stare at them. It looked as if they were counting the Tutsis. But the refugees believed what Mayor Gacumbitsi had told them. They would be safe. In the past, when the Tutsis had been attacked, the churches of Rwanda had been places of refuge. 'They thought it was a safe place to go,' Valentina recalls. 'A church is a respected place. We thought nobody could be killed in a church.'

But Sylvestre Gacumbitsi, along with local military and police officers, had sent orders for all the Hutu men in the district to gather together and march on Nyarubuye church. On 15 April, as many as 7,000 men crowded down the narrow lane towards the church. It was a route many of them took when they went to church on Sundays. Dust rose behind the barefoot peasant army as it marched past banana plantations and maize fields.

A farmer watching from the hillside saw them arrive. 'They were so thick on the ground that not even an ant could have squeezed through,' he remembers. The marching men were all farmers who scraped a living from the overcrowded hills of south-east Rwanda. They were urged on by soldiers and policemen.

Valentina was inside the walls of the church compound when they arrived. First she heard the voices of Tutsi women screaming in panic. The men outside had covered themselves in banana leaves, hiding their faces from the neighbours they were about to attack. People inside began to run back and forth, searching for a hiding place. Valentina became separated from her family. She ran into a room near the diocesan offices.

For a while, nothing happened. The Interahamwe waited outside. The Tutsis watched them from within. Then Mayor Sylvestre Gacumbitsi arrived. He gave orders to the police to open fire. The Hutu peasants lay on the ground as the bullets flew into the compound. Grenades were exploded among the densely packed crowd of Tutsis, splashing blood and flesh onto the walls. All of the survivors remember the terrible noise – the crashing of automatic rifle fire, the explosions, people screaming, babies dropped by their mothers howling. This went on for about twenty minutes. When it ended there was the sound of dying people groaning, and still some of the babies, crawling around in the blood.

Then the order was given for the Hutu peasants to move in and kill. There were many Tutsis still alive, and Gacumbitsi and his cohorts wanted as many Hutus as possible to be complicit in the killing. It was the work of true Hutu patriots. That is what the architects of genocide called it: *work*.

For more than three hours they hacked, slashed and bludgeoned their neighbours to death. Valentina saw them come into the room where she was hiding with other refugees:

'They then started killing, hacking with their machetes, and they kept doing it and I was hiding myself under dead people. Because of the blood that was covering me they thought that I was dead. They were throwing children that they killed on top of me.'

There was a lull in the killing. Valentina thought she might have escaped detection. Then the Interahamwe returned:

'The killers who lived near our house came back to look among dead bodies. There was one of them named Anthony who was the ring leader. He started throwing stones at the bodies to see if there was anyone still alive. They were throwing dead babies on top of bodies to see if anyone was still alive. I got scared and began to plead with them; they then stood me up, smacked me and marched me outside. There were many more, lots of women and men hurt, some of them with parts of their bodies missing. Even my brother who could not walk was dragging himself on the floor to come outside and he was being beaten up all the time.'

Valentina was marched outside, to the grassy knoll in front of the main church. She saw two cars arriving. Gacumbitsi was in one of the vehicles, and was being followed by a pick-up truck on which a group of Interahamwe were sitting. The mayor got out of the car and strode over to where Valentina and other survivors were sitting. By now she was shaking with terror. Gacumbitsi asked why the survivors had not been killed. 'He then told the Interahamwe to pick up their weapons and kill everyone and that there should be no one left. He said they should kill us as they would kill a snake by hitting it on the head.'

Among the Interahamwe were two boys who were neighbours of Valentina. One of them was Ferdinand and the other one Pascal. 'I begged them to have mercy on me and Ferdinand told me that there was no mercy. He then called Anthony, who was talking to Gacumbitsi, to come and kill me. He then hit me with a club on my shoulder and I fell down. He then put his machete on the ground and took the club and smashed my fingers. He hit and hit until the bones were broken and the skin was driven into the ground. Then he picked up his machete and slashed me on the head.'

Valentina passed out. It saved her life. The killers assumed that she was dead and went away. Later she woke up and saw that, of her group, she was the only one still alive. Her brother lay among the dead in front of the church.

She dragged herself into one of the rooms. There were bodies piled everywhere. There was blood too, congealing on the ground, on the walls, everywhere she looked. Valentina lived there for over four weeks. *Thirty days among the dead.*

In the moist, tropical conditions the bodies began to

decompose quickly. The smell brought packs of dogs. 'One time a dog was eating the body next to me and I threw something at him and he ran away. I was always chasing them away whenever they came and they were coming only at night.'

One of Valentina's neighbours, an older girl called Pendo, had escaped from the compound and hidden herself in a banana plantation. As she was hiding she heard vehicles approach and peeked out. She saw Sylvestre Gacumbitsi: 'He was a friend of my father,' she said. 'Gacumbitsi had come to our home. When I saw him I thought that no harm can come to me.'

Pendo emerged from her hiding place. But when Gacumbitsi saw her his face contorted with anger. 'Why are you alive?' he demanded. He ordered his police to grab her and bring her to the truck. Gacumbitsi then took Pendo to the house of a local party councillor. 'He took me into a room and threw me down. Then he raped me,' she said. Then the mayor called the policemen – there were six of them – and told them to rape his friend's daughter. 'We are going to rape you to death,' she remembers him saying.

When the police had finished gang-raping her with their penises they violated her with their truncheons. Then they left her to die. But Pendo dragged herself into the bush where she was found by another Hutu. He was a man of conscience and, seeing the bleeding girl, brought her to his home, and eventually smuggled her out of Rwanda.

With the RPF guerrillas approaching Nyarubuye, Mayor Gacumbitsi and his Interahamwe fled across the border into Tanzania. The RPF soldiers who reached Nyarubuye in mid-May found Valentina and brought her to the makeshift clinic where I would later meet her:

'They told me I was brought there in the back of a van sleeping on a mattress. I could not remember anything myself. When I reached there I did not know where I was because it was the first time I went there. I wanted to scream but could not. I felt pain because the wounds were not healed and I had lost half my fingers and what remained was not healing. I thought everybody in the world was dead. I was waiting to die myself because I did not think I was going to survive.'

~

I reached the churchyard at Nyarubuye as spring turned into summer. The rainwater had already formed into little pools around the mounds of corpses. The smell reached us long before we saw the bodies.

Only once before had I smelt something so appallingly intense. I was about fifteen years of age, back in Cork, and a truck carrying rotting offal drove through the streets in the direction of the city dump. It was summer, the hot summer of 1976, and the stench from the lorry filtered across the narrow streets of the city centre. I gagged then at the smell of putre-fying animal flesh, swollen and fly covered.

The flesh that lay in twisted shapes at Nyarubuye was in a more advanced state of decomposition. The dead were no longer the swollen, blackened figures of the days after slaugh-ter, but were withering away, the skin falling off bones, the expressions on the faces like the faces of fantasy horror, jaws open still in mid-scream.

I can't remember how long we spent there. It was late evening, I remember that, and the sun was setting quickly. Glenn and Tony and David and I. We walked so softly, like people walking through a house late at night, trying not to disturb sleeping children. After a while we learned to look down at our feet every time we moved: bits of bodies, bones, heads, lay everywhere.

Somewhere among the mulch of rotting corpses were the parents and the brother of Valentina Iziribagwaya. In time they would be dumped in a mass grave. Wooden crosses would be placed above them and flowers planted, though most of the dead had nobody left alive to mourn them. With the coming of the rains each season, for year after year, some of the soil in front of the church would be washed away and would reveal pieces of cloth – brightly coloured pinks, yellows and greens, the African shawls of dead Tutsi women – and it would expose too the small bones of children who had died with their mothers, startlingly white amid the red dust.

The killers were gone by the time I arrived. But the survivors like Valentina whom I met at the Rusomo clinic had one name, above all others, that they wished us to remember. *Sylvestre Gacumbitsi.* He was their mayor. There was in their voices still something of the shock of betrayal; they struggled to understand how the man who had been their leader, who had promised them protection, could have become their killer.

I could never feel what the survivors felt about him; his role in their lives had been catastrophic, while I had been simply a witness. But I knew that if we could find him there was a chance of some justice for Valentina, and the murdered thousands of Nyarubuye. What we were seeing in Rwanda inspired rage. It would be wrong to say we felt a responsibility towards the dead. That is too neatly defined a way of putting it. I think it was a matter of instinct. Rwanda was full of situations which tested the limits of your courage. But here there was a chance to use our journalism to hold a killer to account. By that time we also knew that the country had been abandoned by the international community. The extremists knew this too. Wherever Gacumbitsi was hiding he would not be expecting a visit from a BBC television crew.

'He is gone to Tanzania,' one survivor told us. Another said the mayor had gone to the big refugee camp at Benaco, about an hour's drive away in Tanzania. And so we followed his trail down the road to the border, across the corpse-clogged falls at Rusomo and on to the camp at Benaco.

~

There were an estimated quarter of a million refugees in Benaco camp. I had never seen so many people camped out in the open. The camp itself had become a great arena of mud upon which makeshift shelters of blue United Nations plastic lay crowded for mile after mile. Into these the families of the Hutus of Nyarubuye and other parishes were now squeezed. They were a defeated people, and in their midst were men and women who had butchered their neighbours in the genocide.

The surrounding grasslands had been stripped bare. As we entered we passed lines of women carrying piles of wood, the chopped-down remnants of acacia thorn trees. Others queued with their children in long, patient lines to collect water from the temporary wells dug by the UN. White aid workers drove around in their four-by-four vehicles organising basic services for the refugees. I met a man from Texas and asked him if he knew that the 'community leaders' he was dealing with, the people to whom he had entrusted the work of food distribution, were mainly members of the Interahamwe, people like Sylvestre Gacumbitsi. He looked at me with a bewildered expression. No, he didn't know their history. He just had a job to do: feed the people.

In a place so vast, full of the residents of so many different parishes, I wondered if we would ever track down the mayor. Luckily for us the Rwandan obsession with order had been transported across the border. The old power structures were quickly reinstated when the people arrived at Benaco. So the Hutus of Rusomo, including those from Nyarubuye village, had set up camp together under the watchful eye of the mayor. To find Gacumbitsi we simply had to find where the people of

Rusomo were camped, and then ask around until we encountered him.

It took us only a day to find him. I looked recently at the footage of us marching into his compound, surrounded by his flunkies, and demanding answers about his role in the massacre. I can see my face twitching – the eyebrows jumping – like it did when I was a child and scared. Under pressure that old affliction always returns. I remembered that I felt two emotions at that moment: a great deal of fear and boiling anger. And so I made a fierce effort of will to be calm. My questions could be firm, but I could not lose my temper. Apart from being unprofessional it could also prompt Gacumbitsi's supporters to attack. As I strode up and started to ask questions I kept the image of Valentina in my mind.

I had to give Gacumbitsi credit for coolness. He never once gave the appearance of being scared by us. He was clever enough to know that being tracked down by a television crew and accused of genocide on camera wasn't going to make his life any easier, but there was still enough of the politician in him, and the bombastic confidence of the African Big Man, to make him stand his ground. I had the feeling that he cared more about what his supporters would think than the millions who might see the exchange on television.

As I stood directly in front of him I was conscious of his impressive physical presence: Gacumbitsi was a big man, taller and broader than me. It wasn't difficult to imagine him standing in front of a crowd of terrified people – how immensely powerful he must have seemed to them and to the Hutu peasants who were about to do his bidding. The mayor immediately denied that he'd done anything wrong. His conscience was clear. There was no blood on his hands. Him! A mayor! Commit a massacre? The idea was unthinkable.

And then he let something slip, just the smallest indication of how he really felt about the Tutsis. He turned the questioning on me and asked who had been spreading the stories about him. I replied that it was the Tutsi victims of Nyarubuye, the survivors of the massacre.

'Ah, I see. The Tutsis. The Tutsis.' There was venom in his voice. 'The Tutsis. What would you expect them to say? I am a Hutu. They hate me. What would you expect them to say except blame me?'

David insisted that I stay talking to him a little longer so that he could get some cutaway shots. Having accused the man of massacre I wanted to be out of there as soon as possible, but Harrison insisted. He needed the shots.

'All right, old bean. We're done,' he said.

'You can say that again,' I replied.

Gacumbitsi saw that the interview was over and left us. He went off to tend to some chore in the camp. Here he was an important man once again, helping the international aid agencies to dole out food stocks to thousands of his people, deciding who would sleep where, making sure that classes were started for the children, a natural thing for a former schoolteacher to do. The grime of camp life, the air that smelt of shit and smoke all day and night, none of that impinged on his imposing presence. For a man accused of mass murder and rape, he carried himself well.

~

I left Rwanda believing that Valentina Iziribagwaya would die. As I said before, Rwanda was full of dead and dying children in those days; there was no reason to be confident that the emaciated girl with terrible wounds would be an exception. I filed her memory away with my first child of war, Ande Mikail, whom I had seen dying in a tent in Eritrea a decade before, and with all the other children of war whose faces lived with me, but for whom we had been able to do nothing.

That is part of the life of a war reporter. We film them and we leave them. We make the familiar arguments: *If you want to be a humanitarian worker lay down your camera and note-book, join OXFAM . . . If you stop to rescue every wounded child you won't get the story out . . . If you get too close your vision gets blurred, you might become a better human being but your journalism will be crap . . .* Or, as Don McCullin, a long-time hero of mine, put it: *You can't focus with tears in your eyes.*

But Valentina was different. She would come back from the dead.

~

I left the country in the summer of 1994 convinced that Sylvestre Gacumbitsi would never face justice. When I went back two years later there was still no sign of an effective war crimes prosecution. Most of the Big Men who'd planned the slaughter had escaped. Some were encamped with hundreds of thousands of their followers, and large numbers of desperate Hutu civilians, in refugee camps along Rwanda's borders, still staging raids and terrorising the remaining Tutsi population. The lack of international concern over the genocide had now carried over into the criminal justice process.

Then, in 1996, the government of Tanzania, under pressure from the international community, started to empty the camps. The killers of Nyarubuye were sent home. I was sent back to Rwanda by the BBC and went straight away to Nyarubuye. The corpses no longer littered the front of the church and the compound. They had been gathered together and placed in and around the diocesan offices. It was a macabre display, an atrocity exhibition. The new RPF rulers of Rwanda wanted every foreign diplomat, every international journalist and aid worker who came to the country to see the massacre sites. The

328

feelings of survivors did not come into the equation. They were no longer at the mercy of an ethnic dictatorship, but they were still powerless. If the government wanted to stick the decomposed corpses of their loved ones on display for the world to see there was nothing they could do about it.

I met some of the survivors from the clinic at Rusomo. There was a woman there who had shared the small room with Valentina and the other children. I immediately asked after Valentina, assuming that she'd died. No, the woman said, she did not die. Valentina had survived. She had been taken to hospital in the capital and a foreign doctor had done an operation on her hand. They had fixed the cut on her head too.

I couldn't believe what she was saying. 'Are you sure? Are you positive it's the same person?'

Yes, the woman said, there was only one Valentina who was at the clinic. She was alive.

'So where is she now? Where can I find her?' I asked.

'She is back home in Nyarubuye. She lives with an aunt. All of the aunt's children and her husband were killed in the massacre, so she has Valentina now like her own daughter.'

I got directions for the aunt's house and immediately set off on foot up through the village.

The hut was like all village homes, made of mud with a thatched roof, but there were no other houses crowding in, and there was a large clean swept area of ground directly in front which looked out over the valley.

I knocked on the door, still not quite believing what the woman had told me. I wondered how this child could have survived and, if she was still alive, what her mental state would be like. The door was opened by a a tall, handsome woman. Her name was Leoncia, the aunt of Valentina, and yes, she said, her niece would be returning from the fields soon. It was late afternoon and we should have been on the road back to the town where we were sleeping. The Rwandan military escort was worried about the possibility of an Interahamwe ambush.

'We have to wait. This is too important,' I said.

After about twenty minutes some figures appeared from the direction of the banana plantation. In the dusky light I could not make out their features. There were two girls and they were carrying bunches of bananas. As they came closer I strained to see if I could recognise Valentina, but neither of the figures looked like the spectral child I had met two years before.

Soon the two girls were standing in front of the house and I saw that one of them had a deformed hand, a fingerless stump. And when I looked directly into her face I saw Valentina.

She caught my gaze for a second and then looked directly at the ground. There was no smile of recognition. 'Can you ask if she remembers me?' I said to the translator.

He repeated the question in Kinyarwanda.

'Yes, I remember him. I remember also the old man [David Harrison],' she said.

Valentina was unsettled by our arrival. I decided to leave the conversation at that and return the following day. Over the next week I came to see her every day. I interviewed her at length about what had happened at the church. But it was only close to the end, when she had come to trust us, that Valentina softened. That was largely thanks to one of the producers on the trip. Katherine Quarmby is one of those naturally kind people who occasionally appear in the hard world of television. By speaking about everyday things – music, clothes, school, even boys – Katherine managed to unlock the warmth in Valentina.

Valentina was fourteen years old now and already tall and graceful, with a slender face and soft eyes. She was conscious of her maimed hand and used her good hand to cover the ruined one whenever she met us. When it came time for us to leave Valentina was sad. We left her with photographs of us and our families and promises of friendship. 'You will come back?' she said.

Apart from our professional determination not to get involved, foreign correspondents are not good at keeping in touch. Our lives are filled with broken promises. To friends, families, the people we meet on the road. But I swore Rwanda and Valentina would be different.

Year after year Valentina called me back to Rwanda. I saw her grow from the hesitant child of that first returning into a tall, beautiful young woman, confident and determined to be more than a survivor who is pitied. I watched as she left her village school and went to boarding school in another town, and years later listened while she spoke about becoming a doctor so 'that I can heal and not destroy'. I do not have the words to adequately convey to you her courage or humanity.

Once after I'd been to visit her and she ran up and threw her arms around me, a Rwandan friend took me aside. 'Do you know that she tells the children at school that she has a parent who is white, a white father?' I was a bit unnerved at first. I was afraid that someone who had been so hurt would invest so much faith in me. And I thought of her real parents and how much she must have longed for them. At that moment I knew that Rwanda, Nyarubuye, Valentina would be part of my life until I died.

~

In time, the survivors like Valentina turned their minds and bodies to rebuilding their community. There were many challenges, not least the reappearance of the families of the Hutu killers and even some of the Interahamwe who were being allowed out of prison. The government told the survivors that they had to accept this, and Rwanda, with its centuries of autocratic tradition, was still a place where people did what they were told. As one of them put it to me: 'What are we to do? What choice do we have?'

In the years since the genocide, one question has dominated the minds of Valentina and the other survivors of Nyarubuye. Whenever I went there they asked me, 'Where is Gacumbitsi? What is the news of him?' At first I thought it was because they were afraid he would return, that somehow his immense presence could overturn the new, relatively peaceful reality of their lives. But it wasn't that. Valentina and the others wanted justice.

I told them what I knew, and it changed little from year to year. At first he had been in the camp at Benaco and when that was cleared he fled deeper into Tanzania. I heard rumours that he was in Mwanza, the port town on the shores of Lake Tanganyika, and later that he had gone to another camp run by the Tanzanian government. I kept telling them there would be justice some day. They nodded at that. They hoped but they did not really believe.

CHAPTER TWENTY-ONE

Witness

The point of genocide is to dehumanise. Always remember that it's not about another group out there it's about YOU. YOU could be in that situation, someone can decide they don't like Somalis, someone can decide they don't like Irish, or that they don't like white people and you will be in that exactly same position of powerlessness, helplessness and desperation. Always to remember that.

RAKIYAH OMAR, human rights investigator,
to the author, Kigali, 2004

Gacumbitsi was a gifted survivor. He was plausible. He could be charming. I can see how the various international officials he met in the camps would have been impressed. A man to get things done, they would have thought.

In the camps the mayor had rediscovered his old vocation, though it was no longer a question of choice. Sylvestre Gacumbitsi needed to work. The grand days when he controlled the bank accounts of the municipality had ended with the great exodus from Rwanda. And as the years tracked on, and many of his people went home, the mayor saw what was left of his power drain away. Back in Rwanda a Tutsi mayor sat in his old offices. Some of his old staff had been politically rehabilitated and given jobs by the new state. The hated enemy had taken the country, just as he had warned, and it had subverted the Hutus he had once ruled.

There was no question of him going back to Rwanda. He would be arrested and thrown immediately into an over-crowded prison, to wait for years until the Tutsis put him on trial, and eventually passed the sentence of death. They had already shot Froduald Karamira, a big money man for the regime; they took him out into the national stadium in front of a crowd of Tutsis, tied him to a post and put several bullets into him. They'd executed a female prisoner in the same batch. The Pope had complained, and the international community. But there was no certainty that it wouldn't be repeated with Gacumbitsi, should he ever fall into Tutsi hands.

He had stayed first in the camp at Benaco, working with the representatives of the International Red Cross and the United Nations. They must eventually have come to know what kind of man he was: as early as the end of 1994 the UN was well aware that many of Rwanda's mayors had been instrumental in carrying out the genocide. But for a while the situation worked well, for Gacumbitsi certainly, and for the international community. Then the new government in Rwanda decided it wanted to close the camps filled with killers on its borders. Gacumbitsi watched the fearful Hutu peasantry grab their blankets and pots and move homewards, across the Akagera in the direction of Rwanda and Nyarubuye.

But he escaped being sent back. He was still a man of influence and he managed to get out of the camp and flee deeper into Tanzania. He moved east from Benaco across the savannah towards Lake Tanganyika, to the port of Kigoma – just a few miles away from Ujiji, where the Arab slave market once operated, and where Stanley met my old hero, David Livingstone, during the Scramble for Africa.

There was a twice-weekly ferry service from Kigoma down

Lake Tanganyika to Zambia in southern Africa at the time of Gacumbitsi's escape. It was also possible to go across the lake to Congo. But in the late 1990s the traffic would have been entirely in the other direction as thousands of Congolese fled their homeland as the civil war, sparked off by the genocide in neighbouring Rwanda, emptied vast areas of their population. Did Gacumbitsi think of making a run for Tanzania? It's possible. Get to Zambia and you might make it to Zimbabwe next door. The Ethiopian war criminal, Haile Mengistu Mariam, was a guest of the Mugabe regime, and UN investigators of any type would get short shrift in Zimbabwe.

But in Kigoma, Gacumbitsi would have been watched. The Tanzanians were hosting the Rwandan war crimes trials at Arusha, near Mount Kilimanjaro, and they would certainly have been embarrassed had a senior suspect like Gacumbitsi been arrested entering Zambia from their jurisdiction. We must assume that the Tanzanians were happy to wait until the UN was ready to move against the mayor.

~

Almost exactly five years ago to that June day in 1996 when we first tracked down Gacumbitsi in the Benaco camp, I received a call. I was filming in south London when the news came through. David Harrison was on the line:

'They've got him,' he said.

'Got who? Who are you talking about?'

'Gacumbitsi. He was lifted in Tanzania.'

I immediately wanted to call Valentina. But she had no phone. I hoped the people of Nyarubuye would get the news on Radio Rwanda.

On the morning of 21 June, a small aircraft belonging to the United Nations Criminal Tribunal for Rwanda flew out of Arusha to Kigoma. The UN investigators linked up with the Tanzanian police, to whom they handed a warrant for Sylvestre Gacumbitsi's arrest on charges of genocide and crimes against humanity.

'He wasn't shocked when they came. It was as if he had been expecting it; he was almost relieved that it was over and that it was the UN and not the Rwandans who got him,' a UN source later told me.

I felt elated. I also felt relief. After it had walked away from Rwanda in 1994, the international community had a chance to redeem some credibility in the eyes of one small African village.

~

The email came from the office of the prosecutor. It was couched in formal legal language and said the UN prosecutors wanted to use our footage of the aftermath of the massacre and our interview with Gacumbitsi as evidence in his trial. I had heard that our documentary had been influential in making sure that Gacumbitsi was placed on the priority list for arrest by the International Tribunal. If prosecutors were going to use the footage they would also need me to appear in court and testify against Gacumbitsi. 'You've got to verify it,' said Richard Karagyesa, the young, Ugandan-born prosecutor.

I had covered human rights abuses for many years but I'd never been asked to go to court. There were those who believed a reporter was compromised if he went into the witness box for a particular side. Others said we endangered our own lives and those of colleagues by creating the impression that journalists were evidence-gatherers. But I didn't have a moment's doubt about testifying. To me the arguments for doing so far outweighed those against: the Tribunal didn't represent any 'side'; it was an instrument of international justice. My evidence would form part of the record; it would become a small block in the great wall of recorded history. It did not seem right to me that I could be a witness to genocide and then turn away, as if my profession exempted me from any human responsibility.

I also felt, deeply, that I owed it to Valentina and the other survivors – the ones who asked me, every time I went back to Rwanda, if I knew where Gacumbitsi was and who doubted that they would ever see him on trial.

~

The UN police collect me in Nairobi. We travel across the African savannah in an armoured four wheel drive with blacked out windows. I think the security precautions a little overstated but my escort, Jackie, a genial policewoman from Trinidad, assures me it is standard procedure in these cases. The UN is worried about the intimidation of witnesses. The majority of those being called by the prosecution in the Gacumbitsi trial will be appearing as 'protected' witnesses, with their identities and names concealed.

Now that the moment of trial is approaching, after months of waiting, I am starting to feel anxious.

I have just come from Liberia where stoned youths are running wild in the streets. They are looting, raping and killing. They chop their victims into little pieces. One photograph shows a severed head fixed to the front of a car with a cigarette in its mouth. So apart from my worry about the case, I am also feeling a bit weary of Africa. When will this insanity stop?

Nearly ten years have passed since I last saw Sylvestre Gacumbitsi. Back then he had been arrogant and so sure of himself. As we speed towards Arusha I keep trying to picture him in prison. I saw some footage when he was first arrested and indicted. He looked like an African businessman, one of those confident, well-fed-looking men you meet in the Tamarind restaurant or the Muthaiga Club in Nairobi.

But I think that he might have lost some weight since then. In prison the Hutu defendants are allowed free association. I've heard they wander from cell to cell and are allowed to make calls. They are held in a clean and orderly UN facility outside the town. Compared to the fetid, overcrowded jails in Rwanda it is paradisaical. Some of the defendants who are HIV positive are being given anti-retroviral drugs by the UN. All of this is only proper, but it contrasts badly with the experience of the female genocide survivors in Rwanda who were raped and who are now dying from AIDS with no access to such medication.

Only once before have I appeared in court, as a witness in a libel trial involving a man wrongly accused of IRA membership. Although I wasn't the defendant I found the whole experience deeply unnerving. I hated the feeling of exposure, the sarcasm of the lawyers, the grim expression of the judge, all the ludicrous pomposity of the legal profession in full roar. Even the most innocent of men can feel an urge to stand up and scream: 'I'm guilty, your Honour, I did it. Just get me out of here!'

I don't tell the policewoman I feel nervous. I figure anybody who shepherds frightened Tutsi survivors in and out of court every day can do without my little anguish. I am afraid of what the trial might churn up though. I have worked hard at dealing with my memories of Rwanda. Going back regularly and meeting with Valentina and the other survivors helped. You stay in touch because you can see little glimmers of hope and progress. It's small a lot of the time, but if you focus on the individual, like Valentina, you really do notice the changes.

But arriving in Arusha I am ambushed by gloom. The town is crowded with locals and foreign tourists. Jackie drops me off at the hotel and says she will come back later to bring me to meet the prosecutor. 'You are the first witness up for the prosecution, so he wants to prep' you first.' Ahead of me in the queue at check-in are a couple who have come to climb Mount Kilimanjaro. There are other people joining safaris. All around me is a happy buzz. But I don't feel a bit of it:

'Have you seen the Masai on the road? It's just amazing, the way they still dress like they have for hundreds of years.'

'How much do you tip the guides?'

This is the other Africa. The Happy Park. Nobody is hacked to death or raped or starved here. This Africa is full of smiling, friendly Africans. On the road to Kilimanjaro the tourists will pass the turn-off to the UN prison, but their attention will be distracted by the fields full of huge sunflowers, or the Masai herding flocks of sheep, and then they will see the mountain, so beautifully serene, rising out of the plains. They will fall into dreamy contemplation and feel that Africa has touched their souls. When they leave they will carry dreams of Africa, like the dreams I'd known as a child, and they will long to return. I do not begrudge them their ignorance of the crimes revealed in the courtroom on the other side of town. Good for you, I think. Good for you. In time I hope to find that dream of Africa again.

For all my high-minded declarations about international justice, and the private sense of responsibility I feel towards the survivors, I want badly to be elsewhere. There is a line in Günter Grass's novel Crabwalk, *where he talks about German history being like a toilet that won't flush: 'The shit keeps coming back up.' That's what I feel about Rwanda and the genocide.*

People said to me beforehand: 'The trial will give you some closure.' No. That is not the way it works. Nothing is cancelled. You move on, of course. You don't deliberately conjure up the images or the fear of that time. But every now and again in the middle of the night it surprises you, a face from that graveyard flashing out of the darkness.

Jackie comes to pick me up in the afternoon and we drive out of town to a safe house. The armoured vehicle drives into a tiny yard. There are some women standing around. Survivors. But I don't recognise any of them. I am shown into a long, cool room, with bare concrete floors and a sofa where the prosecutor, Richard Karagyesa, is sitting.

He smiles and rises to greet me.

'My man,' he says. His handshake is firm. But he is not very prosecutorial at this moment. He is relaxed, as if my appearance at the trial were a mere formality. I will learn that this ease is very deliberate. Karagyesa knows the kind of evidence he is going to have to produce over the next few weeks; he knows that none of the witnesses will find it easy to relate the things they saw. When he debriefs me he is patient but forensic. He tells me what the procedure will be the following day. I will go into the stand and affirm the footage we shot in 1994. The pictures will be shown to the court. I will affirm that we were present at Nyarubuye and I will give evidence about following Gacumbitsi into Tanzania. Then the defence will cross-examine. 'Just describe what you saw. That's all you have to do,' he says.

Karagyesa makes me feel safe. I feel there is no way he will draw me, or allow me to be drawn by the defence, into dangerous speculation. I start to like this man. The case is more than a career move for him. Karagyesa is as obsessed with genocide as I am. As a prosecutor he has been close to it for several years, sitting with the survivors and taking them slowly through their evidence, painfully building cases against the major killers.

After he is finished he says there are some friends there to see me. We only have a few minutes together; Richard has more prepping to do. I cannot say here who has come from Nyarubuye; for the sake of their safety their identities must remain protected. But the joy of seeing them is hard to describe; we embrace. I think we all find it hard to believe. After a decade the moment of justice is approaching.

Later I meet Elizabeth Jones, an old friend who is in town to research a Panorama *film on Rwanda. We have dinner and I try to listen to what she is telling me about the various other cases before the court. But I can't concentrate. Let's talk about families, I say. So we do. Elizabeth has a child called Daniel. So do I. We go through what sports they both like, how they are getting on at school, what plans we both have for the holidays. It's a conversation of fiercely determined normality.*

Later I ring Anne and she listens while I talk about what happened that day. Then I try to sleep. But it doesn't work. My brain is careering around trying to anticipate how the defence will try to trip me up. I keep remembering Karagyesa's words about only describing what I saw. Objectively I know I only need to stick to the facts as I remember them. But I am thinking also of Gacumbitsi. There is a mix of feelings – half-excited anticipation, half dread.

The following morning the armoured car picks me up and I am driven to the Tribunal headquarters. Irony abounds. In this very building the Hutu leader Habyarimana met the Tutsis of the RPF on the night his plane was shot down. He'd been attending peace talks with the enemy. Peace collapsed. The genocide started. A decade on and his cronies and commanders are being put on trial here. Full circle.

There is no sense of Tanzania's colonial past about this building, which is just as well; it is modern, shiny and antiseptic and provides a perfect atmosphere of calm, the dullness which is essential to the proper practice of law. I am taken along several corridors. At the end there is a security door. I hear buzzing sounds and a click and am shown into the public gallery. This is a long, narrow room which looks into the court through a glass panel. There is a small crowd waiting for the trial to begin and I sit among them. The judges enter. Two men and a woman. The woman is Judge Antonia Vaz, one of the most respected legal figures in Africa. The demeanour of the judges here is nothing like I remember from Ireland or Britain. There is no hint of pomposity. Later I will learn that they are every bit as forensic, but perhaps because of the nature of the crimes they are trying they seem to be that most unusual of species – lawyers with humility.

Richard Karagyesa stands and makes his opening statement for the prosecution. Gacumbitsi is charged with genocide, crimes against humanity, murder and rape. Back in 1994 the survivors had not spoken of rape. They were too traumatised and ashamed. But as the years went on and the huge scale of the sexual crimes became obvious in rising HIV rates, the women began to speak out.

Karagyesa places Gacumbitsi at the heart of the genocidal conspiracy in Nyarubuye. He talks about how the country was taken over by an elite bent on destroying the minority.

As he talks I look down to my left and I see him. He is sitting slightly out of view, shielded by his legal team, a prison guard sits nearby, but the shape is unmistakable. Ten years fly away and I am standing before him once more in that fetid camp. I can only say that he looks exactly the same, although better fed now, dressed in a neat blue suit, his broad forehead shiny under the lights of the court. He cannot see me. He is impassive. Any moment now, I say. Richard is coming to the end of his speech. The laying out of the crimes is almost over. My palms are wet, and I can feel a twitch starting. I fight it. I WILL keep calm.

The first witness for the prosecution is called. I get up to leave the public gallery. A policeman leads the way into court. Crossing from one to another I feel the static surge. The room is crackling with energy. I keep my head focused on the judges to whom I bow and then on the witness box. I don't look at Gacumbitsi. Richard stands to my left with the rest of the prosecution team; the judges are sitting, slightly raised, directly in front of me.

There is a moment's pause while I sit down. The court is silent. Richard speaks:

'Can you please identify the defendant.'

I said that I could see him. Karagyesa asked me to stand and point him out. So I did, pointing at the mayor and looking, for the first time in a decade, on the face of Sylvestre Gacumbitsi. He was not perturbed. He looked straight ahead, as confident as the last time we'd met.

I answered Richard's questions of fact. How we'd travelled to Rwanda and why; what we had seen at Nyarubuye. Then he played the tape of our film. It was the full tape and not the edited version that was broadcast on television. I was struck by the lack of voices. There is little of the usual chatter between cameraman and producer; the camera wanders slowly through the church compound and it sees, everywhere, the dead. It pauses to record the bodies of a family, parents, children, and moves on again to find a mound of corpses – uncountable for they are melting into each other – outside the main church offices.

In a classroom it picks out the body of a mother and her children. They are indoors, out of the rain, and the decomposition is not as advanced. The light is fading now and the camera enters the church where more bodies lie between the pews.

They are schoolboys. They wear the khaki shirt and shorts of Rwandan school children. The head of one has been mashed to nothing. The bodies have left a black, oily imprint on the stone floor.

I am asked to describe what we saw. But as I give evidence I feel my head starting to pound. I am sweating. Because I am back there. 1994. The rot, the stink, the roadblocks, the questions that go and on. My calm is crumbling. But there is *no way out of this dock. Tears come. My throat constricts. I have to stop. I feel all the eyes of the court on me.*

So I reach deep down within. I find the strength from somewhere. I trample on the rising emotions. I recover my composure and finish my evidence.

The defence lawyer comes from Cameroon. He begins genially enough. There are questions about when and why we travelled to Rwanda and who we travelled with. I realise he is setting out to prove that the footage is really a propaganda exercise by the Tutsis of the RPF. His case is that because we were escorted to the massacre site by the guerrillas we were their dupes. He tries to assert that most of the bodies we saw were really killed by the RPF.

Later he becomes indignant. He says that Gacumbitsi is only in court accused of genocide because of the film we made. I am starting to feel more confident now. I would like to say that nothing would please me more. But I tell him that he flatters the BBC. His client is in court, I say, because of the concept of international justice. The judges intervene several times to tell him to speed up his questioning.

He finishes at lunchtime on the second day.

I don't go back to the court to watch the other witnesses. The judges thank me for my assistance but I leave the dock wrung out and exhausted and, for the first time in my life, desperate to get away from the African continent.

Apart from that moment when I was asked to point him out, a dramatic flourish by Richard, I avoid looking at Gacumbitsi. I have seen enough of him. That confidence of his, whether it is real or constructed, makes me mad, and it makes me frightened. I don't know where he gets it from. I can't understand how you can do what he has done and look so at ease. This man is not a psychopath, a creature beyond the scope of logic or moral judgement. He is, or at least was, a Mass-going Catholic, a teacher, a man who went on official

*visits to foreign countries. That is the most unsettling aspect
of this whole bloody business. He isn't from a separate species,
or a candidate for the asylum. Gacumbitsi is a man who loves
power. He is what becomes of us when we crave power above
everything. His crimes came about because he believed that
the Tutsis of the RPF were going to take away that power.*

*'Isn't that extreme,' you might ask, 'to exterminate men,
women, children because you wanted to stay mayor of a
nowhere municipality in a nowhere country?'*

*No. Not when the country has always resolved such issues
by killing the minority. Not when you are brought up with
such violence. Not also when the state from its highest levels
orders the killing and prevents any investigation or conviction.
And not when you regard that minority as vermin. You fear
them so you kill them. You make a world without enemies.
Gacumbitsi was no madman. He followed the logic of his time
and place.*

~

By the end of the 1990s the village had been cleaned up, the
place of slaughter was in the process of being converted into
a genocide museum with the help of international advisers.
The authorities had created an ossuary where the skulls and
bones of the dead might be viewed by visitors; a separate
exhibition had been made of their shoes and clothes. The
process of memorialisation was creating a distance between
the present and the past; Nyarubuye was becoming commodi-
fied, a reduced Auschwitz, disconnected from the terror, a
museum piece for the benefit of foreign visitors.

The study of genocide is now a worldwide industry. We
are addicted to memorialisation because it provides us with a
certain comfort, the luxury of wallowing in sorrow, the shudder of righteous ecstasy that comes from being certain that we

are different, better than the monsters who made Auschwitz, Cambodia, Rwanda. But if war and genocide have taught me anything, it is that we are not at all different.

We, the children of democratised, free-speaking, law-governed societies, are just luckier. Put us in the same shoeless place as the Hutu peasants, subject us to the endless propaganda, the fear drummed up by war, the poverty that will send a man to kill his neighbour for his cattle, the centuries of autocracy – put us there and we will lift the same machetes, become the same monsters.

~

In mid-June 2004, almost a year after I gave evidence, Richard Karagyesa rang me on my mobile. I was walking along the King's Road in London at the time. The voice from Africa jolted me. He was laughing. 'Good news,' he said, 'he's gone down!'

A decade after the genocide Sylvestre Gacumbitsi was convicted of genocide, crimes against humanity and rape and sentenced to thirty years' imprisonment. He will be eighty-seven years old when he is released. (He is appealing against his conviction.)

'Well done, my man. You should be proud,' said Karagyesa.

I didn't feel proud, but I did feel happy for Valentina and the others. I'd doubted for years that the international community would give them justice. But Karagyesa and the other lawyers, and Judge Antonia Vaz and her colleagues, and the great, groaning bureaucracy of the United Nations, had delivered, and in doing so affirmed to the people of Nyarubuye that they mattered in the eyes of the world.

Sylvestre Gacumbitsi and his ilk were what Primo Levi called 'monsters with beautiful words'. Their road, the road of genocide, had taken away the lives of nearly a million of their enemies. I doubt he ever thought he would stand before an international court. Had the genocide happened twenty years ago – as the murdered Hutus of Burundi discovered – there would certainly have been no prosecutions. But something did change after Rwanda and then Bosnia. The decade in which I came of age as a reporter of war became a time of mobilisation for human rights activists and believers in international law.

After Iraq and with the terrible abandonment of Darfur, it is easy to think that international law is bunkum. The powerful or the most ruthless decide how things will work.

I disagree. The infrastructure of international justice is small; the pressures not to investigate the powerful nations of the world for human rights abuse are great. But there is a community of conscience – organised, passionate but also practical – which will not go away. In matters of human rights there isn't the option of despair. You recognise the contradictions, the hypocrisies, the defeats, but you go on. There is no other civilised choice.

~

London, 2004. *Ten years after the slaughter*. Valentina stood on the stage a few yards away from me. She hadn't seen me arrive and climb up the stairs to one side of her. I tapped her on the back. She turned and gave me a huge smile. I reached over and hugged her. Now when she stands up she is taller than me. There was a video playing and the crowd was engrossed. It was a recording of Valentina describing her experiences at Nyarubuye. The hall was full of Rwandans who live in Britain and their supporters. When the video was over I got up and said a few words. I spoke about Valentina and the other survivors and urged people not to forget the victims of the genocide. An MP spoke and then the Rwandan ambassador.

After that we all filed out for tea and biscuits and Valentina was suddenly surrounded; people wanted to embrace her and congratulate her. Her testimony had moved many in the audience to tears.

I was worried for a moment. She had only just come from a remote African village and was now surrounded by an eager metropolitan crowd. I felt protective and wanted to hold the crowd back. But Valentina looked at ease. I stood at the back of the crowd and watched her talking and listening, gracious and polite in the way she had been taught by her mother and father. *They would be so proud of you,* I thought. She was like this because of her own unique personality but also because of those dead parents. They had taught their child to be humane, and their love, the love she described to me whenever she spoke of them, had given her strength.

Valentina stayed a week in London. She was full of wonder and curiosity. She brought a mischievous sense of humour to her first encounters with city life, raising her eyebrows whenever she encountered brusqueness on the part of shopkeepers, her laughter echoing down the long hallways of Tube stations and up the escalators of department stores. She took photographs by the dozen to show the other pupils back at school and reminded me, as if could I ever forget, that she had a family here in London.

On the day she was due to leave I brought her to the airport and she clung to me as the flight was called.

'Would you like to stay?' I asked.

'No. I want to go home to my country,' she said.

It was the best thing I'd ever heard about Rwanda.

CHAPTER TWENTY-TWO

Consequences

It's a goddamn impossible way of life.

ROBBIE ROBERTSON, interviewed by
Martin Scorsese in the documentary
The Last Waltz, 1978

My journalistic life is divided into two parts. Before Rwanda.
After Rwanda. I left Africa after Rwanda. I was due for a
move anyway but the genocide pushed me to go more quickly.

On a perfect southern summer's day at the end of 1994,
Anne and I packed up our belongings and boarded a plane for
Hong Kong. I was now the BBC's Asia correspondent.

We arrived on a grey morning, the week before Christmas. I
was immediately struck by negatives. I noticed how the sewers
stank. The smell swamped us the moment the plane doors
opened. I quailed at the mildewed disarray of the apartment
blocks and factories of Kowloon, where people were squeezed
together like prisoners in tiny cells. I heard a roar and saw a
plane shave the roofs above and I wondered to myself what
on earth I was doing in this place.

We settled into a flat on Jardines Lookout, high over the
harbour, surrounded by tall apartment blocks and constantly
vibrating with the noise of building work. Every evening our

kitchen filled with the smell of garlic powder and steamed rice, funnelled down to us through the mysteries of the dilapidated air-conditioning, a wheezing beast, from the kitchen of our Chinese neighbours.

At least once a week they held a big Mah-Jong party to which many of their extended family came. This produced the strangest noises of all. To the usual coughing and spitting were added shouts and exhortations of various kinds, but the loudest noise was the clack and crash of the little tiles, as they were swept, snapped and slapped around the table.

I would come to be fond of Hong Kong but I would never love the place as I loved Africa. The first few weeks were not propitious. Hong Kong was a travelling post and my patch in Asia extended from the Hindu Kush in Afghanistan all the way to the islands of the South Pacific. I still feel a tinge of exhaustion when I look back at my itinerary in those early days. It set a pattern for the years that followed. It was a time of swift commands to be elsewhere, to be always faster than the opposition; a time of endless plane journeys, lukewarm room service meals gulped down at 2 a.m. after the satellite feed to London; taxis stuck in the mad traffic of Asian cities, and time zones that seemed designed to keep you in a state of permanent waking.

In Africa I had been reporting a story I knew well. Asia was so vast, the territories on my patch so diverse, that it would have taken a lifetime to gather a fraction of the knowledge I had at my command in South Africa. The Asia of the 1990s was an alienating place, where everything happened so much faster than in Africa. After the intensity of human emotion I'd encountered in the previous four years the Asian city seemed brash, shallow and unfriendly. Money dominated every over-heard conversation, and I longed to hear, just once, on a bust-ling Asian street, the sound of African laughter.

The problem, of course, was with me. I could not let Africa

go. I was 'homesick'. I missed the extraordinary intensity of the African experiences. When editors called wanting stories about the Hong Kong economy or some twist in the negotiations with China on the handover, I struggled to be interested.

By contrast Anne loved life in Hong Kong. Compared to South Africa with its multiple security concerns, and the ever-present talk about the 'situation', Hong Kong was a reassuring place to live. The looming handover of power to China gave it just enough edge for her. She took up calligraphy and began to make Chinese friends, and went to the street markets of Mong Kok and the temples on the outlying islands. She brought a Feng Shui man to the apartment and re-arranged the furniture according to his instructions. We could not, she assured me, be the only people in the building who hadn't had a visit from the necromancer.

I brooded in my office and started to look for new wars. There were plenty of them still rumbling on across Asia. Soon I was travelling with the Mujaheddin in Afghanistan and the Tamil Tigers in Sri Lanka; I went into the jungles of the southern Philippines on the trail of Abu Sayaff and spent weeks in Cambodia reporting on the aftermath of Pol Pot's madness. I was chasing after extremes again, that sense of altered being, the 'aliveness' I had felt on the streets of the South African townships. My questing took me far and fast.

My career was taking off. I won awards for my journalism and was getting praise from London. Yet I was struggling to settle. I hated the road but I couldn't live without it. I was agitated and unsettled when I had to sit around in Hong Kong. I felt lonely when I left. I was the living embodiment of that line from the opening scene in *Apocalypse Now* where the leading character says: 'When I was there I wanted to be here, when I was here I wanted to be there.'

Anne would come with me when she could, but had no appetite for the rigours and madness of life in combat zones.

While she explored Hong Kong and fell in love with the gentler elements of the Far East, I watched the rockets fall on Kabul or sat late into the night telling war stories over drinks at a bar on the banks of the Mekong River.

Then something happened which would start a long process of change. Anne and I had gone on a trip together to Vietnam to cover the twentieth anniversary of the end of the war. On the trip we talked about having a baby. We were both keen, even if Anne was understandably nervous about how my peripatetic lifestyle would impact on a child.

'Children need their fathers, you know,' she said.

'I know that,' I replied.

Soon after the Vietnam trip, Anne discovered she was pregnant. And when our baby boy was born on 4 February 1996, I was there to see him open his eyes, and squint warily up at me, taking my measure, I was sure. Daniel Patrick Alexander Keane was born in the Adventist Hospital in Hong Kong. He was a colonial boy, one of the last, before the island reverted to China.

~

The handover of power to China came and went with much ceremony but little in the way of real news. The British left one night and we woke up to see Chinese military helicopters hovering over the Pearl River. Soon afterwards we came to live in London. The idea was that we would 'settle', in other words I would start spending less of my time covering wars, and more in the role of husband and father.

There was less travelling than in my Hong Kong days. But as Anne reminded me: *that wouldn't be hard*. I wanted to be around for my boy as he went from baby to toddler; I knew well the casualty rate among the marriages of foreign correspondents, how the adrenalin-driven quality of life on the road, the excitement and camaraderie, could make the world back home seem flat, so that they could never settle, but kept chasing the elusive charge that only war could give them. That was the way of divorce and possibly death and I didn't want to be one of those casualties.

But I was now drinking much more heavily. I can't pinpoint a precise moment when I realised I wasn't able to stop. Certainly after Rwanda I drank more. But I cannot claim that Rwanda or war was the cause of this accelerating addiction. In Asia I had alternated between dry and drinking periods. I made my first attempts to quit it entirely. But with time the dry periods became shorter. Much later I learned that alcoholism was a progressive disease. In most cases it took its time to take people down. It was like a loan shark. It kept asking for more in return.

Anne could see what was happening to me. I often woke in the mornings with a hangover. The drinking brought on ever-worsening depressions. My ability to exert control was slipping. I could go for weeks without a drink and then, seemingly out of nowhere, the urge to pick up again would become overwhelming. For a man who had prided himself on his powers of control, it was terrifying.

Usually it would happen on the last night of a working trip. Sick and shivering in the morning I would swear never to touch a drink again. Within half an hour I would be raiding the mini-bar for a cure. I also needed more alcohol to get drunk. In the old days it would have taken only a few pints of beer. Now I needed beer and wine and whisky. I began to have my first blackouts. Blackouts have a unique terror, the sense of time and memory being wiped out, waking without any idea where you have been or where you are, scrambling frantically around the edge of consciousness until you remember what country you are in but little or nothing of what has passed in the hours before.

When I was home from trips I tried to white-knuckle. But my ability to stay dry, even for short periods, was ebbing away. I drank in secret. I drank late at night. I waited until everybody was in bed and then slipped the bottle of whisky from the press and sat there on the couch watching late-night television. Alcoholism is the loneliest disease on earth. It shuts out everybody but the drinker and his bottle. I followed a routine familiar to alcoholics. I drank and then gargled with Listerine. I chewed peppermints to hide the smell on my breath; I made sure I was the one who went to the bar to get the drinks so that I could quickly swallow a double whisky before returning to maintain a sober façade at the table.

In all of this, you will ask, did I not remember what had happened to my father? Of course I did. Every damned minute of my drinking life he was there, the old man, sitting by my shoulder, with those lost, sad eyes of his, a warning I could not heed. But I was taken by this thing, far more powerful than my will. I had fallen into a whirlpool, spinning, out of control. I told lies to protect my drinking:

What's that you're drinking?

Oh, just a soda water.

Good man. I don't know how you do it.

Ah, you get used to it, you know.

The lies of alcoholism are small, mean, desperate. You say what you must to protect your relationship with booze.

What must it have been like to live with and try to love such a person? In my case I didn't fall around drunk. I didn't shout and scream. I still worked hard, got to the airport on time, made sure the stories kept flowing to London. There will be many reading this who will say: 'I never saw you drunk. You always seemed a moderate drinker to me.' Which is no reflection on them but a tribute to my powers of control and concealment. But as control waned in the latter stages of my drinking I became a man with a vacant stare, isolated from those I loved.

I once asked Anne what, for her, had been the worst thing about my drinking. 'Emotional absence,' she said. 'You were never there.' It was like living alone, she explained. I might have been physically present in the flat but my mind was always somewhere else.

I tried to quit. But I kept coming back. I tried to drink just a beer or a glass of wine at dinner, two beers at the weekend. There is no greater hell than so-called 'controlled' drinking. The control only works one way. You always want more. You always feel ripped off. You look at the person who nurses one glass of wine and ask yourself: *What is wrong with them?* What is wrong with *them*! There is a pull between what you need and what you know. You are intellectually aware that you have become addicted.

But the desire is so intense it obliterates the will. And all the time, far down inside where nobody can see, your spirit is shrivelling, a little husk of all your dreams and hopes.

~

As the end of the millennium approached I began to experience a sense of dread. I lived in fear every day. By now I wanted terribly to stop. My beautiful son was still only a toddler. He had never seen me drunk and I wanted to get out before he noticed what was happening. He hadn't witnessed rows between me and his mother. That's because we didn't have loud rows. I always retreated into myself, and Anne put the stability of the home first, often at the expense of her own feelings. But in time he would have picked up on the tension; he would have noticed his father's retreats into long silence, his dad's inability to sleep, the odour of whisky and peppermints. Anne kept things going, but I knew that her patience with me was fading.

Late in 1998 the Kosovo crisis erupted. Thousands of Albanian Muslims were being ethnically cleansed by the Serbs under the direction of Slobodan Milosevic, and I was sent first to the border of Macedonia and from there to Albania. I watched the refugees roll across the border on tractors and by foot, frightened and desperate people leaving behind their burning homes, preyed on now by Albanian bandits and corrupt officials. At night in the local hotel, and on the roof of our rented house, I drank with old friends from other wars. We swapped stories and speculated about the coming NATO invasion – all of us caught up in the power of this new drama.

We knew that when that war ended there would be a lull, and then there would be another drama and the same media faces would turn up, relieved for the renewed sense of purpose they had been given and glad for the fellowship of the road; *alive* again, yes, that's the word, *alive*. On and on it would go, from war to war to war, only now and again faces would vanish – like Miguel and Kurt killed in Sierra Leone, or Bill, dead from drugs and drink. We would gather at memorial services in St Bride's on Fleet Street, dressed in unfamiliar suits, people out of place brought face to face with the unalterable consequence of war.

I came back from Kosovo and went on a long-planned holiday with some old friends from Ireland. I'd never been on a holiday with my male friends before. But they were people I'd known in Ireland for years; I felt safe around them. John King and his brother Padraig lived near me in Ardmore, where we kept a cottage. John was a marine biologist with a gentle sense of humour and a sense of reassuring normality about him. Father Dick O'Riordan was a priest from Cork who worked in the South African squatter camps. He had performed my marriage ceremony back in 1986, shortly after he was deported from South Africa for anti-apartheid activities. He was back in the squatter camps now and the trip to Spain was a welcome break from the daily struggle of his work.

They were men with whom I did not need to keep up appearances. I knew that they cared about me for the sake of friendship, not because of who I was or what I might be able to do for them. Working and drinking had pulled me away from my friends. The idea of this trip was that we would reconnect.

We planned to travel through northern Spain to the pilgrim's town of Santiago de Compostela. But the more we travelled the more I longed to be back in the mountains and close to the war in the Balkans. I listened constantly to the World Service for news from Pristina and Kukes, and while my friends were sleeping off the late night before, I was on my mobile harrying London to send me back. My face twitched and I drummed my fingers on the table. Every day I woke sick with a hangover. My stomach heaved, sweat rolled down my face, and my brain felt light and heavy, light and heavy. The first curing drink tasted like acid but it stopped the shaking, calmed me down and allowed me to face the day.

One morning in a café in Santiago, surrounded by pilgrims who'd walked all the way from northern France, I ordered a beer and sat down to read the paper. It was full of reports that NATO troops would soon invade Kosovo. 'Why am I here,' I cursed, 'stuck in the north of Spain when I should be there.' I pictured my colleagues who would all be at the war before me. I drank my beer and ordered another.

I took a sip of the second beer and felt my throat constrict. It had nothing to do with the beer as such; it still tasted the same, but as I drank I felt an upwelling of emotion. Tears came into my eyes and the choking sensation in my throat grew stronger. I had to get up and leave the café and find a place where I would not be seen.

The streets were filling up with demonstrators. A big anti-war rally had been called for that day. People were beating drums and blowing whistles. There were placards with the symbol of the white dove of peace. I could see my Irish friends in the distance, and remembered that I had arranged to meet them for lunch. I ducked into an alleyway. I began talking sternly to myself. *Get a grip, Keane. Get a hold of yourself.* I leaned against the wall and wrapped my arms tight together, embracing myself. I rocked back and forth, back and forth, like a man consoling the bereaved. *What's happening?*

What was happening? The booze was not working. I couldn't get a feeling of escape or ease. The warm rainbow had gone and I was panicky. I took half an hour to calm down. I walked the back streets until the shaking gradually stopped. Then I sought out my friends.

John and Dick O'Riordan were relaxing over a drink in a bar near the square. I looked at how easy they were with alcohol. They sipped glasses of wine. They told jokes and laughed. I didn't join them. The idea of raising another glass to my lips made me want to retch. After a sleepless, panic-tormented night I left Spain for home.

~

I returned to London to an empty house: Anne and Daniel were away on holiday in Ireland. The night I came back I took a bottle of whisky to the attic and sat staring out over the roofs of west London. I knew that I would not be able to sleep. I felt panic. I felt sorry for myself. The illusion of control was finally gone. I just waited until the dawn, and then I went downstairs and played the telephone messages from the night before.

I heard Anne's voice. 'Please call us. We are worried about you. Your son wants to hear your voice.' There was a sad weariness in Anne's voice which cut through the fug of my hangover. *Your son wants to hear your voice.* My son. The child I love, whose existence I swore meant more to me than anything on earth.

I have heard other drinkers talk about the moment they reached a moment of clarity. In my case it was a gift given to me by those I love, Daniel and Anne. I only played the message once but I heard the voice all morning. Later I picked up the phone and called a friend who put me in touch with another friend, who in turn put me in touch with a man who could show me a way out of drinking.

In the end there was no big drama but a lot of pain as I started to live without the protection of alcohol. The professionals who helped me told me I was an angry man. Anger from long ago, anger directed at a father who had been crippled by anger himself. 'Face it and move on,' they told me. With the help of other alcoholics I gave up drinking. I made alcohol part of my past tense. It stays that way on a daily basis. That was more than six years ago. I was lucky. The majority who are struck with this disease don't make it.

I do wonder if it was something in my genes that responded so powerfully to booze. My father once said he was born with a bottle of stout in his mouth. His father before him and a few other relatives had been touched by the powerful lure of alcohol. The experts would say I was in the category of those susceptible to developing an alcohol problem, the children of alcoholics who, through their genes or the circumstances of childhood, find themselves repeating the madness in which they grew up. In the end the why didn't matter. In fact it could easily have become another rationalisation, an excuse for where I found myself. All that mattered was stopping.

In my early days of sobriety I was told by a counsellor that I had a chance to stop the cycle. I needn't die like my father did. Nor did I need to pass on my unhappiness to my own son: 'That history can stop here and now. It can become a different history.'

~

A friend asked me one day what I would say to my father if I could see him for one last time. I didn't know then but with time and the settling of things I have found what I want to say. If I could see him now – and I wish so much that I could – I would tell him so many things:

I have a photograph of you, one of the few of us together. It sits on the mantelpiece next to a Waterford crystal bowl we were given for our wedding. It was taken in Belfast on that last trip. I am leaning back on the couch, smiling. You are leaning forward, and you seem happy. There is a knowing look in your eyes as if you at last have the measure of yourself and are not too upset by what you've learned. You look like a man who has started to accept himself.

That was the day Robbie the driver from the Belfast office took you on a trip to the city centre. You backed some horses, one of those immensely complicated triple bets you were so fond of, and took us to a Chinese restaurant with the profits. When the waiters were surly and slow you put on this deep, lordly voice and denounced them: 'Can we have service, PLEASE! If it isn't too much trouble.' I think that they believed you were quite mad. But they hurried up with the food after that.

We lost each other soon afterwards. That was my choice. You would have come back again and again. That was your nature. Forget about what happened. Make a new start. But I was running too fast. Now that I have travelled down part of your road I see you differently. I do not use the word 'forgive' for it implies the notion of sin. You were no sinner. And by God, as you said often enough, we've had enough sin in our Irish past.

In our lives both of us did things that caused hurt and none of that is undone. We cannot erase facts. But I know that in your own way you tried to make amends. You reached for kindness when you could. So do I on a daily basis. What am

*I trying to say here? Just that I was more like you than you
ever knew. I looked like you, spoke like you, walked like you,
loved the poetry you loved, and was touched by the same
lonely moments.*

*For the longest time I was angry with you. I was so sure
you were responsible for my sorrows. And when I didn't blame
you I blamed your background. I blamed the hard times you
grew up in, that country of poverty, struggling to get over the
Civil War; I blamed de Valera and his grey-faced crew and the
Church which suffocated its people; I blamed Listowel and its
streets full of pubs, and our national culture of drinking. Have
I left anyone, anything, out?*

*But where did all that get me? You can guess, Da. The place
the blame game always takes us, around and around in circles.
If you were here in front of me now I would embrace you and
hold on forever. And I would tell you that you should not feel
guilty on my account.*

*No way. Whatever I have screwed up in my life I have done
myself. I believe, my dear father, you did the very best you
could. My mother too. You both came at things with big hearts.
Neither of you set out to fail. You both taught me that staying
true to what your heart tells you is the best path, if not always
the easy one. I think of what Derek Mahon calls 'everything
pertaining to the good and the true'.*

*We pass on what we learn, and from both of you I learned
that kindness is the greatest virtue.*

*So when I am being the 'wise father', an unaccustomed role,
I advise Daniel of some few things that he may wish to carry
with him. I tell him that what matters above all the rest is to
be kind and to look out for the weak.*

*I wish you were here this minute. I would love you to see
Daniel. He looks like his mother – fair hair and blue eyes –
and he is gentle like her too. But he has the Keane sense of
mischief and he makes me laugh a lot. We have fun together;*

we play football in the park across the road in the evenings, and go to movies and fish and swim on holidays. You would be pleased to know that the drama teacher at his school says he has a real talent for acting. Naturally, I told him how great you were on stage, and as I said it I knew that I could be proud of you without qualification.

The other day I came into the room and found Daniel looking at the picture from Belfast. 'I wish I had been alive then,' he said.

I asked him why.

'Because I would have stopped Éamonn from smoking and then he wouldn't have died so young,' he answered.

You see, I told him you died from smoking. Which is part of the truth. There will be time for other truths later on. All that matters is that he is growing up in happiness and with so much love.

When he asks me what you were like, I tell him you were a good man, a man who did his best and a man who never stopped trying. Anne found your funeral mass card recently. I noticed that the Serenity prayer was printed on the front.

> God grant me the Serenity
> To accept the things I cannot change . . .
> Courage to change the things I can
> And Wisdom to know the difference.

I heard later you loved that prayer. So do I. We have so much to talk about. There was a lot written about you after you died. Brendan Kennelly wrote a poem about you; he captured the artist in you so well:

> With what ease the man could conjure
> People, images, scenes to please the blood.
> He was a pure artist, celebrant – loner

Yet few could charm a company as he could.
The child that most men kill he nurtured in the heart
And to the end remained a vulnerable lover
Paying the price of fierce fidelity to art.

That was an important part of the truth of what happened to you. In Listowel I saw that they had inscribed those words into a memorial on the town square. You would have been delighted with that, to be so honoured in your own place. So many people come up to me in Listowel to say how much they loved you. In the old days I resented them for forcing their idealised version of you on me. But I see now that that was a vital part of you, the charming romantic who stopped to joke and talk with whoever was passing. I knew other sides to you, just as those who love me know of my imperfections, but they don't cancel out the good. Anyway, Da, we are all of us a mix of many things, trying to be better.

More than anything I miss you. So much that when Daniel asks about you, there is a lump in my throat and I sometimes need to turn away. Last summer I visited your grave. I went on my own. You are buried with your mother and father, Hanna and Bill, and your Aunt Juleanne and Uncle Dan. There were some children playing at the entrance to Gurtenard Wood at the end of the graveyard, but they were quiet and after a few minutes they disappeared in the direction of the River Feale. It was a silent afternoon in the country. A schoolboy was fast asleep between two headstones. I didn't pray or say anything. I just stood there and thought of you. If you were here now, Da, I would put my arms around you and repeat over and over. I love you.

EPILOGUE

A Last Battle

You could scream
Because mankind is mad.
But you, of all people, should not.

'Calling To Order', CZELAW MILOSZ

I was sober but I was still going to the wars. A counsellor said once: 'I think you go to these war zones because you are a survivor. You want to replicate the experience of surviving as a child again and again. It validates you.'

That is part of it, I'm sure. But I think I also sought out war because conflict was part of my inner being: I had grown up with and was comfortable with it. On an objective level I could understand that the fear and tension of my childhood had damaged me; but I was drawn back relentlessly to the familiar, seeking the pulsing anxiety I had first experienced lying awake, waiting for my father to come home.

Looking around I couldn't help but notice that a lot of people who did my job had come from fractured homes. Ego was a big part of it too, of course; it is with many journalists. Covering war brought me plenty of praise and awards for my work – always welcome in the chronically insecure world of television news.

But here a big caveat is in order: there was another force at work which doesn't fit so easily into the more obvious psychological definitions. For all the cynicism, glory-chasing and hunger for adrenalin of the world in which I operated, I still believed passionately in the ideals I grew up with. From my parents, and from that great teacher, Jerome Kelly, I learned two simple truths: the weak need protecting; the powerful need to be challenged.

There is nothing radical there, nothing that wouldn't be described as self-evident by any supporter of human rights; no inspiration that isn't shared by many of my colleagues, and nothing, absolutely nothing, that makes me any more 'moral' a witness than anybody else. We are judged, rightly, by the standards and consequences of our work, not by the motives that propel us; hence my great unease when people, with the kindest motives, refer to me as 'a voice of conscience', as if that were something unusual in journalism. I don't believe it is. I have often felt I have been a very imperfect witness. I have struggled with the limits of my own courage, and been painfully aware that I have not come close to getting the whole story. But I always console myself with that line of Kant's: 'Out of the crooked timber of humanity, nothing straight was ever made.'

Jerome Kelly would have put it another way: 'Just do your best, boy.'

But doing my best can no longer involve continually going to the wars. I am becoming a journalist of the aftermath. This is for two reasons. Firstly, I want to spend more time on investigative work. Digging away to unearth unpalatable truths takes time, something the daily grind of hard news does not allow for. But my most pressing reason has to do with family life. It was brought home to me forcefully by the deaths of several colleagues in Iraq and later the killing by the Israeli Defence Force of my friend, the brilliant young film-maker James Miller. He was the best of men, not a glory-seeker or a man to take needless risks. If James can be killed, it can happen to any of us, I thought.

~

If Santiago was my turning-point in relation to alcohol, then Iraq finally changed the way I felt about war. It wasn't a Damascene conversion. I had been working towards quitting war zones ever since I got sober. But Iraq was to me a different kind of war. It was the first time since Belfast where I had felt a seething hatred simply because of who I was, the way I looked, the place I came from.

On that first night we slept in the desert. We'd planted our feet on Iraqi soil an hour before, tentatively entering the abandoned customs post and finding that the looters had been there before us; they materialised out of the desert within hours of the allied capture of Baghdad and the forecourt was now strewn with the detritus of the recently fallen empire. There were old files, photographs, a grenade launcher, tea cups and a faded velvet couch upon which had been placed a huge portrait of Saddam, a black-and-white photograph taken in the 1980s, some time between the genocide of the Kurds and the invasion of Kuwait.

There were white pigeons too. They fluttered in a long cage near the VIP room, where visiting foreigners had once waited while Saddam's secret policemen checked their passports.

In a room near the kitchen some journalists had found a dog. Abandoned by the fleeing border guards, it barked and scratched from behind a closed door until one of the drivers, a burly Iraqi who was making his first visit home since the war began, opened the door and the skinny, terrified cur slunk out. It looked at us imploringly and whined but the driver kicked out and the dog jumped and ran skittering in panic down the corridor and away into the desert.

Glenn remonstrated with him. 'Go easy, man. It's not Saddam's dog.' Astonished by this outburst the driver laughed, and waddled away to tell his colleagues about the sentimental Westerner. On the surface Glenn Middleton was an unlikely friend: a white South African male who loved the wild outdoors, disdained any intellectual conversation, generally divided the world into irreconcilable camps of goodies and baddies, lived for deep-sea fishing, and whistled relentlessly – arguably the most infuriating habit in a travelling companion. But I had gone to hell and back with Glenn.

I knew also that he was fiercely loyal, generous and unfalteringly kind, this last the most important human instinct of them all. We had been on the road together for more than a decade; we had come through the violence of the South African townships and the terror in Rwanda. In that central African country we had both witnessed the most extreme kinds of human behaviour, from the horror of genocide to the bravery of peacekeepers faced with overwhelming odds, and we had come away traumatised. When the request to cover the war in Iraq came, Glenn was the first person I called. Like me he was married with children; he wasn't reckless, no war junkie determined to prove his name at any cost.

Now he busied himself filming the looters at the warehouse. The arrival of our convoy had sent the other looters scattering. From a distance our armoured Land Rovers and four-by-four vehicles must have seemed like the advance column of an invading army grinding up from Amman. Then the journalists began to loot. They took small keepsakes: passport stamps, uniforms thrown off by the fleeing border guards, a few pots and pans from the kitchen where the half-eaten meals of the previous occupants lay on a small, filthy table.

There were, still, a handful of looters in a food warehouse beyond the border post. They were local Bedouin and had come in from their camps to plunder the stockpiles of rice and maize which had until recently been used to feed the guards. Noticing that we carried no weapons the Bedouin smiled when we approached. But then one of them, a boy aged about ten, rushed up to one of our drivers and whispered something.

'He says we must go now. Go back to the other side,' said Najib.

'He says bandits will be here and it's not safe.' The word passed quickly among the other drivers. Soon they were gathered in a cluster around the vehicles. Some had been uneasy about the journey from the outset.

Like us they'd sat on the roof of our mud house near the border for weeks, watching the helicopters filled with special forces shuttle north, night after night. Another driver, a friend of Najib's, had been killed when he stopped to use the phone in a village outside Baghdad. The public phone office was situated next to the Mukhabarrat – secret police – building. The same Tomahawk missile took out both buildings and killed everybody inside.

The arguing voices grew louder. I could tell that in spite of his own fears Najib was trying to calm the others. He was a man who enjoyed his creature comforts. The VIP room looked tempting, with its plush couches and carpets, a far more tempting prospect for the night than a cold desert floor. We had planned to spend the night at the deserted border post. Travelling on to Baghdad at that hour was impossible. There was still fighting on the road ahead and in the darkness any convoy of unknown vehicles would be a likely target for allied aircraft, Iraqi guerrillas or any one of the British, Australian or American special forces operating in the Western Desert.

Najib was still arguing passionately with one of the drivers, a large surly Jordanian who had a reputation for complaining and whose nervousness at being in Iraq was now rippling through the ranks of the others. I suddenly saw Ian walk across to the group. At just over five feet tall he was an unlikely looking special forces soldier. But Ian Watt had spent eighteen years in the SAS and he had the quiet assurance of a man who had been tested to the limits of endurance and discovered that he could go beyond them and survive. He spoke to the drivers. The volume of the conversation dropped. Then Ian listened to each of them speak. After a few minutes he came back to where I was standing.

'They're not happy to be here overnight. They think we'll have our throats cut in our sleep by the Bedouin. Scared shitless of the Bedouin, they are. I told them there was no problem. The Bedouin only want to strip this place down. That's why the kid was sent to put the frighteners on us. But it's not worth arguing with them. There's no way they will stay here. Let's go into no-man's land and kip there. Then come first light we'll be up and away.'

We turned around and drove out of Iraq once more, back across the mile or so of desert until we found a spot within clear sight of the last Jordanian military post. Anybody who wished to cut our throats now would have to do so under the eyes of the Jordanian border guards.

We lay in a huddle behind the vehicles, wrapped in our sleeping bags, but shivering from the sharp cold of the desert night. I lay on my back, listening to Najib snore. He was asleep on the roof of his vehicle and with every exhalation of breath it seemed to shudder under his vast bulk. Some of the others moved about restlessly in their sleep. Far to the west I heard shots ring out. I sat up. A voice spoke out of the darkness:

'It's some arse playing with his pistol. Nothing to worry about. Go back to sleep.' Ian was awake too.

I lay back on the ground and counted stars and recited some poetry to myself. I sometimes use it as a prelude to sleep, like reading a story to myself:

> *Every particle of dust on a patch of earth*
> *Was a sun-cheek or brow of the morning star;*
> *Shake the dust of your sleeve carefully –*
> *That too was a delicate, fair face.*

When I was a teenager I memorised favourite lines from 'The Ruba'iyat of Omar Khayyam'. Written in the eleventh century in the time of the Abbasid Caliphs of Baghdad it is hauntingly beautiful. It came back readily and seemed appropriate to the place and hour in which I now found myself.

I could not sleep because I was afraid. We had waited for weeks to get across this border and now that Saddam's statue had been dragged from its plinth in Baghdad we could at last move. But there was still fighting for other cities and small battles were taking place in different parts of the desert. The war was not over and ours was the first convoy to travel into Iraq since the border guards fled. I never like to be the first journalist along a newly opened route. I had too many memories of close calls in Rwanda and Afghanistan and already this war had killed several colleagues, one of them shot when he drove in behind the invading army a fortnight before.

I'd called Anne on the satellite phone the previous night. Everything was fine, I said. The road ahead was in allied hands. The Iraqi army was a beaten force. What else was I going to say? Yes, the Iraqi army has fled but there could be any number of freelance lunatics out there with guns and grenades itching to blow the heads off any Westerners they meet? On the road you keep that kind of bad news from the people at home. You hope your voice doesn't give anything away.

But Anne is a good translator. She has been under fire herself as a journalist. Once she was caught in the open in a Belfast graveyard when a Loyalist gunman opened up with a pistol and grenades. Three people were killed around her. In South Africa she'd reported from the townships at the height of the violence. The friends of mine who'd been killed doing their job were friends of hers too. So does she really believe me when I reassure her about how safe everything is? Or does she go along with this because neither of us can deal with the possibility of what is hugely, screamingly obvious: that at any point along this road I could be killed. 'Don't worry. Everything will be fine.' I say it. I am sure that at some stage in the conversation she says it back to me. Back and forth. Reassurance. The necessary fiction.

I nodded off eventually and was woken by a gentle prod in the ribs. 'Good morning, ladies.' It was Ian with mugs of hot coffee. The first light had appeared on the desert horizon, a sliver of vermilion slowly changing to a paler orange. Then a flurry of movement. I called a military contact back in London.

'Any word of what's happening?' I asked.

'It's hard to say. They are on the run everywhere. Be careful around Ramadi. There's been a lot of fighting there.'

Maps came out and over a final cup of coffee Ian briefed the group: 'I will go in the lead vehicle. If we get hit we try to keep going. We try to drive through the ambush. Whatever happens don't just stop and sit there scared shitless. Keep moving if it's at all possible.' I didn't ask him if he was armed. But I hoped to God he was. They could argue all they want about journalists and armed bodyguards at academic seminars back in London; on the road to Baghdad I wanted as many odds in my favour as possible.

I squeezed in beside Glenn. He fell asleep almost instantly. We drove past the border post. A group of American special forces soldiers had appeared there overnight. They checked our passes and waved us through. Ahead lay hours of emptiness. An hour or so into Iraq we came across a bus that had been bombed from the air and shredded by cannon fire; we peered inside and saw trails of blood along the seats and floor. The bodies had been removed immediately and buried nearby according to Muslim tradition. We never found out who had been riding on that bus, whether civilians or soldiers or foreign Jihadis. Whoever it was had died terribly. An hour after that we saw men walking towards us out of the desert. They wore desert camouflage, some of them were in shorts, most had beards. They looked like the South African commandos I remembered from the war in Angola.

'It's the Aussie SAS,' said Ian. We were waved through.

'Easy,' I thought to myself. A cakewalk to Baghdad.

And then the desert became farmland. The dreary sand gave way to irrigated fields and date palms. Villages appeared and we saw our first Iraqis. Then, seeing what had suddenly appeared on the road ahead, my heart erupted. I grabbed the walkie-talkie. 'Ian. A roadblock. *There's a fucking roadblock up ahead.*'

His voice came back, calm, but noticeably more intense than usual:

'I can see the roadblock. Calm down. We go through nice and easy.'

Somebody had taken a mechanical digger and dumped several huge piles of dirt, each higher than a normal man's height, at intervals along the road to create a chicane. Who made the roadblock? Not the allies. We hadn't seen a Western soldier for several hours.

As we came closer I scanned the road from left to right. If we were hit there was no way out. On each side the road fell away sharply into fields. Any vehicle trying to drive across country would overturn and be shot to pieces in the process. Suddenly two figures appeared to our right. One carried an automatic rifle, the other shouldered a rocket launcher.

'Oh dear Jesus, no!' I shouted the words without thinking.

As the lead car approached the chicane the gunman waved frantically. Ian's voice crackled on the walkie-talkie:

'No panic now, boys. None. Just keep your heads. Leave space between the vehicles.'

Ian's car stopped in the middle of the road. We were a few yards behind him, enough distance to turn and run, we hoped. But run where? The road behind us was choked with other media vehicles travelling in the same convoy. If shooting started there *would* be panic, a snarl of cars crashing into each other, toppling over the ditch, bursting into flames. I thought of Mutla Ridge in the last Gulf War and all those Iraqi conscripts carbonised in their vehicles as they tried to escape.

At that moment I was convinced that I was about to die. Never in my time as a reporter was the conviction so clear or so absolute. I would die there within the next few minutes. I saw myself flat on my back gasping for air but with the blood gushing out of my mouth with every dying pulse of my heart. And I didn't feel the promised calm of acceptance I've sometimes heard survivors of battle speak of. I was unbearably scared. My life did not flash before me. But the faces of my loved ones did. I saw Anne at home in the kitchen making a cup of tea. I saw Daniel as I'd last seen him when I went to kiss him goodnight before I left for Iraq: him sitting up in bed asking: 'When will you be back, Dad?'

'Soon, love. Soon. Now off to sleep.'

The gunman walked up to the lead car. The other one with the rocket launcher stood well back, eyeing the line of vehicles. Ian rolled his window down. The gunman came closer. Then a white hand emerged through the window, palm open in the gesture of friendship. The gunman seemed to pause. In this pause I heard Najib mumbling. He was praying. Then the gunman offered his hand. White and brown hands shook. I heard the gunman laugh and saw him slap the roof of the car. Then he stood back and waved us all through.

I gasped loudly. Then all of us in the car started cheering. We were alive!

Once before, in Rwanda, we had managed to turn back out of an ambush. I felt now what I'd felt then, an extraordinary surge of joy, adrenalin and optimism sweeping together through my body. As we were going through another chicane the gunman waved and smiled:

'*Salaam Aleikum!*' I called out.

'*Aleikum Salaam!*' he responded.

Ian reckoned later that they 'were just locals', a civil defence committee who'd armed themselves to protect their homes from the looting which had erupted everywhere around Baghdad. Had they been Saddam Fedayeen or foreign Jihadis there would have been no pleasantries. They would simply have opened up from the side of the road the moment we were within range.

There were more roadblocks after that and many men with guns. On the road into Baghdad the ground trembled and in a field to our left we saw an airstrike turn a factory building into a riot of flame and smoke. We pulled over into an abandoned garage. The drivers went off to find a local, somebody to ask about the safest routes into the city. There was another blast, closer now, and the air thickened with the smell of burning plastic. We drove onto a ring road, past the first American tanks, and saw a body doubled over in the road, bloated in the heat like a Michelin man; further on the body of a donkey, swollen too and stinking. Everywhere there were pieces of twisted metal and glittering seas of broken glass. Gunfire echoed around the streets.

Several times we were turned back because of shooting. I will never forget that scene. The insane comedy of all those journalists in their four-by-fours – at least thirty vehicles, probably many more – racing up and down side streets, blocking each other, nearly crashing a hundred times, behaving like madmen, which in truth was the only way to behave in such a place, at such a time. A squad of US Marines was moving up towards the city centre and we followed behind them. Some of them waved and smiled. Others looked wary. One gave me the finger.

'And fuck you too,' I screamed in reply. I knew he couldn't hear me, which was why I was brave enough to say it.

At the Palestine Hotel reporters and technicians were camped out on the roof. There were hundreds of us, new arrivals who looked enviously on the old hands who'd been here through the bombing, itching to be out and earning our own glory. The American network star, Dan Rather, held court in one corner, surrounded by fawning acolytes. I saw one American reporter sweep in from the desert dressed in a tank commander's battle suit.

There was much of this: men playing at war. And there was the other crew – myself included – who looked at them scornfully, but realised in our hearts that we weren't much different, only a little more discreet in our excitement. There were lights, cameras and, across the city, the thump and crackle of action as American units fought 'the last' of Saddam's Fedayeen.

~

That first afternoon in Baghdad I sat drinking coffee on the roof of the Palestine Hotel when shooting erupted on the other side of the building. Never had I heard so much sustained fire. I ran with Glenn, down the back stairs and out the front, rushing in the direction of the gunfire. As we came around the corner I could see US Marines blazing away with their M16s, firing at some buildings directly across the Tigris. 'This way, head down, this way,' Glenn shouted, and I raced after him to the cover of an American armoured personnel carrier.

Then I noticed that there were reporters and cameramen everywhere. They were wandering into the free-fire zone between the Marines and the river. Others were crouched beside prone Marines, filming them where they lay. 'Would you look at them. What a circus,' shouted Glenn.

My ears were battered from the noise. Then it stopped. Whatever, whoever, had been in the building on the other side of the river was either pulverised into thousands of tiny pieces or had fled soon after the firing started. The Marines pulled back towards the road beside the hotel, most of them slumping to the ground, laughing and cursing among themselves. They were red-faced, sweating, most of them breathing heavily as if they'd been on a long run. 'Now wasn't that something like fuckin' fun,' said a big-eared, shaven-headed boy.

I spent about three weeks in Iraq as the Americans watched their occupation unravel at speed. In Baghdad we drove to hospitals where the nurses carried AK-47s and bodies were being buried in the gardens, where a man moved from grave to grave, watching as bodies were disinterred and trying to find the familiar features of his son among the decomposing corpses. He didn't cry until the end when they told him his son definitely wasn't there. I'd followed the US Marines when they took Saddam's home town of Tikrit, sitting in a tea room the morning after the fall and watching young boys from Arkansas and Idaho clean their weapons while 'American Pie' blasted from the speakers of a reporter's personal stereo; one of them didn't look a day over seventeen and he cleaned his M16 with a toothbrush, singing along to Don McClean: *So bye bye, Miss American Pie/ Drove my Chevy to the levee/ But the levee was dry/ Singing this'll be the day that I die/ This'll be the day that I die . . .*

The boy look so innocent, but lethal. His squad commander was a sergeant named Joe from Sacramento, California, who told me he'd split up from his wife before coming to Iraq but that she still allowed him to talk to his three-year-old son on the phone. 'I think the kid really loves me. You know. I think he really does. He said it on the satellite phone last night. Isn't that something?'

In Babylon I met some more of these Marines, who told Ian and myself they'd killed so many Iraqis in Nasariyah that they'd stopped counting. They were full of bravado. I think the dusty emptiness of Iraq scared the hell out of them. 'I'd waste the whole fucking country,' a boy from Hawaii said. Ian, who knew war and killing, walked away in disgust at that.

In al-Hilla I went to the local hospital and saw the victims of allied cluster bombs. There were young children with arms and legs missing, others with their bellies sliced open by shrapnel, big stains seeping through their bandages, blood and pus from wounds gone septic. There was one blonde little girl whose foot had been blown off. She smiled at us and then looked away. Before we left the room I looked back in at her. Before she saw me looking, I caught her expression staring out the window. They had what seemed like ancient stares, these children: already wise about war and killing in a way you and I would never be.

There was a time coming down from Tikrit when we drove into a battle about five miles north-west of Baghdad. The Americans had tanks fighting up ahead and helicopters were rocketing some buildings in an industrial estate. We had to turn to go the long way around, through the countryside, to get back to Baghdad. Eventually we found ourselves in a traffic jam near a pontoon bridge. The cars edged forward with excruciating slowness. I looked out of the window of the car and saw immediately to my left a crowd of locals carrying stacks of assault rifles and rocket launchers out of a building.

The policeman who usually controlled the building stood by. Then one of the Iraqis came up to the window and smiled at me. I smiled back. Then he drew his index finger across his throat and smiled again. Suddenly the drone of helicopters filled the air and two marine gunships came up the river. They passed us at eye level and must have seen the crowd looting the police station. But they kept moving. The traffic freed up. We got out of there. Later Ian said that being stuck in the jam on the bridge was his worst moment of the trip, so sure was he that the gunships would return and fire on the looters.

We left Iraq on a bright April morning, travelling back on the road upon which we had entered. By the time we reached the Jordanian border a sandstorm had closed in, and we drove the last miles enveloped by red dust, sure that we were hidden from any who would do us harm. There were many journalists who did not survive Iraq. As I write, the conflict in the Middle East is still killing reporters, cameramen, drivers and translators. The resident correspondents live as virtual prisoners behind high walls.

~

When the call came to return to Iraq I told my editor that I would not go. I didn't make up excuses, I just told him that I was no longer prepared to take that chance. It was too dangerous. He didn't try to persuade me, or criticise my decision. He actually said he understood.

Instead I planned a documentary on the links between big business interests and the civil war in the Congo. The war in the Congo was over, a peace was holding, and it would be safe enough to go and do some digging around. I went back to Sudan to report on the refugee camps, twenty-one years after I had first gone there. But even that involved a degree of unpleasant risk. Being sober and happy wouldn't count for much if I was dead. So I made myself a new rule: I would try to avoid places where the bullets were flying. And I would make far fewer trips. Shouldn't I have done that years ago? Of course. But my adult life has been about finding the courage to change. It takes time but I am getting there.

How do I feel when I see a colleague in a flak jacket standing in the middle of a free-fire zone? I do feel a momentary pang. It is loss, of a kind. I know that. But I don't *need* to be there any more. Things have shifted inside me. Let others chase the sound of gunfire. There are other battles to fight: one need not always go to wars to report on human rights.

These days I don't struggle to stay at home. I cherish the life I have. The rewards of change come in such unexpected ways; the way a child leans against you when he is tired, and knows, instinctually, that you will be there to hold him when he falls asleep; the look in the eyes of the woman who knows you can be relied on to keep promises.

But I am not always calm or serene; I am not 'resolved' or 'redeemed'. I am still prey to sad moods, flashes of anger, dissatisfactions I cannot assuage or understand. Perhaps the change is that I'm learning to live with it.

~

I am writing these last few lines in Johannesburg on a clear winter's night. I have just come from dinner with my oldest, best friend Milton and his beautiful wife Dr Dorcas Nkosi, and their children Kgotsile and Ditha. Milton and I spent the night remembering the craziness and magic of those other South African days, and we spoke about the ones who were lost and thanked God we were here now, two middle-aged storytellers who had survived.

I am in a hotel room on my own now. But I will go to bed sober and wake up without fear. I don't feel the old loneliness of the road. I will be going home tomorrow. And besides they are all with me now, in every place I wake up in these days: Anne and Daniel, Valentina, my beloved parents Maura and Éamonn. All of these people, alive or dead, are with me.

ACKNOWLEDGEMENTS

In Ireland I am grateful firstly to my mother, Maura, and siblings Niamh McAllister and Niall O'Shea for their love and continuing support. I owe a warm debt to the Keanes of Listowel, Paul Hassett of Cork and the extended Keane and Hassett families who have shared their stories and hospitality over the years. My cousin Conor Keane has been a stout friend and read the manuscript carefully, making wise suggestions. A particular thanks is owed to Mary Keane, widow of John B, for her great help over the years and Denis Keane, my father's brother, for his friendship.

In London I want to thank my tenacious and protective agent, David Godwin, my patient and insightful publisher, Michael Fishwick, Kate Hyde, and Kate Johnson who worked with such sensitivity and insight on the manuscript. I owe a debt to my colleagues at the BBC, in particular Mike Robinson and Darren Kemp at Panorama, Kevin Bakhurst on the Ten O'Clock News and Jane Beresford at Radio 4; gratitude also to the camera geniuses Fred Scott and Glenn Middleton who were with me on the road in all the wrong places; thank you as well to my bosses Adrian Van Klaveren, Jonathan Baker, Vin Ray, Malcolm Downing and Richard Sambrook, especially Richard for his example of courage in the face of adversity.

Big thanks as well to: my dear friend Nijm Jara for his wisdom over many cups of coffee; John Lynch, Ireland's best actor and the best friend a man could have; Bill Whelan, musician and bringer of fun; Patrick Brown of the Canadian Broadcasting Corporation who was steering me in wise directions from way back; to Brendan Halligan, Cormac Liddy and Billy Kelly of the Limerick Leader, and Paul Dunne and Mick O'Kane of the late and very great Irish Press, and Shane Kenny and David Davin Power at RTE.

For the chapter dealing with my father's childhood (and the filming of the movie *The Field*) I must acknowledge a particular debt to the work of Gus Smyth and Des Hickey who wrote my uncle's biography "John B – The Real Keane", Mercier Press, Cork, 1992.

On a more personal level a special thanks to Nicholas Wilson and Andy Molyneaux in Dublin for the kindness and friendship they gave to my father. And I am grateful too to Dr Tony Humphreys, Rob Greene and Gordon Duncan without whose counsel so much might have been lost. To my great friends John and Paula King in Ardmore, and to Tony Gallagher, the Moloneys, Keatings and Padraigh Keevers I want to acknowledge my everlasting delight in sharing your company. Most of all thanks to Anne and Daniel and our new arrival Holly Mei. You give me so much, a gift every day of my life.

Grateful acknowledgement is made to all the authors and publishers of copyright material which appears in this book, and in particular to the following for permission to reprint material from the sources indicated. Although we have tried to trace and contact all copyright holders before publication, we will be pleased to correct any inadvertent errors or omissions.

Andre Brink: extracts from *Rumours of Rain* (Minerva, 1994) and from *An Instant in the Wind* (Minerva, 1991), reprinted by permission of The Random House Group Ltd. **Raymond Carver**: lines from 'Miracle' from *All Of Us: The Collected Poems* (first published in Great Britain by The Harvill Press, 1996), © Tess Gallagher 1996, reprinted by permission of The Random House Group Ltd and International Creative Management, Inc. **C P Cavafy**: lines from 'Voices' from *Collected Poems of C P Cavafy* translated by Rae Dalven (Hogarth Press, 1961), copyright © C P Cavafy, reprinted by permission of The Estate of C P Cavafy, The Random House Group Ltd and Rogers, Coleridge and White Ltd, 20 Powis Mews, London W11 1JN. **Hugh Cudlipp**: from *Publish and Be Damned!: the Astonishing History of the Daily Mirror* (Andrew Dakers, 1953), reprinted by permission of Lady Cudlipp. **Paul Durcan**: lines from 'Daddy, Daddy' from *Daddy, Daddy* (Blackstaff, 1990), reprinted by permission of the author, c/o Rogers, Coleridge & White Ltd, 20 Powis Mews, London W11 1JN. **J Anthony Gaughan**: from *Listowel and Its Vicinity* (Mercier Press, 1973), reprinted by permission of the author. **Seamus Heaney**: lines from 'Requiem for the Croppies' from *Door Into the Dark* (1969), reprinted by permission of the publishers, Faber & Faber Ltd. **Patrick Kavanagh**: lines from 'If Ever You Go to Dublin Town' from *Collected Poems* edited by Antoinette Quinn (Allen Lane, 2004), reprinted by kind permission of the Trustees of the Estate of the late Katherine B Kavanagh, through the Jonathan Williams Literary Agency. **John B Keane**: lines from 'Many Young Men of Twenty', from 'The Street', and from 'My Father', all from *The Street and Other Poems* (Mercier, 2003), copyright © John B Keane 1961, reprinted by permission of Mercier Press Ltd, Cork; also extracts from his plays *Sharon's Grave* (Progress House, 1960/ Mercier, 1995) and from

INDEX

EK refers to Éamonn Keane, and FK to Fergal Keane.

P.S.

Ideas,
interviews
& features ...

About the author

About the book

Read on

From Our Own Correspondent

Travis Elborough talks to Fergal Keane

This memoir is dominated by your father, but there are also a number of other father figures, men like Father Jerome, running throughout the book. I wondered if this was something you yourself noticed while writing it. Did the process of writing about your father possibly make you reflect on some of the other prominent men in your life?

That was really only something I noticed after writing it. It certainly wasn't something I was conscious of while working on it, but then reading it afterwards I did come to see that a lot of my life has been a search for strong male figures to lean on. But curiously enough, probably one of the most defining figures, if not *the* most defining person in my childhood and a real source of strength, was my grandmother.

You write about once being very angry with your father. Did you find writing the book a cathartic experience?

I found it a very painful book to write, particularly the last letter to my father. That was very, very cathartic, but halfway through writing it I found that the tears were streaming down my face. It just came right from inside. It was really a letter to myself; it's a letter one writes to read aloud to recognise what part of him is in me. Cathartic, I suppose, is one word to use, but in another way it's really a kind of excavation.

Did writing the book, then, produce more questions than resolutions?
I suppose what I felt was that there's this great myth that one is finally realised as a human being, that there is a great moment of catharsis. I don't believe that is the case at all. I think that it is an ongoing process, certainly in my experience anyway, and that the book has been part of that process. I'd say that it has left me quite raw emotionally, very raw, especially having put it out there because I am also left with lots of other people's reactions to it, which in turn has made me consider how I've reacted to it myself.

Did examining your relationship with your father change your own relationship with your own son, Daniel, or was it perhaps more the other way round?
It was the other way round. The experience of being a parent and of recognising how difficult it is – that really helped me to see him differently. Being a parent produced so many different emotions.

You write, 'I cannot understand my grandparents, or my father, without looking at the country they lived in,' and later state that it was your experiences in Northern Ireland that bred your hatred of tribalism. Do you think your Irishness helped you as a foreign correspondent to empathise with your subjects in any way? There's a section in the book, for instance, ▶

❛ The last letter to my father was really a letter to myself; the letter one writes to read aloud to recognise what part of him is in me. ❜

3

LIFE
at a Glance

BORN

London, 6 January 1961

EDUCATED

Presentation College,
Cork

CAREER

Limerick Leader, Irish
Press Group, *RTE News*,
BBC News

FAMILY

Married to Anne Flaherty,
with two children, Daniel
and Holly Mei

LIVES

West London

From Our Own Correspondent *(cont.)*

◄ where you josh about oppression with
your South African friend Milton.
I was, I should point out, doing that in a
highly sardonic way. I think there is a
tendency on the part of some Irish people
to overplay that. There's a kind of Irish
exceptionalism abroad at the moment that
I absolutely loathe with every fibre of my
being – this notion that we are uniquely
placed to understand the suffering of the
world because things have happened to
our great grandparents. I don't believe that
to be the case. What I do believe is that one
of the things we do have, and I think this is
one of our national traits, is a great gift for
communication. My empathy came from
my parents – that was a very particular family
thing. But in terms of communication and an
oral storytelling tradition, that is definitely
rooted in my Irishness.

**Poetry is clearly very important to you and
features prominently in the book. Do you
write poetry yourself?**
I do write poetry, though at the moment I
only write for myself, and I do absolutely
adore poetry, it's my version of praying.

**One of the things that struck me reading
your book, actually, was that while you
make it plain how oppressive the Catholic
church was in Ireland during your youth,
in places like South Africa Catholic priests
appear frequently to have been an
enormous force for good.**
Well, for me in Ireland there was also Father
Jerome, who had a huge influence on my life.

So I think what I would say is that while I feel a deep anger over what the church was allowed to do in Ireland, I've been able to separate that out from individuals. I do, however, think that the missionaries who set out for Africa from Ireland in the 1950s and 60s – and who probably thought they'd never see the place again – who went and lived in the villages with the local people and learned the local languages and stayed there for years, well, there is something in what they did that a lot of the latter-day would-be saviours of Africa with their 4 x 4s could do well to learn from.

You claim that you've made yourself a new rule to avoid places where the bullets are flying, but are there occasions when —
Are there occasions when I get a twinge? Of course there are. It's a bit like drinking. There are moments on a hot summer's day when I see someone with a cold pint of beer and think that would be nice. The difference is that now I don't have the impulse to follow that desire to its logical conclusion, whether it's going to war or going out drinking again.

Do you wonder, with advances in modern technology allowing local people like Salam Pax, the Baghdad blogger, to report on events on the ground, if the golden age of the foreign correspondent has passed? Or, conversely, is it that in a world of embedded war reporting and corporate news channels they are now more necessary than ever before?
I think the latter. There is now a tyranny of ▶

From Our Own Correspondent *(cont.)*

◄ whining, nasal clones, all sounding like each other, all writing like each other, all over-describing, with a kind of *faux* enthusiasm, a *faux* drama. There are, of course, some very notable exceptions. But I do believe that the emphasis on storytelling has been diminished in favour of sensationalism with the corporatisation of broadcasting.

With that in mind, what advice would you give to anyone wanting to become a foreign correspondent today?
Read. Read. And Read. And then get yourself an air ticket somewhere far away and a little strange, and go.

Who do you read?
Journalists? Jon Swain, John Simpson. At the moment I am reading Robert Lowell's *Letters* and Anne Applebaum's *Gulag*, but in fiction I like Chekov, Murakami; I like a lot of American writers: Faulkner, Fitzgerald, Raymond Carver, Don DeLillo, Philip Roth. With Carver there's a shared background in alcohol and rootlessness. Back in early 1990, when I had a mental breakdown, I was given a present of *A New Passage to the Waterfall* which had just come out and I kept it with me through that winter, and I still have that copy, and in many ways it was just a lifeline for me. It's so beautifully written and so full of hope. And I am a great believer in hope.

After all that you have seen, are you still optimistic about the world?
Despite the evidence and despite my own

> ❝ I absolutely adore poetry, it's my version of praying. ❞

intellectual arguments with it, yes, I find I am. When I get up in the morning, I am just naturally curious and excited about the world.

Your task as a journalist has been to bear witness to the events. Have you ever felt compelled to take a more active political role?
It's something that many people have asked me. But the answer, in the party political sense, is no. But how do we define the political? I am involved in campaigning for human rights, and the struggle for human rights is something that overrides any political party or group.

You advise Daniel to 'be kind and look after the weak'. Would you describe this as your motto?
I guess it is my motto. The thing that I believe in most as I've got older is kindness. I think it is the greatest human virtue, for much else follows from it. It's very hard to find a mean-spirited person who is kind. ∎

> ❛ The thing that I believe in most as I've got older is kindness. ❜

A Writer's Life

When do you write?
I write very early in the morning before the rest of the house has risen. It's the only quiet time of the day. I am usually exhausted by the end of the day so night writing isn't an option.

Where do you write?
I write in my studio in the attic of the house. I have a lovely old Indonesian desk and am surrounded by books. I also waste a great deal of time looking out over the rooftops of West London and dreaming.

Why do you write?
Because I have to. I couldn't imagine a life without writing. It is at the heart of me.

Pen or computer?
Pen for the notes that precede the writing, computer for the writing.

Silence or music?
Silence.

What started you writing?
An urge to be heard. It comes from very far back in childhood.

How do you start a book?
It always starts with an idea that refuses to go away. I have lots of ideas. Some die a natural and deserved death. The ones that become books cling like barnacles to the brain.

And finish?
With great relief and a strangely bereft

feeling. Also a somewhat scared feeling as I wait for my agent and publishers to give their views.

Any writing rituals or superstitions?
None.

Which living writer do you most admire?
Philip Roth.

Who or what inspires you?
I am usually inspired by the example of individuals I have encountered in my travels. But the strongest inspiration for me these days is a close friend, Roman Halter. Roman survived Auschwitz and came to Britain. He is an accomplished artist and a wonderfully humane and good man.

What's your guilty reading pleasure?
I love sneaking upstairs on the pretext of working and lying on the bed with a book far above the tumult of the house. ■

In the Bone Shop of the Heart: Writing *All of These People*

By Fergal Keane

IT BEGAN AS A very different book. Two years before writing a word I'd sat in the offices of my publisher and announced that I was going to write a book about the state of the world. If they felt any nervousness about that portentous declaration the assembled editors kept it well hidden. 'It'll be a book about the world as I see it, and of course my own life as a foreign correspondent,' I said.

I started plotting the chapters soon after, and within a month began writing. I had planned to start with Iraq and finish somewhere in Africa, the former because it was the most recent war I'd covered, the latter because I regard the continent as my spiritual home. Along the way I planned to reflect on 'big' themes like poverty, conflict resolution, the spread of democracy, while trying to give a flavour of what life was like on the road in some of the world's more dangerous locations.

It was the latter ambition which put paid to the original book. A little context is needed here:

By the time I started to write I had been nearly five years sober. The end to drinking had been followed by a commitment to abandon active war zones. My life had changed dramatically. I wasn't just sober but I had two young children. But as I tried to describe my life as a foreign correspondent – the pressures of the road, the impulses and influences which drove me to desperate places – I found I could not advance without talking about alcoholism or about the world in which I had grown up.

And so I went back to the beginning, to the physical and emotional landscape of childhood, finding that, as Yeats put it, 'I must lie down where all the ladders start/in the foul rag and bone shop of the heart.'

It was an extraordinarily difficult book to write. Not because I had to quarry for memories but because they were still so vivid. They flooded back and gave me many restless nights. There is a common assumption that writing which raises the ghosts of the past will prove cathartic. I do not believe this to be true. Not for me. The ghosts came and still come. For me writing and talking about the past does not expunge its pain. But they do help me to accept what has been and gone. Acceptance is the key word. Pain that was sharp and insistent, a spur to the old life of running and insecurity, became a dull ache, a presence I've learned to live with.

When the book was published I did experience twinges of panic. What would people think? I visualised newspaper headlines that screamed: 'BBC Man's Drunken Hell!'

With the exception of one witless headline in Ireland, 'I Won't Die from Drink Like My Dad, Says Fergal', and another which spoke of 'The Sins of the Father' (when in ▶

> ❛When the book was published I did experience twinges of panic. What would people think? ❜

11

In the Bone Shop *(continued)*

◄ fact the book repudiates the notion of parental 'sin'), the tone was sober. In Britain the worst was a suggestion from the *Guardian* that I was either very brave or very foolish to be talking about my alcoholism. Why is it foolish to talk publicly about a disease that is killing tens of thousands of people?

Several colleagues did call me to express astonishment. 'I never knew you had a drinking problem!' they declared. Then the letters started to come. Some were from people who had known my parents in their youth. Others were from fellow alcoholics or the children of alcoholics. They mattered more to me than anything any critic could say – good, bad or indifferent. Without exception the letters were warm and supportive. Many of the correspondents shared details of their own struggle. They were people in alcohol and drug treatment centres or going to their first AA meetings. I salute them for the courage they have discovered in themselves.

There were unexpected reunions with long-lost friends. The daughter of a family I'd lived near as a child came to a reading in Edinburgh. I am sure our hugs and exclamations surprised the others in the book-signing queue. Old schoolmates called to say they had read the portrait of my late headmaster, Brother Jerome Kelly, and recognised the man I described. One of them reminded me of something he had told us and that I'd forgotten. Speaking to assembly one morning he declared: 'Remember, lads, that the world out there is full of people who

> ❝ The letters from fellow alcoholics or the children of alcoholics mattered more to me than anything any critic could say. ❞

want to walk on other people. That is not what you are learning here. That is not how to behave.'

A woman sent me a photograph of my parents on the day they were engaged. I looked into their faces and saw innocence and hope, nothing yet mortgaged away. I believe it was the same person who said she'd been part of a guard of honour from my mother's school at the church when they married. 'They were so happy looking. It was a great day,' she wrote.

A man wrote to tell me he had helped my father when he was trying to get sober. This was towards the end of his life. 'He really tried hard to get it, you know.'

As far as non-fiction is concerned, I believe I have written the last of the story of my father and myself. Both he and my mother still inspire me, of course, but in different and more mysterious ways than I could have imagined before I wrote this book. More than anything I cherish their bravery and humanity. I would never have been able to say that before making the journey this book describes. ∎

> ❝ As far as non-fiction is concerned, I believe I have written the last of the story of my father and myself. ❞

Have You Read?

Other books by Fergal Keane

The Bondage of Fear: A Journey Through the Last White Empire

As the BBC's Southern Africa correspondent, Fergal Keane witnessed South Africa's transition from a racist oligarchy to a democracy. In this riveting book, based on his encounters with the white Parliamentarians, the Afrikaner bitter-enders, members of the black radical left; the Zulus, soldiers, spies, killers, and the leading figures in the ANC, Keane perceptively and compassionately charted the final days of the last white empire.

Season of Blood: A Rwandan Journey

Winner of the Orwell Prize for best political book of 1995, Keane's impassioned eyewitness account of the genocide of Rwanda's Tutsi minority by Hutu extremists remains a searing indictment of man's inhumanity to man, and of the international community's failure to halt mass murder.

Letters to Daniel: Dispatches from the Heart

'Letter to Daniel' was an emotional message to his newborn son that Keane wrote for BBC radio's long-standing *From Our Own Correspondent* programme. This volume contains many of Keane's other vintage dispatches, including a similarly evocative and moving piece on his late father.

Letters Home
Another fine collection of Keane's broadcasts and columns from the horrific war zones of Sierra Leone, Kosovo and Rwanda.

....

A Stranger's Eye: A Foreign Correspondent's View of Britain
After years covering the world's conflict zones, at the turn of the millennium Keane turned his attention to the country in which he was born but where, until then, he had never lived. From Glasgow to Leeds, London, Cornwall, Wales and the very fringes of the United Kingdom in County Tyrone, he found a surprising and little-known world of poverty, exclusion and alienation as disturbing and compelling as anything he'd encountered across the globe. ■

If You Loved This,
You Might Like ...

River of Time
Jon Swain

News from No Man's Land:
Reporting the World
John Simpson

The Kindness of Strangers:
An Autobiography
Kate Adie

From Our Own Correspondent
edited by Tony Grant

My Ear at His Heart
Hanif Kureishi

Patrimony
Philip Roth

And When Did You Last See Your Father?
Blake Morrison

Father and Son
Edmund Gosse